Contents Continents and Poles 3

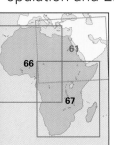

Europe

Topographic map _____ 42–43

European Union _____ 43

Wealth _____ 43

Climate and Ecosystems _____ 44

Farming, Energy, and Minerals _____ 45

Industry and Environmental issues _____ 46

Population _____ 47

France _____ 48

Benelux, Germany, Alps _____ 49

Spain and Portugal _____ 50

Italy _____ 51

Asia

Countries, Land and Water _____ 52

Climate and Ecosystems _____ 53

Farming, Energy, Minerals, and Industry _____ 54

Population and Environmental issues _____ 55

Northern Eurasia _____ 56–57

Southern Asia _____ 58

China and Japan _____ 59

South East Asia _____ 60

The Middle East and North Africa _____ 61

Africa

Countries, Land and Water _____ 62

Climate and Ecosystems _____ 63

Farming, Energy, Minerals, and Industry _____ 64

Population and Environmental issues _____ 65

North and West Africa _____ 66

South and East Africa _____ 67

Oceania

Countries, Land and Water _____ 68

Climate and Ecosystems _____ 69

Farming, Energy, Minerals, and Industry _____ 70

Population and Environmental issues _____ 71

Australia _____ 72

New Zealand _____ 73

North America

Countries, Land and Water _____ 74

Climate and Ecosystems _____ 75

Farming, Energy, Minerals, and Industry _____ 76

Population and Environmental issues _____ 77

Canada, Greenland, USA, Mexico and the Caribbean _____ 78–79

South America

Countries, Land and Water _____ 80

Climate and Ecosystems _____ 81

Farming, Energy, Minerals, and Industry _____ 82

Population and Environmental issues _____ 83

South America _____ 84–85

The Poles

The Arctic Ocean _____ 86

Antarctica _____ 86

Index _____ 87-96

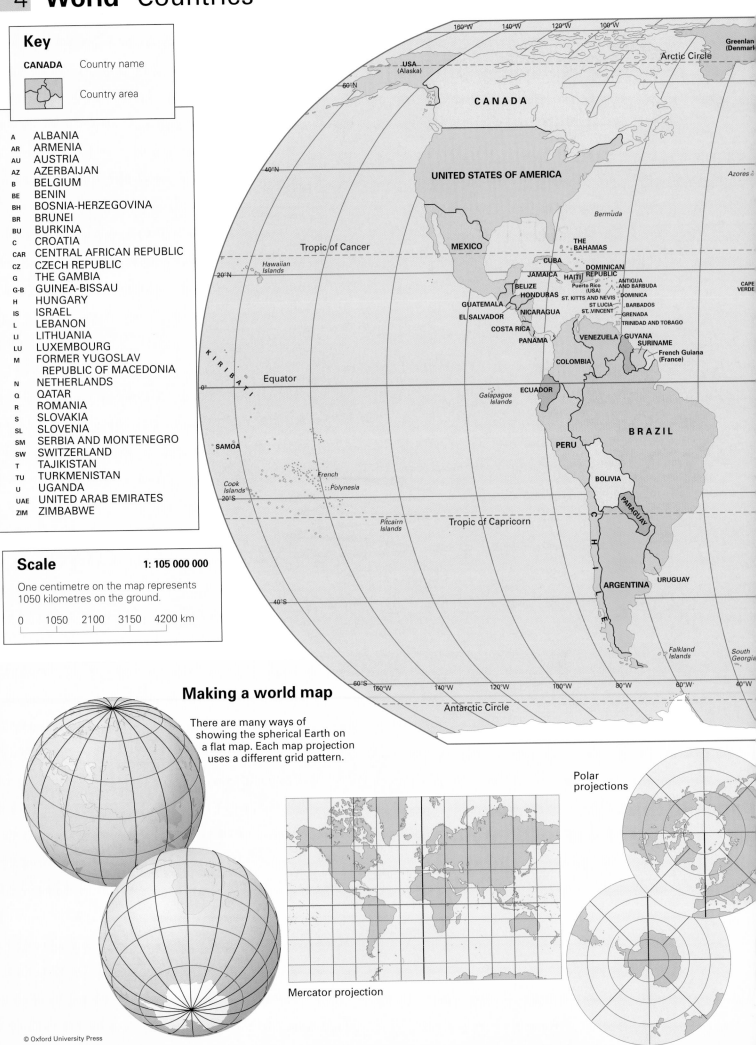

Key

CANADA   Country name

Country area

A	ALBANIA
AR	ARMENIA
AU	AUSTRIA
AZ	AZERBAIJAN
B	BELGIUM
BE	BENIN
BH	BOSNIA-HERZEGOVINA
BR	BRUNEI
BU	BURKINA
C	CROATIA
CAR	CENTRAL AFRICAN REPUBLIC
CZ	CZECH REPUBLIC
G	THE GAMBIA
G-B	GUINEA-BISSAU
H	HUNGARY
IS	ISRAEL
L	LEBANON
LI	LITHUANIA
LU	LUXEMBOURG
M	FORMER YUGOSLAV REPUBLIC OF MACEDONIA
N	NETHERLANDS
Q	QATAR
R	ROMANIA
S	SLOVAKIA
SL	SLOVENIA
SM	SERBIA AND MONTENEGRO
SW	SWITZERLAND
T	TAJIKISTAN
TU	TURKMENISTAN
U	UGANDA
UAE	UNITED ARAB EMIRATES
ZIM	ZIMBABWE

Scale

1: 105 000 000

One centimetre on the map represents
1050 kilometres on the ground.

0   1050   2100   3150   4200 km

Making a world map

There are many ways of
showing the spherical Earth on
a flat map. Each map projection
uses a different grid pattern.

Polar
projections

Mercator projection

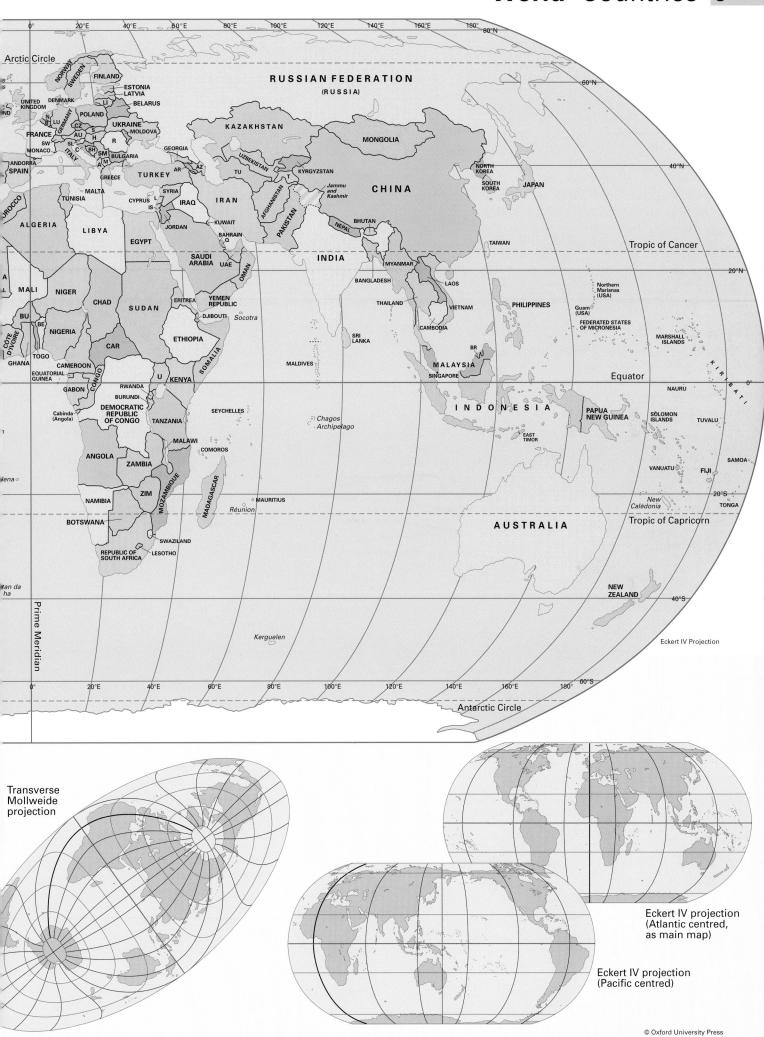

Arctic Circle

RUSSIAN FEDERATION
(RUSSIA)

NORWAY
SWEDEN
FINLAND
ESTONIA
LATVIA
UNITED
KINGDOM
DENMARK
BELARUS
POLAND
UKRAINE
FRANCE
MOLDOVA
MONACO
GEORGIA
ANDORRA
SPAIN
BULGARIA
GREECE
TURKEY
AR
AZ
MOROCCO
MALTA
TUNISIA
CYPRUS
SYRIA
IS
IRAQ
ALGERIA
LIBYA
JORDAN
EGYPT
KUWAIT
BAHRAIN
Q
SAUDI
ARABIA
UAE
OMAN
MALI
NIGER
CHAD
SUDAN
ERITREA
YEMEN
REPUBLIC
DJIBOUTI
Socotra
BU
BE
NIGERIA
CAR
ETHIOPIA
COTE
D'IVOIRE
TOGO
GHANA
CAMEROON
SOMALIA
EQUATORIAL
GUINEA
U
KENYA
GABON
CONGO
RWANDA
BURUNDI
DEMOCRATIC
REPUBLIC
OF CONGO
TANZANIA
Cabinda
(Angola)
SEYCHELLES
MALAWI
ANGOLA
ZAMBIA
COMOROS
MOZAMBIQUE
MADAGASCAR
ZIM
NAMIBIA
MAURITIUS
Réunion
BOTSWANA
SWAZILAND
REPUBLIC OF
SOUTH AFRICA
LESOTHO

KAZAKHSTAN
MONGOLIA
UZBEKISTAN
KYRGYZSTAN
TU
T
Jammu
and
Kashmir
AFGHANISTAN
PAKISTAN
CHINA
NORTH
KOREA
SOUTH
KOREA
JAPAN
NEPAL
BHUTAN
IRAN
TAIWAN
INDIA
MYANMAR
BANGLADESH
LAOS
THAILAND
VIETNAM
PHILIPPINES
Northern
Marianas
(USA)
Guam
(USA)
FEDERATED STATES
OF MICRONESIA
SRI
LANKA
CAMBODIA
MARSHALL
ISLANDS
MALDIVES
BR
MALAYSIA
SINGAPORE
Chagos
Archipelago
NAURU
INDONESIA
PAPUA
NEW GUINEA
SOLOMON
ISLANDS
TUVALU
EAST
TIMOR
SAMOA
VANUATU
New
Caledonia
FIJI
TONGA
AUSTRALIA
KIRIBATI

St Helena

Tristan da
Cunha
Prime Meridian

NEW
ZEALAND

Kerguelen

Eckert IV Projection

80°N
60°N
40°N
Tropic of Cancer
20°N
Equator
Tropic of Capricorn
20°S
40°S
60°S

0° 20°E 40°E 60°E 80°E 100°E 120°E 140°E 160°E 180°
0° 20°E 40°E 60°E 80°E 100°E 120°E 140°E 160°E 180°

Antarctic Circle

Transverse
Mollweide
projection

Eckert IV projection
(Atlantic centred,
as main map)

Eckert IV projection
(Pacific centred)

© Oxford University Press

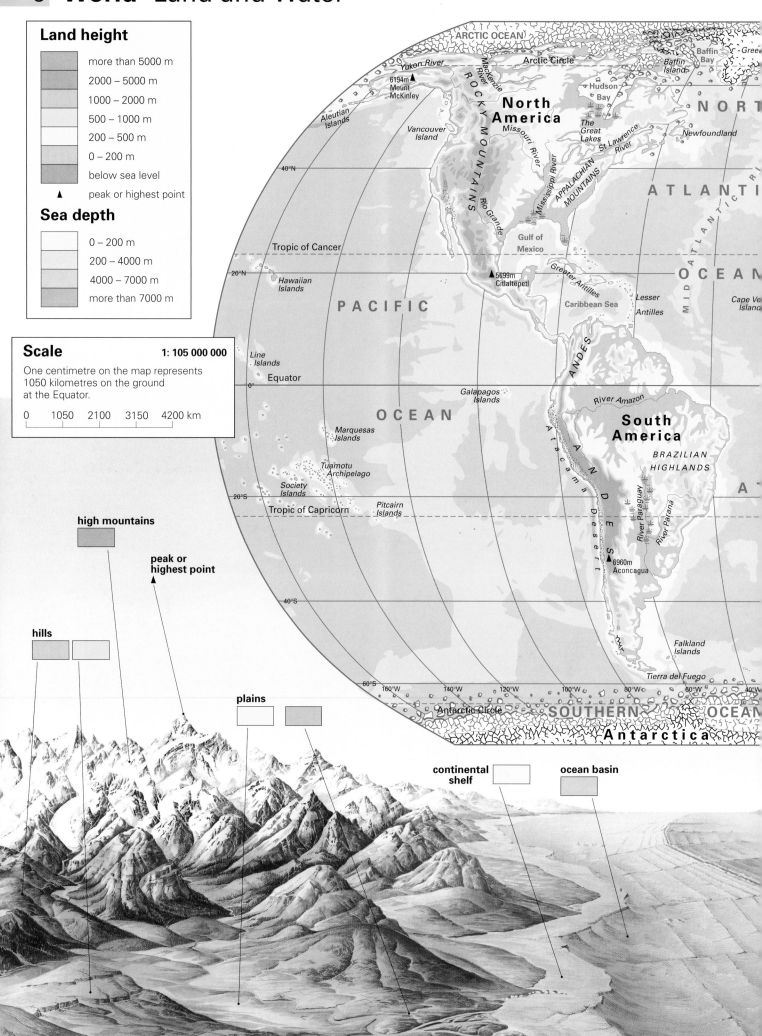

Land height

- more than 5000 m
- 2000 – 5000 m
- 1000 – 2000 m
- 500 – 1000 m
- 200 – 500 m
- 0 – 200 m
- below sea level
- ▲ peak or highest point

Sea depth

- 0 – 200 m
- 200 – 4000 m
- 4000 – 7000 m
- more than 7000 m

Scale   1: 105 000 000

One centimetre on the map represents
1050 kilometres on the ground
at the Equator.

0   1050   2100   3150   4200 km

high mountains

peak or highest point

hills

plains

continental shelf

ocean basin

ARCTIC OCEAN

Arctic Circle

Baffin Bay

Gree

Baffin Island

Yukon River

Mackenzie River

Hudson Bay

NOR

6194m ▲ Mount McKinley

R O C K Y   M O U N T A I N S

Aleutian Islands

Vancouver Island

North America

Missouri River

The Great Lakes

St Lawrence River

Newfoundland

ATLANTI

40°N

Mississippi River

APPALACHIAN MOUNTAINS

OCEAN

Tropic of Cancer

20°N

Rio Grande

Gulf of Mexico

MID ATLANTIC RIDGE

Hawaiian Islands

▲ 5699m Citlaltépetl

Greater Antilles

Caribbean Sea

Lesser Antilles

Cape Ver Island

PACIFIC

Line Islands

Equator 0°

Galapagos Islands

River Amazon

Marquesas Islands

OCEAN

South America

BRAZILIAN HIGHLANDS

A

Tuamotu Archipelago

A N D E S

Society Islands

20°S

Pitcairn Islands

Tropic of Capricorn

Atacama Desert

River Paraguay

River Paraná

40°S

▲ 6960m Aconcagua

Falkland Islands

Tierra del Fuego

60°S 160°W 140°W 120°W 100°W 80°W 60°W 40°W

Antarctic Circle

SOUTHERN   OCEAN

Antarctica

OXFORD
Practical

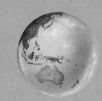

ISBN 0 19 832162 7 (hardback)
ISBN 0 19 832161 9 (paperback)

1 3 5 7 9 10 8 6 4 2

Printed in Singapore

Acknowledgements

The publishers would like to thank the Telegraph Colour Library for permission to reproduce the photograph on page 8.

Cover image: Tom Van Sant / Geosphere Project, Santa Monica, Science Photo Library.

The illustrations are by Chapman Bounford, Hard Lines, and Gary Hinks.

2 **Contents** The World, The British Isles

The World

Countries — 4–5
Land and Water — 6–7
Climate and Ecosystems — 8–9
Earthquakes and Volcanoes — 10–11
Population — 12–13
Development and Interdependence — 14–15
Environment and Pollution — 16–17

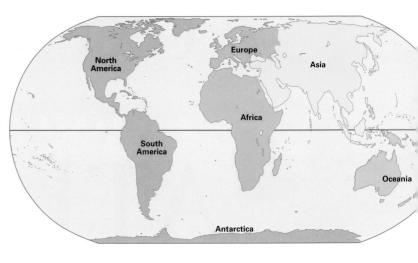

The British Isles

Countries — 18
Land and Water — 19
Climate — 20–21
Population — 22
Farming and Industry — 23
Energy — 24
Communications — 25
Pollution — 26
Scenery and Conservation — 27
Topographic map — 28
Orkney and Shetland Islands — 29
Scottish Highlands and Islands — 30–31
Northern Ireland — 32
Southern Scotland — 33
Northern England — 34–35
Wales — 36
English West Midlands — 37
South East England — 38–39
South West England — 40–41

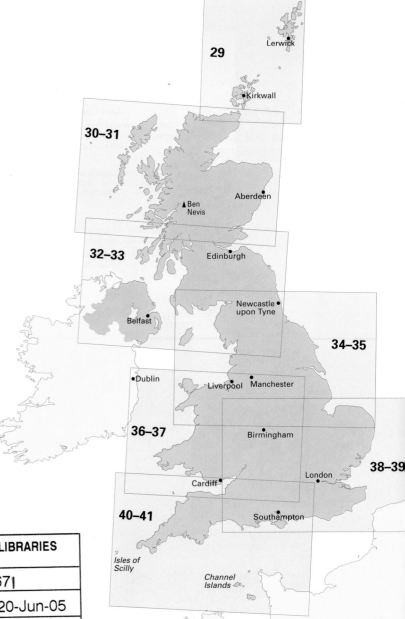

Maps that show general features of regions, countries or continents are called **topographic maps.**
These maps are shown with a light band of colour in the contents list.

For example:

South West England

© Oxford University Press

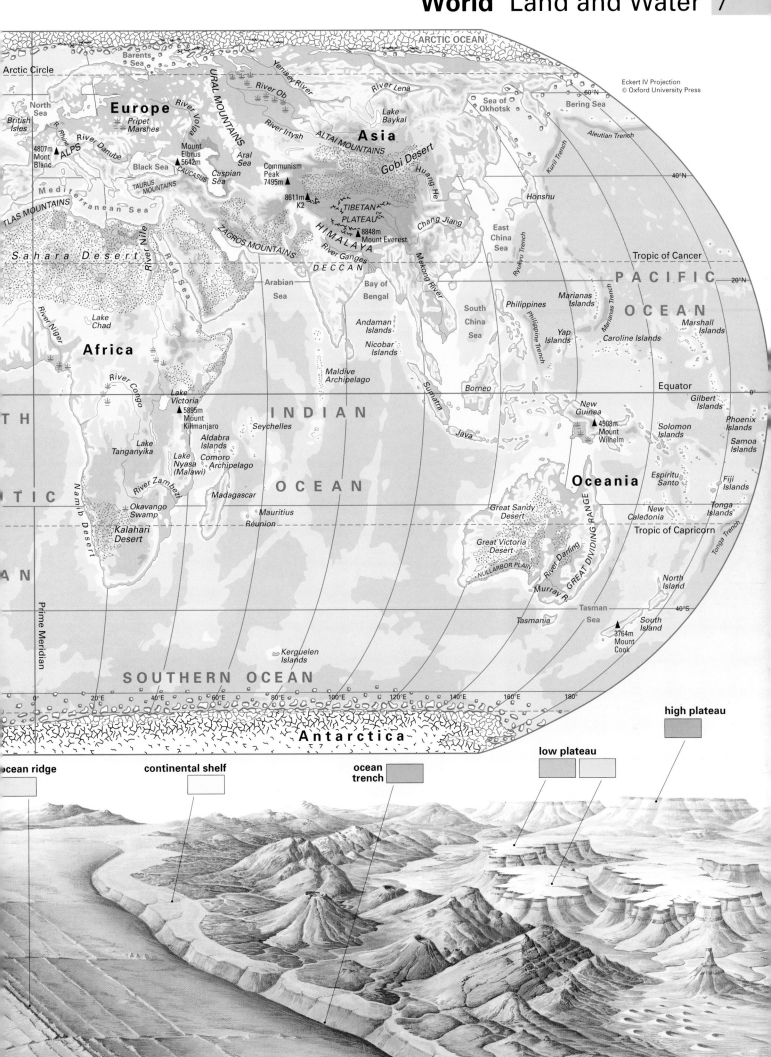

ARCTIC OCEAN

Arctic Circle

Barents Sea

Europe

URAL MOUNTAINS

Yenisey River

River Ob

River Lena

60°N

Sea of Okhotsk

Bering Sea

Eckert IV Projection
© Oxford University Press

North Sea

British Isles

Pripet Marshes

River Volga

River Irtysh

Asia

ALTAI MOUNTAINS

Lake Baykal

Aleutian Trench

Kuril Trench

40°N

R. Rhine
River Danube

4807m Mont Blanc ▲ ALPS

Mount Elbrus ▲5642m

Aral Sea

Communism Peak 7495m ▲

Gobi Desert

Huang-He

Honshu

Black Sea

CAUCASUS

Caspian Sea

8611m ▲ K2

TIBETAN PLATEAU

Chang Jiang

East China Sea

TAURUS MOUNTAINS

M e d i t e r r a n e a n   S e a

ATLAS MOUNTAINS

ZAGROS MOUNTAINS

HIMALAYA

▲8848m Mount Everest

Mekong River

Ryukyu Trench

Tropic of Cancer

River Nile

Red Sea

River Ganges

D E C C A N

P A C I F I C

20°N

S a h a r a   D e s e r t

Arabian Sea

Bay of Bengal

Marianas Islands

Marianas Trench

O C E A N

River Niger

Lake Chad

Andaman Islands

South China Sea

Yap Islands

Philippine Trench

Caroline Islands

Marshall Islands

Africa

Nicobar Islands

Philippines

River Congo

Maldive Archipelago

Equator

Gilbert Islands

0°

Lake Victoria

▲5895m Mount Kilimanjaro

I N D I A N

Borneo

New Guinea

▲4508m Mount Wilhelm

Solomon Islands

Phoenix Islands

Seychelles

Sumatra

Lake Tanganyika

Aldabra Islands

Java

Espíritu Santo

Samoa Islands

Lake Nyasa (Malawi)

Comoro Archipelago

O C E A N

Oceania

Fiji Islands

River Zambezi

Madagascar

New Caledonia

Tonga Islands

ATLANTIC

Okavango Swamp

Mauritius

Réunion

Great Sandy Desert

GREAT DIVIDING RANGE

Tropic of Capricorn

Namib Desert

Kalahari Desert

Great Victoria Desert

River Darling

North Island

Tonga Trench

NULLARBOR PLAIN

Murray R.

Tasman Sea

Tasmania

South Island

3764m Mount Cook

40°S

Prime Meridian

Kerguelen Islands

S O U T H E R N   O C E A N

0° 20°E 40°E 60°E 80°E 100°E 120°E 140°E 160°E 180°

Antarctica

high plateau

low plateau

ocean ridge

continental shelf

ocean trench

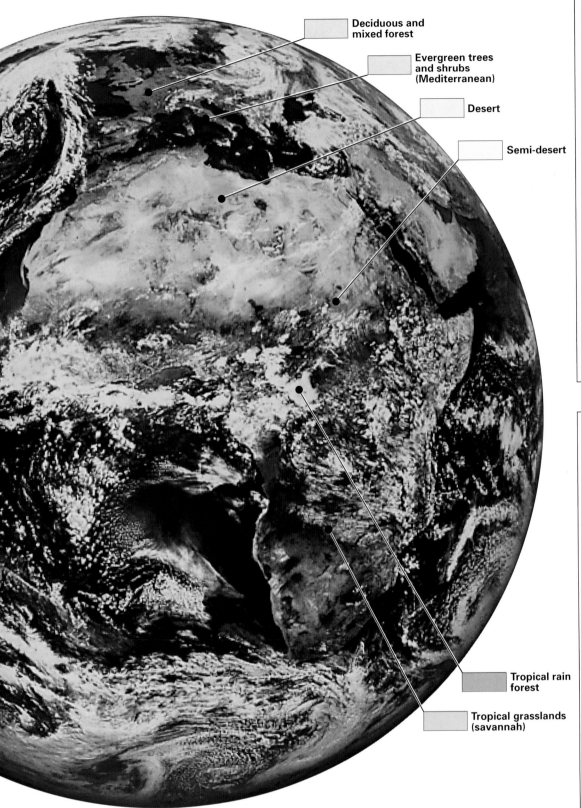

Deciduous and mixed forest

Evergreen trees and shrubs (Mediterranean)

Desert

Semi-desert

Tropical rain forest

Tropical grasslands (savannah)

Climatic regions

Hot tropical rainy

rain all year

monsoon

dry in winter

Very dry

with no reliable rain

with a little rain

Influenced by the sea: warm summers, mild winters

with dry summers (Mediterranean type)

with dry winters

with no dry season

Cool

with dry winters

rain all year

Cold polar

no warm season and fairly dry

Mountain

height of the land strongly affects the climate

Ecosystems

Vegetation types are those which would occur naturally without interference by people

Coniferous forest

cone bearing trees

Deciduous and mixed forest

leaf shedding and coniferous tress

Tropical rain forest

many species of lush, tall trees

Tropical grasslands (savannah)

tall grass parkland with scattered trees

Thorn forest

low trees and shrubs with spines or thorns

Evergreen trees and shrubs

plants and small trees with leathery leaves

Temperate grasslands

prairies, steppes, pampas and veld

Semi-desert

short grasses and drought-resistant scrub

Desert

sand and stones, very little vegetation

Tundra

moss and lichen, with few trees

Ice

no vegetation

Mountains

thin soils, steep slopes and high altitude affects type of vegetation

A Meteosat view of the Earth recorded by a geostationary satellite positioned 36 000 km above the intersection of the Prime Meridian and the Equator

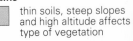

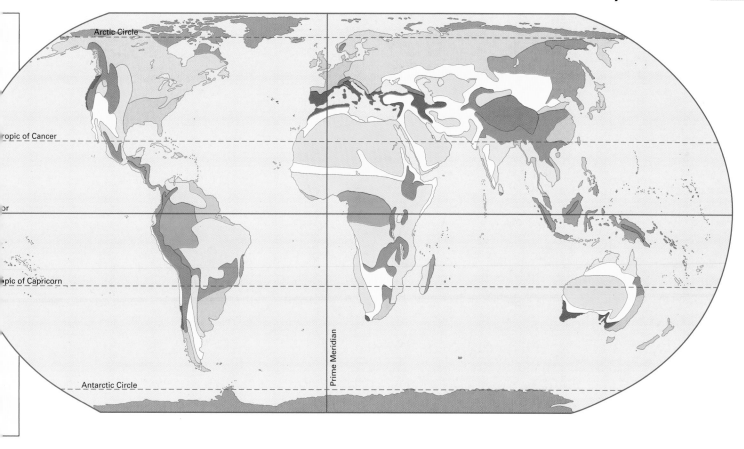

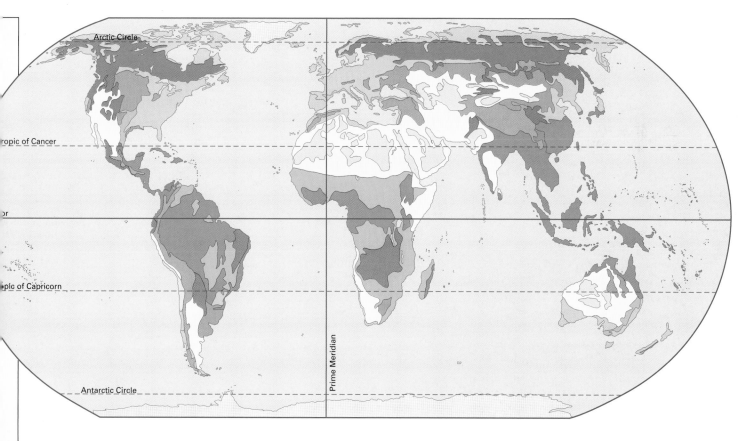

Scale

1: 190 000 000

One centimetre on the map represents
1900 kilometres on the ground
at the Equator.

0   1900   3800   5700 km

Eckert IV Projection   © Oxford University Press

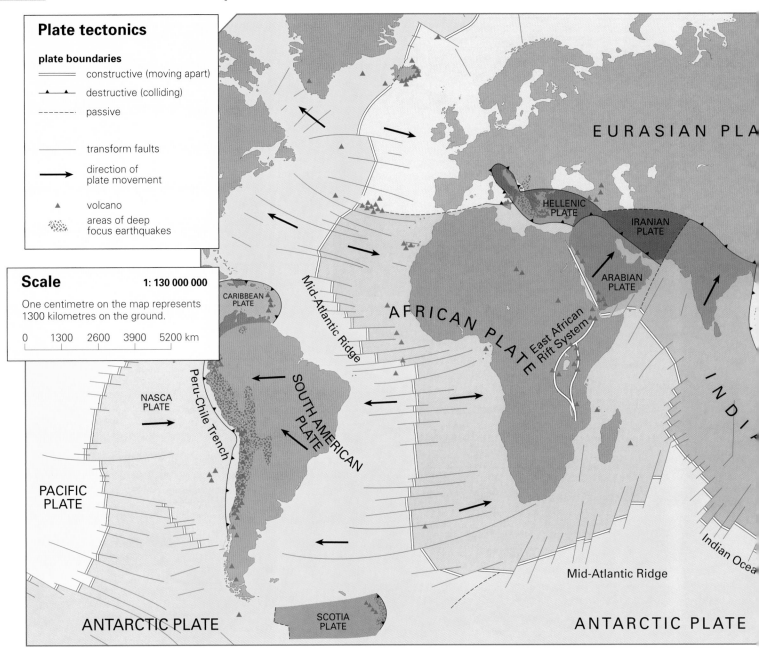

Plate tectonics

plate boundaries

═══	constructive (moving apart)
▲──▲	destructive (colliding)
- - - -	passive
———	transform faults
➜	direction of plate movement
▲	volcano
⣿	areas of deep focus earthquakes

Scale
1: 130 000 000

One centimetre on the map represents 1300 kilometres on the ground.

0   1300   2600   3900   5200 km

EURASIAN PLATE

HELLENIC PLATE

IRANIAN PLATE

ARABIAN PLATE

Mid-Atlantic Ridge

CARIBBEAN PLATE

AFRICAN PLATE

East African Rift System

INDIA

NASCA PLATE

Peru-Chile Trench

SOUTH AMERICAN PLATE

PACIFIC PLATE

Mid-Atlantic Ridge

Indian Ocean

ANTARCTIC PLATE

SCOTIA PLATE

ANTARCTIC PLATE

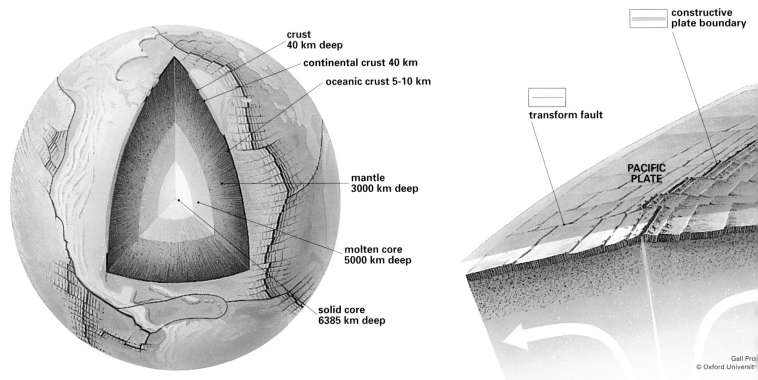

crust 40 km deep

continental crust 40 km

oceanic crust 5-10 km

mantle 3000 km deep

molten core 5000 km deep

solid core 6385 km deep

constructive plate boundary

transform fault

PACIFIC PLATE

Gall Projection

© Oxford University

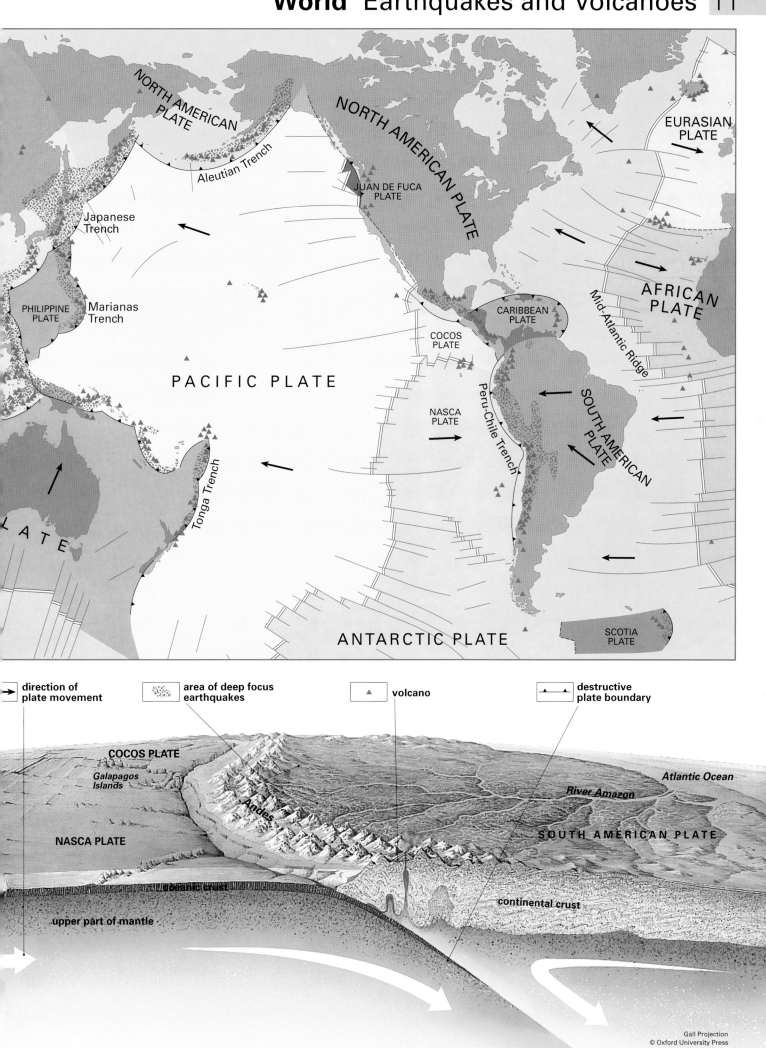

NORTH AMERICAN PLATE

NORTH AMERICAN PLATE

EURASIAN PLATE

Aleutian Trench

JUAN DE FUCA PLATE

Japanese Trench

PHILIPPINE PLATE

Marianas Trench

PACIFIC PLATE

CARIBBEAN PLATE

COCOS PLATE

AFRICAN PLATE

Mid-Atlantic Ridge

NASCA PLATE

Peru-Chile Trench

SOUTH AMERICAN PLATE

...LATE

Tonga Trench

ANTARCTIC PLATE

SCOTIA PLATE

→ direction of plate movement

area of deep focus earthquakes

▲ volcano

destructive plate boundary

COCOS PLATE

Galapagos Islands

Andes

NASCA PLATE

Atlantic Ocean

River Amazon

SOUTH AMERICAN PLATE

oceanic crust

continental crust

upper part of mantle

Gall Projection
© Oxford University Press

Population density

number of people
per square kilometre

high		more than 50
moderate		6 – 49
sparse		1 – 5
very low		less than 1

○ major cities and built up areas of at least 3 000 000 people

— international boundary

Scale

1: 105 000 000

One centimetre on the map represents 1050 kilometres on the ground at the Equator.

0   1050   2100   3150   4200 km

Population structure of the World

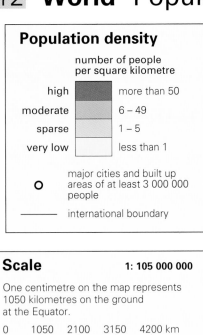

Age

Males   Females

percent of the population in 2004

In 2004 the total world population was approximately 6 372 493 257.

World urban and rural population, 2003

rural   urban

Population, 2004

millions of people

Europe 728	Asia 3875	Africa 885	North America 510	South America 365

Oceania 33

Land areas

thousands of square kilometres

Europe 10 498	Asia 44 387	Africa 30 335	Oceania 8503	North America 24 241	South America 17 832	Antarctica 13 340

World population growth
Past growth (1AD to 2000)

Green Revolution: development of new varieties of cereals such as rice, wheat, and maize increasing food production in many countries

Revolutions in Medicine and Sanitation: many diseases eliminated or reduced

Industrial and Agricultural Revolutions in Europe and North America: technological advances in food production, distribution and exchange for industrial goods

Black Death: bubonic plague spread from Central Asia devastating the populations of China and Europe

1AD 100 200 300 400 500 600 700 800 900 1000 1100 1200 1300 1400 1500 1600 1700 1800 1900 2000

Seattle

Montréal
Toronto
Detroit   Boston
Chicago   New York
                 Philadelphia
San Francisco   Washington DC

Los Angeles
          Phoenix
          Dallas   Atlanta
Monterray Houston
                     Miami

Tropic of Cancer

Guadalajara Mexico City

Equator

Bogotá

Lima

Tropic of Capricorn

Rio de Janei
São Paulo

Santiago Buenos Aires

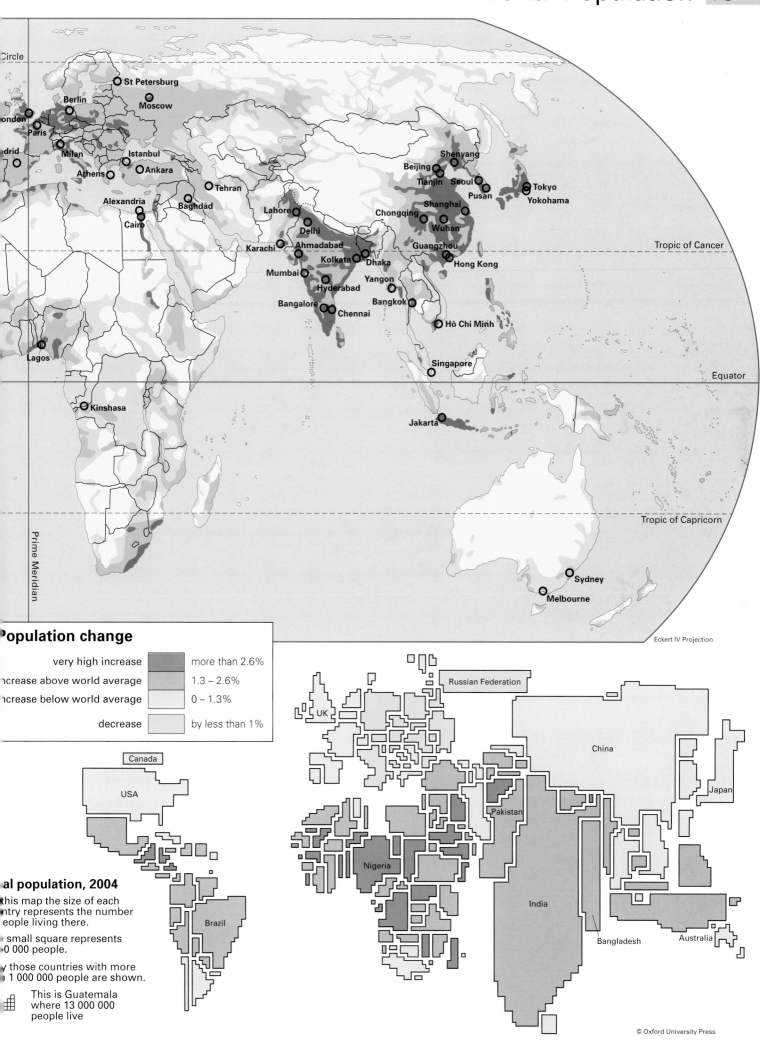

St Petersburg

Berlin
Moscow

ondon
Paris

drid
Milan
Istanbul
Athens
Ankara

Tehran

Alexandria
Baghdād
Cairo

Shenyang
Beijing
Tianjin
Seoul
Pusan
Tokyo
Yokohama
Shanghai
Chongqing
Wuhan
Lahore
Delhi
Karachi
Ahmadabad
Kolkata
Dhaka
Guangzhou
Hong Kong
Mumbai
Yangon
Hyderabad
Bangalore
Chennai
Bangkok
Hồ Chí Minh
Singapore
Jakarta

Tropic of Cancer

Equator

Lagos

Kinshasa

Tropic of Capricorn

Prime Meridian

Sydney
Melbourne

Eckert IV Projection

Population change

very high increase		more than 2.6%
ncrease above world average		1.3 – 2.6%
ncrease below world average		0 – 1.3%
decrease		by less than 1%

Russian Federation

UK

China

Canada

Japan

USA

Pakistan

al population, 2004

this map the size of each
ntry represents the number
eople living there.

small square represents
0 000 people.

y those countries with more
1 000 000 people are shown.

Nigeria

India

Brazil

Bangladesh

Australia

This is Guatemala
where 13 000 000
people live

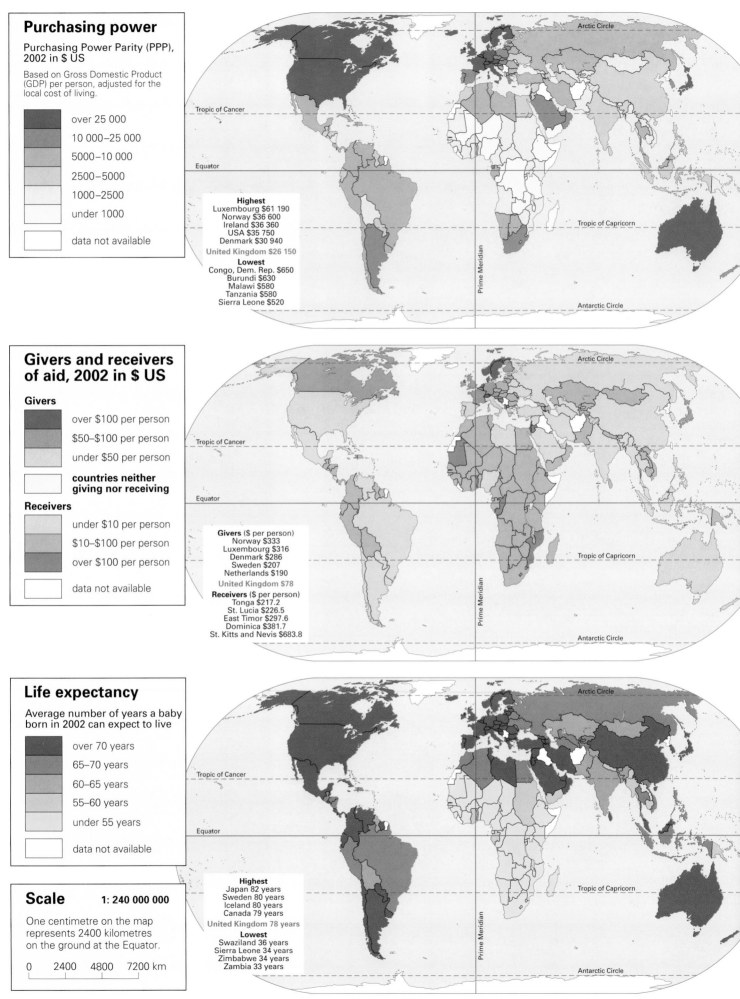

Purchasing power

Purchasing Power Parity (PPP), 2002 in $ US

Based on Gross Domestic Product (GDP) per person, adjusted for the local cost of living.

- over 25 000
- 10 000–25 000
- 5000–10 000
- 2500–5000
- 1000–2500
- under 1000
- data not available

Highest
Luxembourg $61 190
Norway $36 600
Ireland $36 360
USA $35 750
Denmark $30 940
United Kingdom $26 150
Lowest
Congo, Dem. Rep. $650
Burundi $630
Malawi $580
Tanzania $580
Sierra Leone $520

Givers and receivers of aid, 2002 in $ US

Givers
- over $100 per person
- $50–$100 per person
- under $50 per person
- **countries neither giving nor receiving**

Receivers
- under $10 per person
- $10–$100 per person
- over $100 per person
- data not available

Givers ($ per person)
Norway $333
Luxembourg $316
Denmark $286
Sweden $207
Netherlands $190
United Kingdom $78
Receivers ($ per person)
Tonga $217.2
St. Lucia $226.5
East Timor $297.6
Dominica $381.7
St. Kitts and Nevis $683.8

Life expectancy

Average number of years a baby born in 2002 can expect to live

- over 70 years
- 65–70 years
- 60–65 years
- 55–60 years
- under 55 years
- data not available

Highest
Japan 82 years
Sweden 80 years
Iceland 80 years
Canada 79 years
United Kingdom 78 years
Lowest
Swaziland 36 years
Sierra Leone 34 years
Zimbabwe 34 years
Zambia 33 years

Scale   1: 240 000 000

One centimetre on the map represents 2400 kilometres on the ground at the Equator.

0   2400   4800   7200 km

Eckert IV Projection

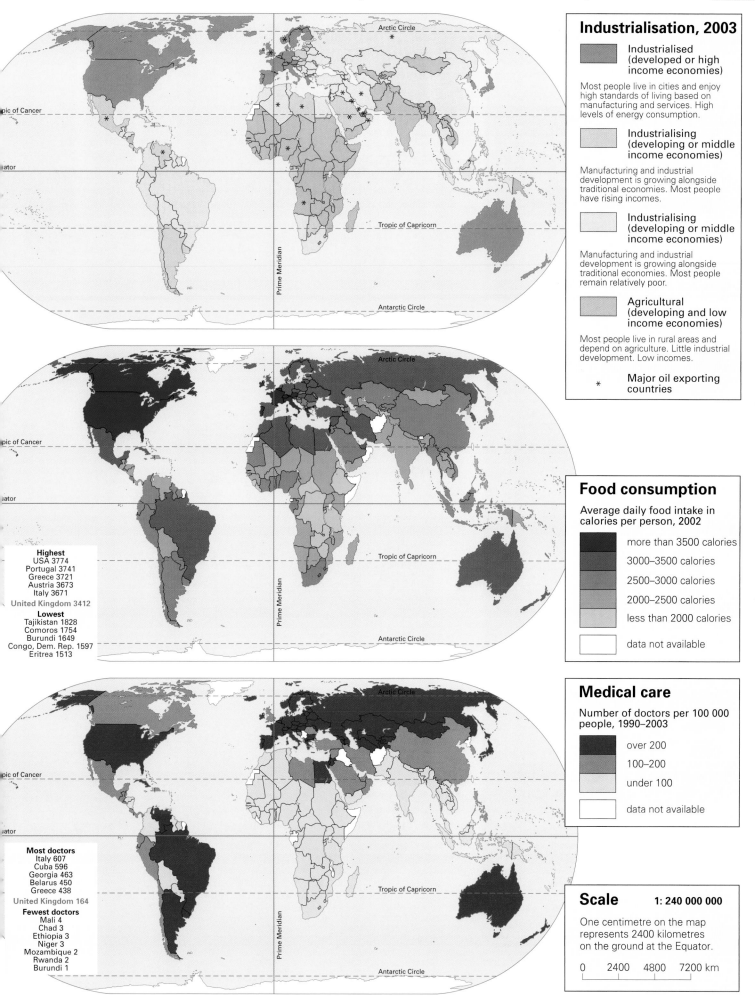

Industrialisation, 2003

Industrialised (developed or high income economies)

Most people live in cities and enjoy high standards of living based on manufacturing and services. High levels of energy consumption.

Industrialising (developing or middle income economies)

Manufacturing and industrial development is growing alongside traditional economies. Most people have rising incomes.

Industrialising (developing or middle income economies)

Manufacturing and industrial development is growing alongside traditional economies. Most people remain relatively poor.

Agricultural (developing and low income economies)

Most people live in rural areas and depend on agriculture. Little industrial development. Low incomes.

* Major oil exporting countries

Food consumption

Average daily food intake in calories per person, 2002

- more than 3500 calories
- 3000–3500 calories
- 2500–3000 calories
- 2000–2500 calories
- less than 2000 calories
- data not available

Highest
USA 3774
Portugal 3741
Greece 3721
Austria 3673
Italy 3671
United Kingdom 3412
Lowest
Tajikistan 1828
Comoros 1754
Burundi 1649
Congo, Dem. Rep. 1597
Eritrea 1513

Medical care

Number of doctors per 100 000 people, 1990–2003

- over 200
- 100–200
- under 100
- data not available

Most doctors
Italy 607
Cuba 596
Georgia 463
Belarus 450
Greece 438
United Kingdom 164
Fewest doctors
Mali 4
Chad 3
Ethiopia 3
Niger 3
Mozambique 2
Rwanda 2
Burundi 1

Scale   1: 240 000 000

One centimetre on the map represents 2400 kilometres on the ground at the Equator.

0   2400   4800   7200 km

Eckert IV Projection   © Oxford University Press

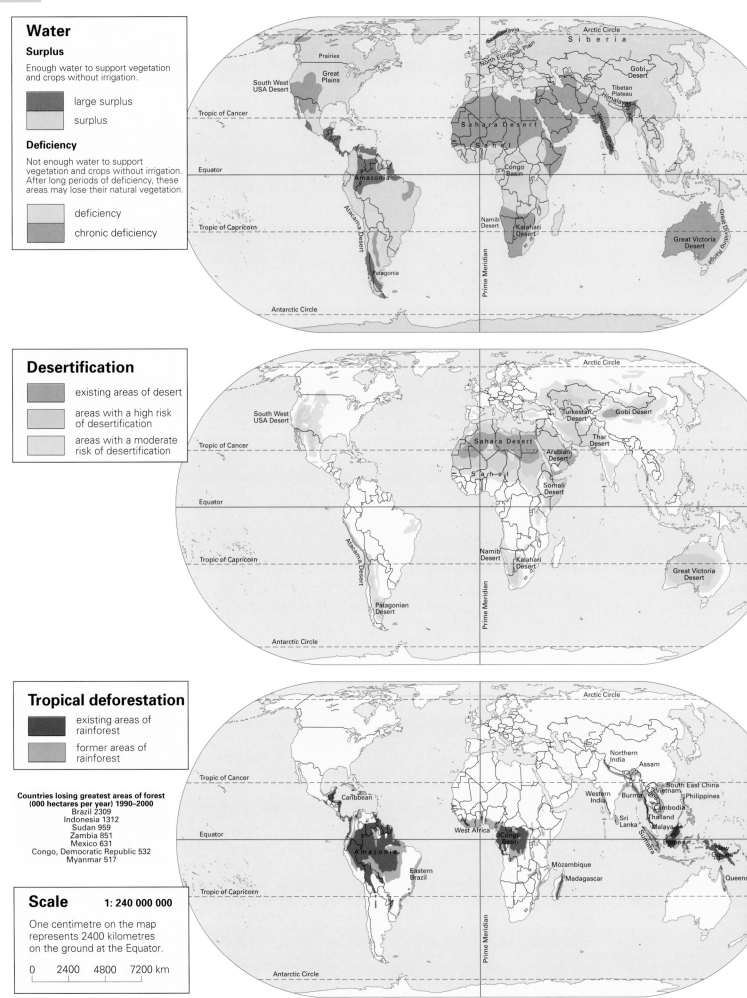

Water

Surplus

Enough water to support vegetation and crops without irrigation.

- large surplus
- surplus

Deficiency

Not enough water to support vegetation and crops without irrigation. After long periods of deficiency, these areas may lose their natural vegetation.

- deficiency
- chronic deficiency

Desertification

- existing areas of desert
- areas with a high risk of desertification
- areas with a moderate risk of desertification

Tropical deforestation

- existing areas of rainforest
- former areas of rainforest

Countries losing greatest areas of forest (000 hectares per year) 1990–2000
Brazil 2309
Indonesia 1312
Sudan 959
Zambia 851
Mexico 631
Congo, Democratic Republic 532
Myanmar 517

Scale   1: 240 000 000

One centimetre on the map represents 2400 kilometres on the ground at the Equator.

0   2400   4800   7200 km

Eckert IV Projection

© Oxford University Press

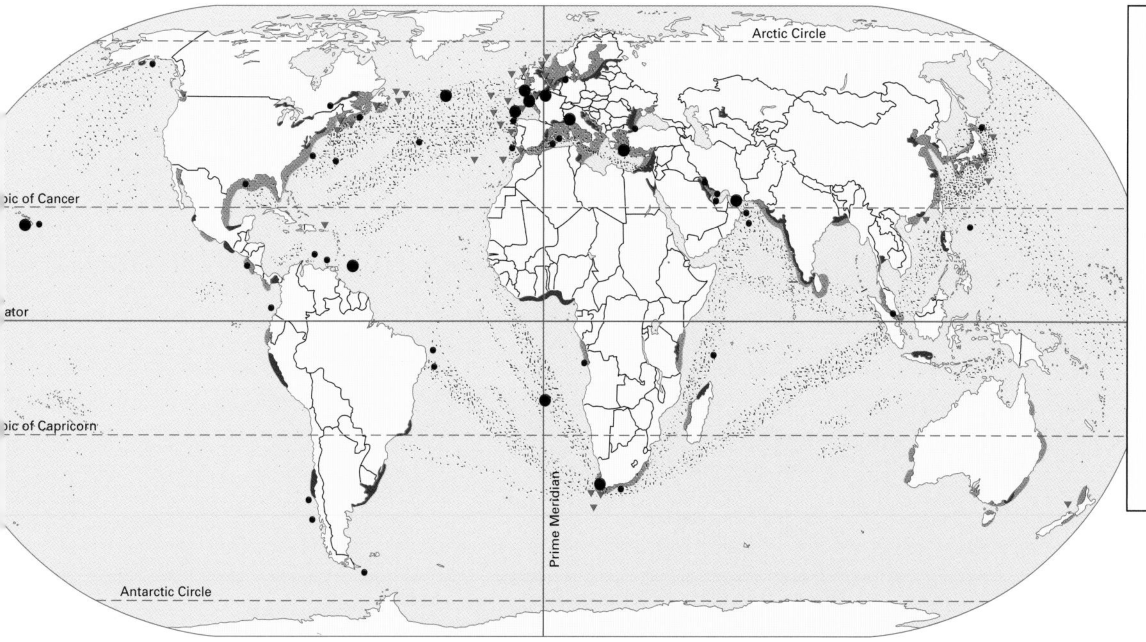

Sea pollution

Oil spills

● over 100 000 tonnes

• under 100 000 tonnes

Oil slicks

pollution from routine tanker and other shipping operations

Other sea pollution

areas severely polluted for all or part of the year

areas persistently affected by pollution

▼ deep sea dump sites

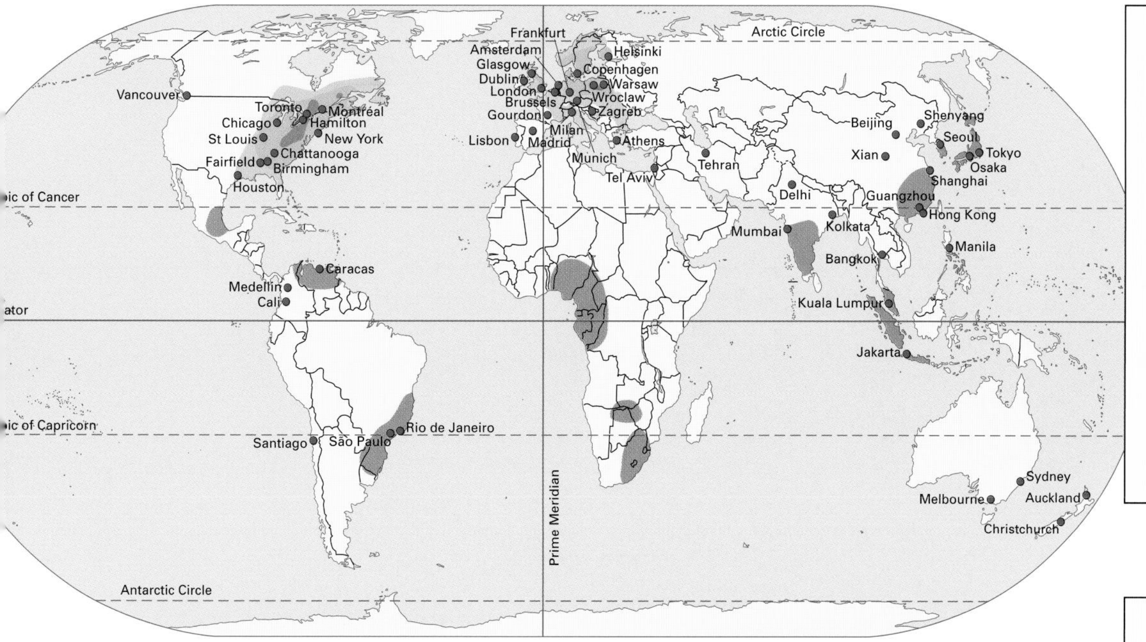

Acid rain

Areas of acid rain deposition

A pH scale measures acidity. 'Clean' rain water is slightly acidic with a pH of 5.6

pH less than 4.2 (most acidic)

pH 4.2 – 4.6

pH 4.6 – 5.0

other areas where acid rain is becoming a problem

Air pollution

● cities where sulphur dioxide emissions are recorded and exceed recommended levels

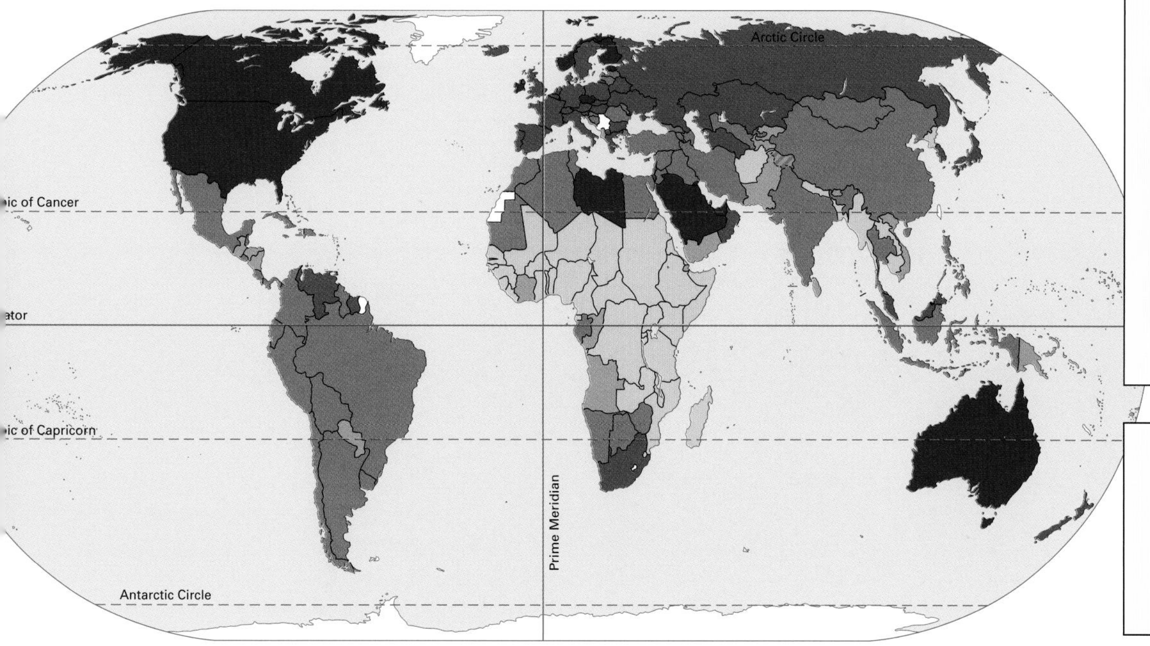

Acid rain map labels: Vancouver, Toronto, Montreal, Hamilton, Chicago, St Louis, New York, Fairfield, Chattanooga, Birmingham, Houston, Caracas, Medellin, Cali, Santiago, São Paulo, Rio de Janeiro, Frankfurt, Amsterdam, Glasgow, Dublin, London, Brussels, Gourdon, Lisbon, Madrid, Milan, Munich, Copenhagen, Helsinki, Warsaw, Wroclaw, Zagreb, Athens, Tel Aviv, Tehran, Delhi, Mumbai, Kolkata, Bangkok, Kuala Lumpur, Jakarta, Beijing, Xian, Shenyang, Seoul, Tokyo, Osaka, Shanghai, Guangzhou, Hong Kong, Manila, Sydney, Melbourne, Auckland, Christchurch

---

Global warming

Carbon dioxide emissions in tonnes per person, 2000

Global warming is caused by adding 'greenhouse gases' (carbon dioxide, methane, CFCs) to the atmosphere

over 10.0

5.0–10.0

1.0–5.0

0.5–1.0

under 0.5

data not available

Scale   1: 240 000 000

One centimetre on the map represents 2400 kilometres on the ground at the Equator.

0   2400   4800   7200 km

Eckert IV Projection

© Oxford University Press

Map labels: Arctic Circle, Tropic of Cancer, Equator, Tropic of Capricorn, Antarctic Circle, Prime Meridian

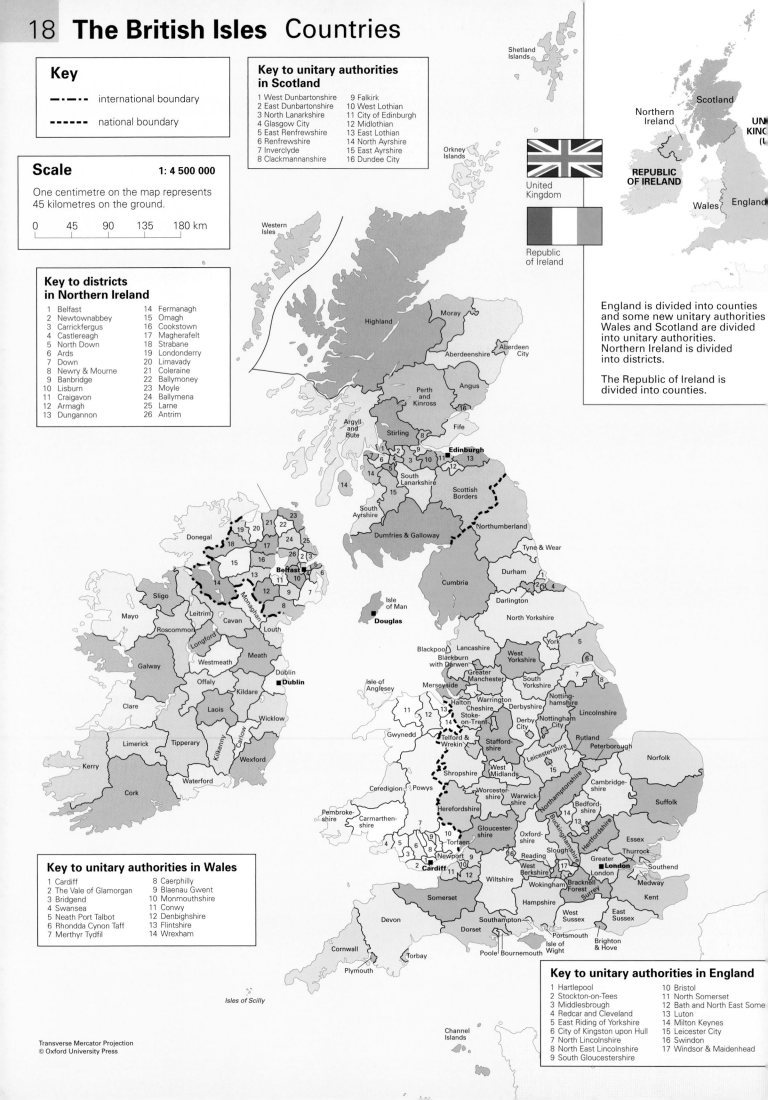

Key

—·—·— international boundary

- - - - - national boundary

Scale

1: 4 500 000

One centimetre on the map represents 45 kilometres on the ground.

0   45   90   135   180 km

Key to unitary authorities in Scotland

1 West Dunbartonshire
2 East Dunbartonshire
3 North Lanarkshire
4 Glasgow City
5 East Renfrewshire
6 Renfrewshire
7 Inverclyde
8 Clackmannanshire
9 Falkirk
10 West Lothian
11 City of Edinburgh
12 Midlothian
13 East Lothian
14 North Ayrshire
15 East Ayrshire
16 Dundee City

Key to districts in Northern Ireland

1 Belfast
2 Newtownabbey
3 Carrickfergus
4 Castlereagh
5 North Down
6 Ards
7 Down
8 Newry & Mourne
9 Banbridge
10 Lisburn
11 Craigavon
12 Armagh
13 Dungannon
14 Fermanagh
15 Omagh
16 Cookstown
17 Magherafelt
18 Strabane
19 Londonderry
20 Limavady
21 Coleraine
22 Ballymoney
23 Moyle
24 Ballymena
25 Larne
26 Antrim

Key to unitary authorities in Wales

1 Cardiff
2 The Vale of Glamorgan
3 Bridgend
4 Swansea
5 Neath Port Talbot
6 Rhondda Cynon Taff
7 Merthyr Tydfil
8 Caerphilly
9 Blaenau Gwent
10 Monmouthshire
11 Conwy
12 Denbighshire
13 Flintshire
14 Wrexham

Key to unitary authorities in England

1 Hartlepool
2 Stockton-on-Tees
3 Middlesbrough
4 Redcar and Cleveland
5 East Riding of Yorkshire
6 City of Kingston upon Hull
7 North Lincolnshire
8 North East Lincolnshire
9 South Gloucestershire
10 Bristol
11 North Somerset
12 Bath and North East Some
13 Luton
14 Milton Keynes
15 Leicester City
16 Swindon
17 Windsor & Maidenhead

United Kingdom

Republic of Ireland

England is divided into counties and some new unitary authorities Wales and Scotland are divided into unitary authorities. Northern Ireland is divided into districts.

The Republic of Ireland is divided into counties.

Transverse Mercator Projection
© Oxford University Press

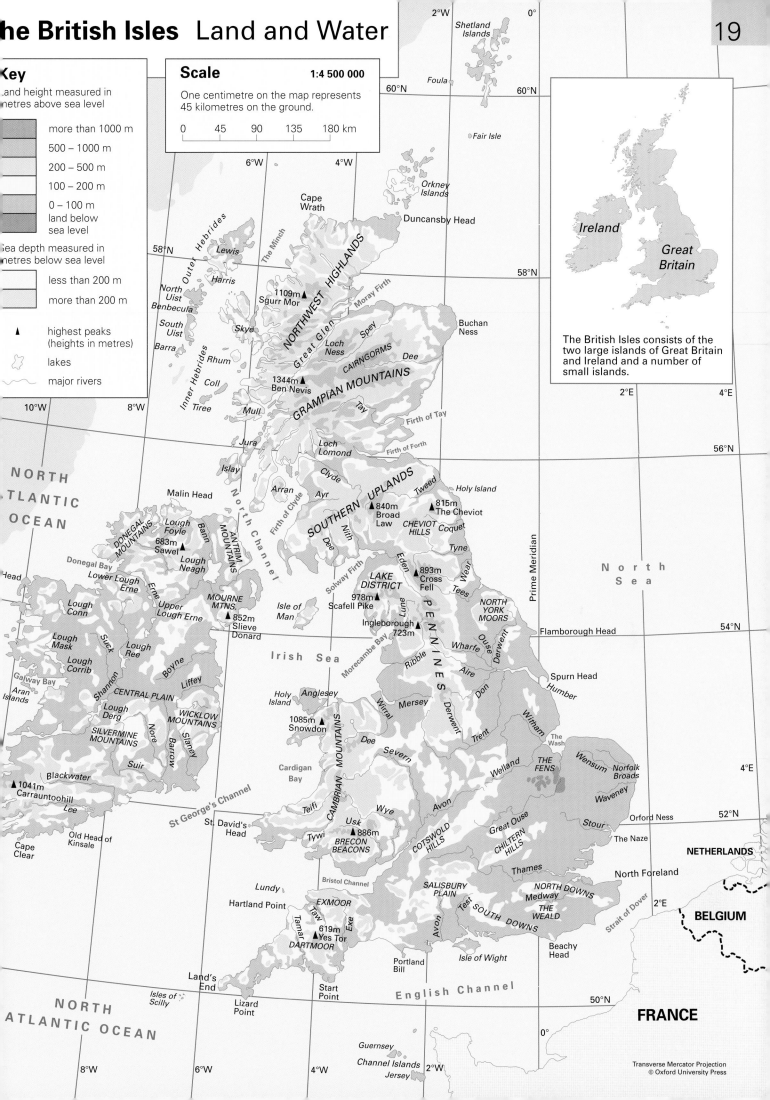

Key

Land height measured in metres above sea level

- more than 1000 m
- 500 – 1000 m
- 200 – 500 m
- 100 – 200 m
- 0 – 100 m
- land below sea level

Sea depth measured in metres below sea level

- less than 200 m
- more than 200 m

- ▲ highest peaks (heights in metres)
- lakes
- major rivers

Scale

1:4 500 000

One centimetre on the map represents 45 kilometres on the ground.

0   45   90   135   180 km

The British Isles consists of the two large islands of Great Britain and Ireland and a number of small islands.

Ireland *Great Britain*

Transverse Mercator Projection
© Oxford University Press

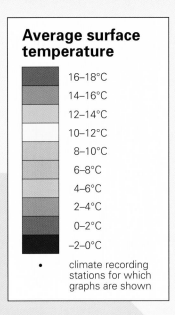

Average surface temperature

	16–18°C
	14–16°C
	12–14°C
	10–12°C
	8–10°C
	6–8°C
	4–6°C
	2–4°C
	0–2°C
	–2–0°C
•	climate recording stations for which graphs are shown

Scale 1: 8 000 000

One centimetre on the map represents 80 kilometres on the ground.

0   80   160   240 km

January temperature

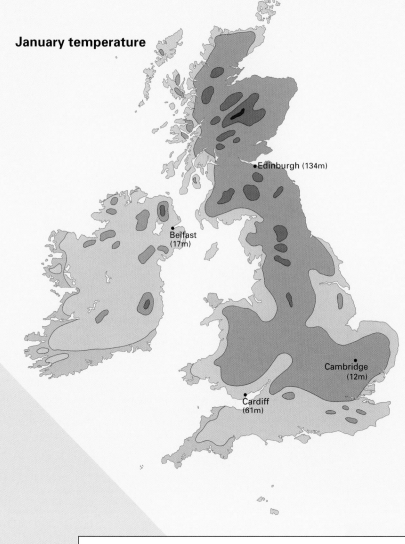

July temperature

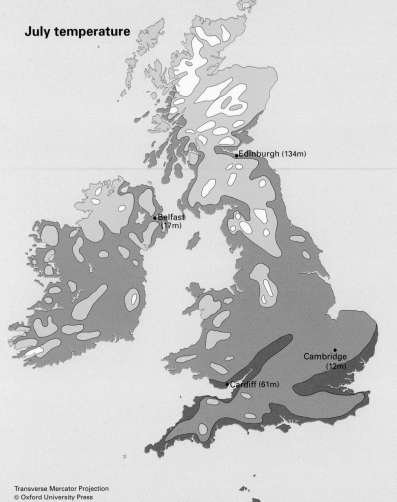

Transverse Mercator Projection
© Oxford University Press

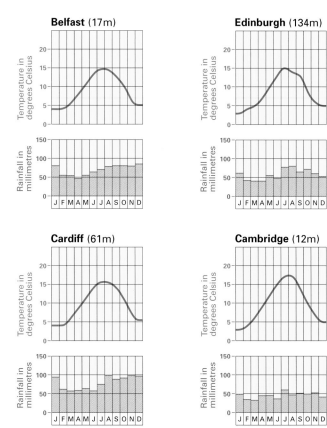

Belfast (17m)

Temperature in degrees Celsius

Rainfall in millimetres

J F M A M J J A S O N D

Edinburgh (134m)

Temperature in degrees Celsius

Rainfall in millimetres

J F M A M J J A S O N D

Cardiff (61m)

Temperature in degrees Celsius

Rainfall in millimetres

J F M A M J J A S O N D

Cambridge (12m)

Temperature in degrees Celsius

Rainfall in millimetres

J F M A M J J A S O N D

Average annual rainfall

- more than 2400 millimetres
- 1200 – 2400 millimetres
- 800 – 1200 millimetres
- less than 800 millimetres
- • climate recording stations for which graphs are shown

Drought and flood

- inland areas in regular danger of flooding
- coastal areas in regular danger of flooding
- areas in regular danger of drought

Scale 1: 8 000 000

One centimetre on the map measures 80 kilometres on the ground.

0   80   160   240 km

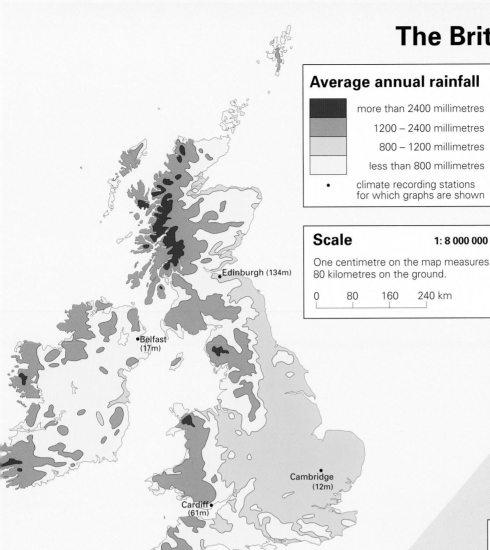

•Edinburgh (134m)

•Belfast (17m)

Cambridge (12m)

Cardiff• (61m)

Scale 1: 16 000 000

One centimetre on the map represents 160 kilometres on the ground.

0   160   320   480 km

water cycle

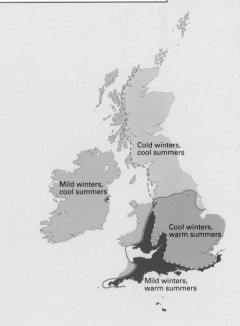

precipitation

clouds

rain

snow

ndensation

ice

aporation

lake

groundwater

river

sea

Arrows show movement of water or change from one state to another.

Cold winters, cool summers

Mild winters, cool summers

Cool winters, warm summers

Mild winters, warm summers

Climate regions

- ----- average January temperature (4°C)
- ——— average July temperature (16°C)

Transverse Mercator Projection
© Oxford University Press

Population structure of the United Kingdom

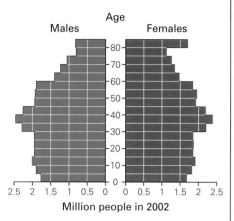

Age

Males   Females

Million people in 2002

Population density, 2002

- ■ more than 1000 people per square kilometre
- ■ 500–1000 people per square kilometre
- ■ 100–500 people per square kilometre
- ■ less than 100 person per square kilometre

- – – – international boundary
- ——— national boundary
- ——— county, unitary authority, or district boundary

Major cities

- ● with more than 6 million people
- ● with 1 million people
- ● with between 400 000 and 1 million people
- • with between 100 000 and 400 000 people

Scale   1: 8 000 000

One centimetre on the map represents 80 kilometres on the ground.

0   80   160   240 km

British Isles population data

United Kingdom	Overall population density 244 people per square kilometre
Republic of Ireland	Overall population density 55 people per square kilometre

Total population 2002
England	50.0 million people
Wales	2.9 million people
Scotland	5.1 million people
Northern Ireland	1.7 million people
United Kingdom	59.7 million people
Republic of Ireland	3.9 million people

Population change

Change in population in each county, region or district, 1982 – 2002

very large increase	■	(more than 20%)
large increase	■	(10–20%)
small increase	■	(less than 10%)
small decrease	□	(less than 10%)
large decrease	■	(more than 10%)

- – – – international boundary
- ——— national boundary
- ——— county, unitary authority, or district bounda

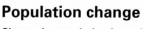

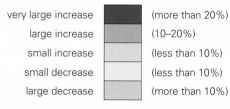

Transverse Mercator Projection
© Oxford University Press

Farming, forestry and fishing

mostly livestock farms (cattle are kept for meat)

mostly hill farms (sheep are kept for meat and wool)

mostly dairy farms (cows are kept for milk)

mostly arable farms (crops are grown)

**Many farms in Britain are mixed farms.
Farmers grow crops and keep animals.**

🌲 forestry (trees are planted for wood)

✳ market gardening (fruit and vegetables are grown)

no farming (built-up areas)

⛴ fishing port

main fishing grounds

‒ ‒ ‒ international boundary

Scale   1: 8 000 000

One centimetre on the map represents
80 kilometres on the ground.

0   80   160   240 km

United Kingdom employment structure

The number of people employed in each activity , 2003

Primary activity
agriculture, farming, fishing,
mining, and quarrying

Secondary activity
manufacturing industry

Tertiary activity
energy and water supply,
construction, transport
and other services

Quaternary activity
information services

0 1 2 3 4 5 6 7 8 9 10 11 12 13
million people

Industry and business

major industrial area

• office and business centre

‒ ‒ ‒ international boundary

—— national boundary

Central Lowlands
Glasgow •Edinburgh

Belfast

Newcastle
Tyneside

Dublin

Greater Manchester
Merseyside
Manchester

Leeds
West Yorkshire
South Yorkshire

East Midlands

Birmingham
West Midlands

South Wales
Cardiff Bristol

Greater London City of London
Croydon

Southampton

sverse Mercator Projection
xford University Press

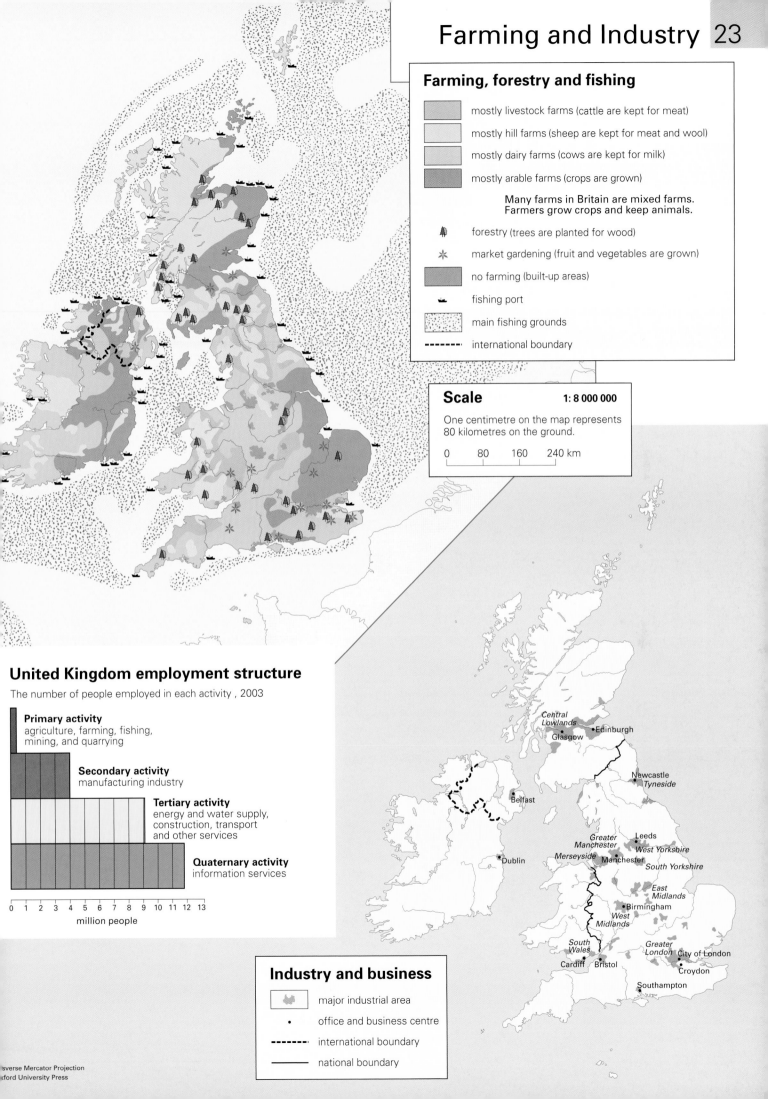

Key

- ● largest coal mines
- ⚒ gas field
- ── gas pipeline
- ⚒ oil field
- ── oil pipeline
- ⬤ largest oil refineries

Largest power stations

- ▲ burning coal, oil, or gas
- ▲ burning peat
- ▲ using water power
- ▲ using nuclear power
- △ using wind power

- ─ ─ exploration boundary
- ▪ ▪ ▪ international boundary
- ── national boundary

Scale

1: 5 750 000

One centimetre on the map represents 57.5 kilometres on the ground.

0   57.5   115   172.5   230 km

UNITED KINGDOM SECTOR

NORWAY

Magnus
Tern
Statfjord
Brent
Ninian
North Alwyn

Shetland Islands

Foinaven

Bruce
Frigg
Beryl

NORWEGIAN SECTOR

Orkney Islands

Birch

Claymore
Piper
Scott

N o r t h
S e a

Shin

Conon
Kilmorack
Peterhead
Affric
Glenmoriston

Forties

Tummel
Breadalbane
Cruachan
Sloy

Fulmar

DANISH SECTOR

Longannet
Torness
Grangemouth
Cockenzie
Hunterston

A t l a n t i c
O c e a n

Windy Standard

Ellington
Blyth Harbour

UNITED

Hartlepool
North Tees
Teesside

Owenreagh
Ballylumford

KINGDOM

REPUBLIC OF IRELAND

Isle of Man

Heysham

Ravenspurn

Lanesboro
Shannon Bridge

Leixlip
North Wall
Poolbeg
Pollaphuca

South Morecambe

Eggborough
Ferrybridge
Saltend
West Sole

IRISH SECTOR

Wylfa
Dinorwig

Coal Clough
Kellingley
Killingholme
South Killingholme

Pickerill

DUTCH SECTOR

Moneypoint
Ardnacrusha
Tarbert

Eastham
Stanlow
Harworth
West Burton
Cottam
Thoresby

Hewett
Leman

Indefatigable

Great Island

Connah's Quay
Fiddler's Ferry

Ratcliffe-on-Soar

Mynydd Cemmaes

Marina
Aghada
Inniscarra
Whitegate

Penrhyddlan
Llidiart-y-waun

Rugeley
Daw Mill

Sizewell

NETHERLANDS

Kinsale Head

Milford Haven
Pembroke
Blackmill
Aberthaw

Tower

Didcot

Shell Haven
Barking
Coryton
Tilbury
Kingsnorth

Hinkley Point

Fawley

Dungeness

BELGIUM

Delabole
Cold Northcott

Wytch Farm

Carland Cross

Channel Islands

F R A N C E

A t l a n t i c
O c e a n

The British Isles

to the
Faroe Islands

Lerwick

Roads, airports, ferries

────	motorway
────	major road
✈	international airport
●────	car ferry route and port
----	international boundary

Bergen

Haugesund

Stavanger

NORWAY

Göteborg

SWEDEN

DENMARK

Esbjerg

Hamburg GERMANY

Inverness

Aberdeen
Dyce Aberdeen

Rosyth

Glasgow M9
M8 Edinburgh

M74

Londonderry Coleraine

Larne Stranraer

Belfast Newcastle

Sligo Belfast

M1

Galway

REPUBLIC
OF IRELAND

UNITED
KINGDOM

M6

Newcastle

Middlesbrough

Dublin Dublin

Dun Laoghaire

Holyhead Liverpool

Manchester M62

Kingston
upon Hull

Grimsby

Tiree

East Midlands

Amsterdam

NETHERLANDS

Cork

Rosslare

Birmingham

Stansted Felixstowe

Hook of Holland

Sullom
Voe

Fishguard

M1

Swansea

M4

Luton

Harwich

Rotterdam

Heathrow

Gatwick

Dover

Zeebrugge

BELGIUM

M5

Poole Portsmouth

Plymouth

Newhaven

Calais

Penzance

Dieppe

Cherbourg

le Havre

Jersey

Caen

Roscoff

St-Malo

FRANCE

Railways, ports

────	main railway
●	terminal or major junction
⚑	major ports
	built-up area
	land over 200 metres
	land under 200 metres
----	international boundary

Inverness

Aberdeen

Dundee

Forth Edinburgh

Glasgow

Londonderry

Larne Stranraer

Sligo Belfast

Newcastle
upon Tyne

Tees and
Hartlepool

Leeds

Liverpool Manchester

Kingston
upon Hull

UNITED
KINGDOM

Sheffield

Grimsby and
Immingham

REPUBLIC
OF IRELAND

Dublin

Nottingham

Leicester

Norwich

Holyhead

Birmingham

Rosslare

Cork Fishguard

Milford
Haven

Cardiff Bristol

London

Dover Channel
Tunnel

Folkestone

Southampton Calais

Weymouth

Penzance

FRANCE

Santander

Bilbao

SPAIN

Scale   1 : 8 000 000

One centimetre on the map represents
80 kilometres on the ground.

0   80   160   240 km

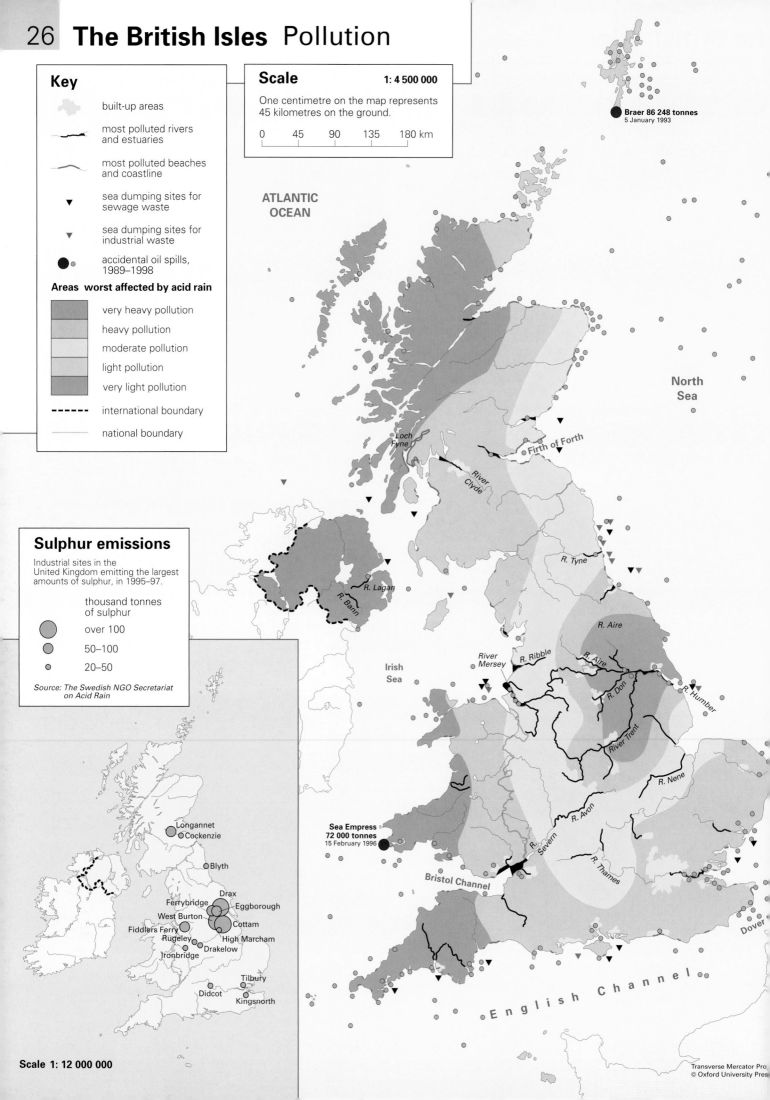

Key

- built-up areas
- most polluted rivers and estuaries
- most polluted beaches and coastline
- ▼ sea dumping sites for sewage waste
- ▼ sea dumping sites for industrial waste
- ● ○ accidental oil spills, 1989–1998

Areas worst affected by acid rain

- very heavy pollution
- heavy pollution
- moderate pollution
- light pollution
- very light pollution
- - - - - international boundary
- ———— national boundary

Scale

1: 4 500 000

One centimetre on the map represents 45 kilometres on the ground.

0   45   90   135   180 km

Sulphur emissions

Industrial sites in the United Kingdom emitting the largest amounts of sulphur, in 1995–97.

thousand tonnes of sulphur

- ● over 100
- ● 50–100
- ● 20–50

Source: The Swedish NGO Secretariat on Acid Rain

ATLANTIC OCEAN

North Sea

Irish Sea

Braer 86 248 tonnes
5 January 1993

Loch Fyne

Firth of Forth

River Clyde

R. Tyne

R. Lagan

R. Bann

R. Aire

River Mersey

R. Ribble

R. Aire

R. Don

R. Humber

River Trent

R. Nene

Sea Empress
72 000 tonnes
15 February 1996

R. Severn

R. Avon

R. Thames

Bristol Channel

Dover

English Channel

Longannet
Cockenzie

Blyth

Drax
Ferrybridge   Eggborough
West Burton   Cottam
Fiddlers Ferry
Rugeley   High Marcham
Drakelow
Ironbridge

Tilbury

Didcot
Kingsnorth

Scale 1: 12 000 000

Transverse Mercator Pro
© Oxford University Press

National Parks

- National Park
- land over 200 metres
- land under 200 metres
- major built-up area
- ------ international boundary
- —— national boundary

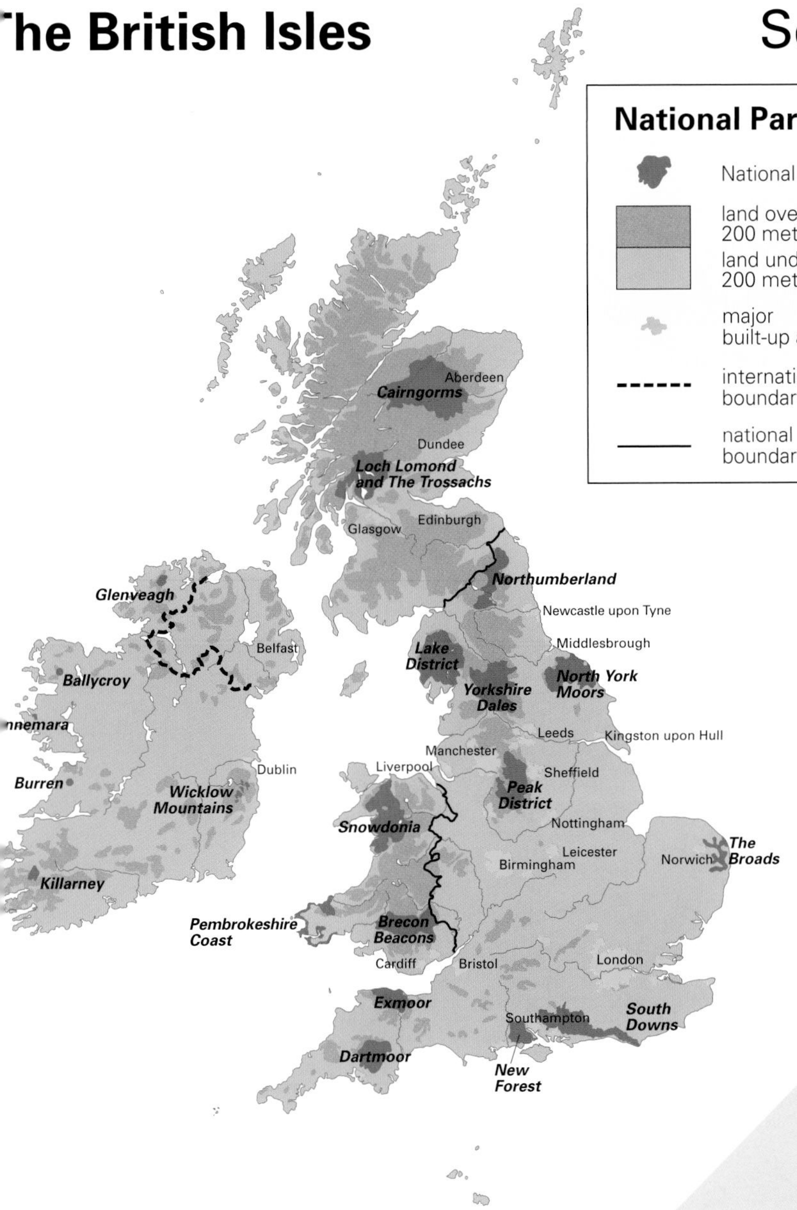

World Heritage Sites

Sites and monuments of world-wide natural (★) and cultural heritage (★), considered to be of such exceptional interest and value that their protection is agreed by international cooperation.

National Parks map labels:

Cairngorms
Aberdeen
Dundee
Loch Lomond and The Trossachs
Edinburgh
Glasgow
Glenveagh
Belfast
Northumberland
Newcastle upon Tyne
Ballycroy
Middlesbrough
Lake District
Yorkshire Dales
North York Moors
nnemara
Burren
Dublin
Wicklow Mountains
Liverpool
Manchester
Leeds
Kingston upon Hull
Sheffield
Snowdonia
Peak District
Nottingham
Killarney
Leicester
Birmingham
Norwich
The Broads
Pembrokeshire Coast
Brecon Beacons
Cardiff
Bristol
London
Exmoor
Southampton
South Downs
Dartmoor
New Forest

World Heritage Sites labels:

The Heart of Neolithic Orkney
St Kilda
Giant's Causeway
New Lanark
Old and New Towns of Edinburgh
Hadrian's Wall
Durham Castle/Cathedral
Archaeological Ensemble of the Bend of the Boyne
Liverpool Maritime Mercantile City
Fountain's Abbey/Studley Royal Park
Saltaire
Derwent Valley Mills
Castles/Town Walls of King Edward
Ironbridge Gorge
Blenheim Palace
Tower of London
Blaenavon
Bath
Kew Gardens
Maritime Greenwich
Stonehenge/Avebury
Canterbury Cathedral
Dorset and East Devon Coast
Westminster Palace/Abbey

Scale

1 : 8 000 000

One centimetre on the map represents 80 kilometres on the ground.

| 0 | 80 | 160 | 240 km |

Other protected areas

- Areas of Outstanding Natural Beauty (England, Wales, Northern Ireland); National Scenic Areas (Scotland)
- Heritage Coast (England and Wales); Coastal Conservation Zones (Scotland); Conservation designated coast (Northern Ireland);
- major built-up area
- ------ international boundary
- —— national boundary

Other protected areas map labels:

South Lewis, Harris and North Uist
Wester Ross
Ben Nevis and Glen Coe
Jura
Upper Tweeddale
Antrim Coast and Glens
Sperrin
North Pennines
Mourne
Nidderdale
Forest of Bowland
Anglesey
Clwydian Range
Lincolnshire Wolds
Norfolk Coast
Lleyn
Shropshire Hills
Suffolk Coast and Heaths
Wye Valley
Cotswolds
Gower
North Wessex Downs
Chilterns
Surrey Hills
Kent Downs
Cranbourne Chase
High Weald
Blackdown Hills
Bodmin Moor
Dorset
Isle of Wight
Tamar Valley

sverse Mercator Projection
ford University Press

Key

– – – –	international boundary
——	national boundary
═══	motorway and main road
——	railway
✈	main airport
〜	river
🝊	lake
▲	peak or highest point

towns

⬠	built-up areas
■	largest towns
●	large towns
•	other towns

Land height

measured in metres above sea level

	more than 1000 m
	500 – 1000 m
	200 – 500 m
	100 – 200 m
	less than 100 m
	land below sea level

Scale   1: 4 500 000

One centimetre on the map represents
45 kilometres on the ground.

0   45   90   135   180 km

© Oxford University Press
Transverse Mercator Projection

Key

- – – – county or unitary authority boundary
- motorway and main road
- railway
- ⊕ main airport
- river
- lake
- ▲ peak or highest point

owns

- • other towns

Land height

measured in metres above sea level

- 200 – 500 m
- 100 – 200 m
- less than 100 m

cale

1: 1 000 000

centimetre on the map represents
ometres on the ground.

10   20   30   40   50 km

NORTH

ATLANTIC

OCEAN

Herma Ness

Haroldswick

Unst

Point of Fethaland

Yell Sound

Yell

Fetlar

▲ 449m

Esha Ness

Out Skerries

St Magnus Bay

Whalsay

Muckle Roe

Symbister

Papa Stour

Mainland

SHETLAND ISLANDS

Walls

Bressay

The Deeps

Lerwick

Scalloway

417m

Foula

Sumburgh Head

Fair Isle

Mull Head

Papa Westray

North Ronaldsay

Westray

Sanday

Westray Firth

Rousay

Eday

Brough Head

Stronsay

Stronsay Firth

Shapinsay

Stromness

Mainland

Kirkwall

ORKNEY ISLANDS

Scapa

Ward Hill

479m ▲

Scapa Flow

Rora Head

Hoy

South Ronaldsay

North Sea

Pentland Firth

Dunnet Head

Stroma

Duncansby Head

Strathy Point

John o' Groats

Thurso

Halkirk

Kirkwall

Transverse Mercator Projection
© Oxford University Press

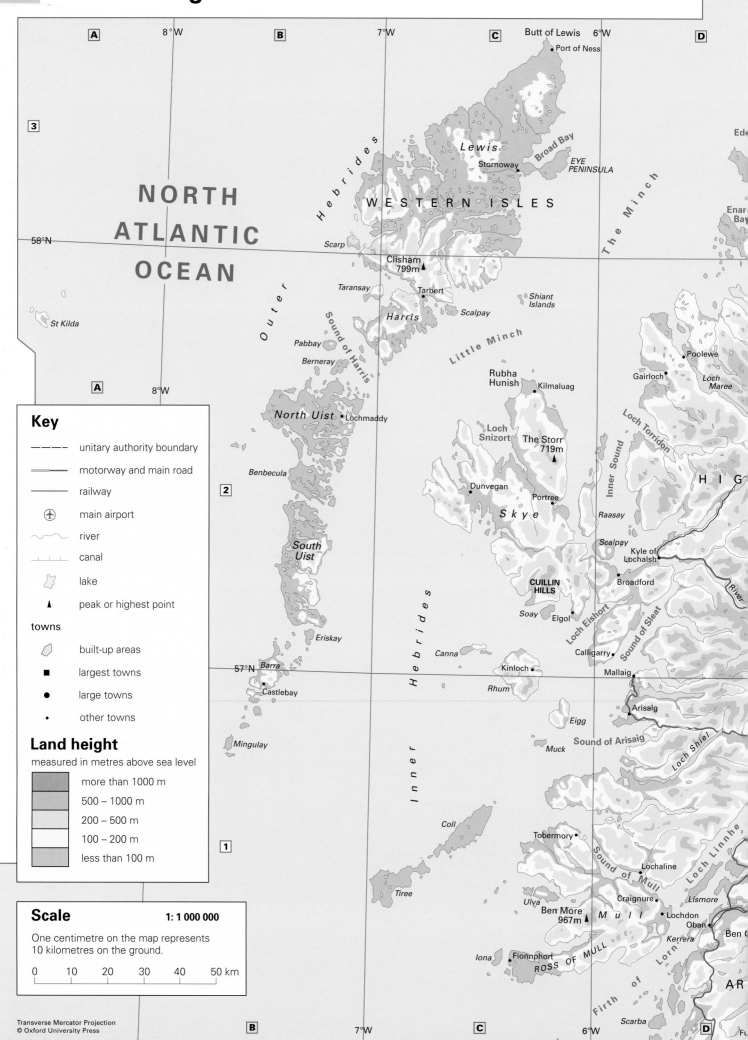

A   8°W   B   7°W   C   Butt of Lewis   6°W   D
• Port of Ness

3

NORTH
ATLANTIC
OCEAN

Hebrides

Lewis

WESTERN ISLES

• Stornoway

Broad Bay

EYE
PENINSULA

The Minch

Enar
Bay

58°N

Scarp

Clisham
799m ▲

Taransay   Tarbert •   *Scalpay*

Harris

Shiant
Islands

St Kilda

Outer

Pabbay

Berneray

Sound of Harris

Little Minch

Rubha
Hunish   • Kilmaluag

Pooleue •

Gairloch •   Loch
Maree

A   8°W

Loch Torridon

North Uist   • Lochmaddy

Loch
Snizort   The Storr
719m ▲

HIG

2

Benbecula

• Dunvegan

Portree •

Inner Sound

Raasay

Scalpay

*South
Uist*

Skye

Kyle of
Lochalsh •

CUILLIN
HILLS

Broadford •

Hebrides

Eriskay

Soay   Elgol •

Loch Eishort

Sound of Sleat

57°N   *Barra*

Canna

Calligarry •

River

Kinloch •

Mallaig •

Castlebay •

Rhum

Arisaig •

Mingulay

Inner

Eigg
•   Sound of Arisaig

Loch Shiel

Muck

Coll

Tobermory •

Hebrides

Lochaline •

Ulva   Craignure •   Lismore •

Tiree   Ben More
967m ▲   *Mull*   Lochdon •   Ben (
Oban •

Kerrera

Iona   Fionnphort •   ROSS OF MULL   AR

Firth   Scarba

of

Lorn

B   7°W   C   6°W   D   Fi

Transverse Mercator Projection
© Oxford University Press

Key

- – – – – unitary authority boundary
- —————— motorway and main road
- —————— railway
- ✈ main airport
- 〜 river
- ⊦⊦⊦⊦ canal
- 🝖 lake
- ▲ peak or highest point

towns

- ⬠ built-up areas
- ■ largest towns
- ● large towns
- • other towns

Land height

measured in metres above sea level

- more than 1000 m
- 500 – 1000 m
- 200 – 500 m
- 100 – 200 m
- less than 100 m

Scale

1: 1 000 000

One centimetre on the map represents
10 kilometres on the ground.

0   10   20   30   40   50 km

North Sea

SCOTLAND

Relief and place names (selected):

Wrath
Ben Hope 927m
Strathy Point
Dunnet Head
Stroma
John o' Groats
3°W
Thurso
Halkirk
Wick
961m Ben Klibreck
Loch nan Clar
Kinbrace
Morven 705m
Lybster
998m Ben More Assynt
River Thurso
River Helmsdale
Helmsdale
inn Dearg
31m
Loch Shin
Lairg
Brora
Bonar Bridge
Dornoch
Tarbat Ness
Dornoch Firth
Tain
rr Mór
1046m Ben Wyvis
Invergordon
Cromarty
Cromarty Firth
Moray Firth
River Meig
Dingwall
Nairn
Forres
Branderburgh
Lossiemouth
Burghead
Elgin
Portknockie
Buckie
Cullen
Portsoy
Banff
Rosehearty
Fraserburgh
R. Spey
Macduff
Fochabers
Aberchirder
Turriff
Keith
River Deveron
Peterhead
Buchan Ness
Rothes
Huntly
Inverness
Charlestown of Aberlour
R. Beauly
Dufftown
Ellon
River Nairn
Grantown-on-Spey
River Spey
MORAY
Drumnadrochit
Oldmeldrum
Loch Ness
ABERDEENSHIRE
Inverurie
River Don
Invermoriston
Aviemore
River Don
Dyce
ABERDEEN CITY
Aberdeen
MONADHLIATH MOUNTAINS
Fort Augustus
CAIRNGORMS
Kingussie
Newtonmore
1244m Cairn Gorm
Aboyne
River Dee
Invergarry
Ballater
Banchory
Braemar
57°N
Loch Lochy
GRAMPIAN MOUNTAINS
1155m Lochnagar
Stonehaven
Ben Alder 1148m
River North Esk
m Nevis
Loch Ericht
PERTH AND KINROSS
Laurencekirk
Inverbervie
ANGUS
Blackwater Reservoir
River Isla
Milton Ness
Loch Rannoch
Ben Lawers 1214m
Brechin
Montrose
Loch Tay
Pitlochry
River South Esk
Kirriemuir
River Tay
Aberfeldy
Blairgowrie
Rattray
Alyth
Forfar
Loch Tay
Coupar Angus
SIDLAW HILLS
Arbroath
Tyndrum
Ben More 1174m
Loch Earn
River Tay
DUNDEE CITY
Carnoustie
Crianlarich
Loch Earn
Crieff
River Earn
Perth
Dundee
ally
COTLAND
BUTE
Loch Katrine
Callander
Auchterarder
Newburgh
St Andrews
FIFE
Auchtermuchty
Cupar
Crail
Tarbet
Ben Lomond 974m
OCHIL HILLS
M90
Glenrothes
Anstruther
Loch Lomond
STIRLING
Dunblane
CLACKMANNAN-SHIRE
Kinross
Loch Leven
Buckhaven
River Forth
4°W
3°W
2°W

Key

- **–·–··–** international boundary
- **– – –** national boundary
- **– · – · –** county, district or unitary authority boundary
- motorway and main road
- railway
- ✈ main airport
- river
- canal
- lake
- ▲ peak or highest point

towns
- built-up areas
- ■ largest towns
- ● large towns
- · other towns

Land height
measured in metres above sea level

- more than 1000 m
- 500 – 1000 m
- 200 – 500 m
- 100 – 200 m
- less than 100 m

Transverse Mercator Projection
© Oxford University Press

Belfast · Edinburgh

REPUBLIC OF IRELAND

NORTHERN IRELAND

Malin Head
INISHOWEN PENINSULA
Slieve Snaght 615m
Tory Island
Tory Sound
Errigal Mountain 752m
Creeslough
Buncrana
Lough Swilly
Lough Foyle
Portrush
Portstewart
Coleraine
COLERAINE
River Bush
Ballymoney
Ballycastle
MOYLE
Rathlin Island
Rathlin Sound
Fair Head
Mull of Kintyre
North Channel
Corsewall Point
Stranraer
Portpatrick
ANTRIM MOUNTAINS
BALLYMONEY
River Bann
River Main
BALLYMENA
Ballymena
LARNE
Larne
Island Magee
Carrickfergus
CARRICKFERGUS
NEWTOWNABBEY
Newtownabbey
Bangor
NORTH DOWN
Donaghadee
Newtownards
ARDS
Strangford Lough
ARDS PENINSULA
Downpatrick
St John's Point
Newcastle
Slieve Donard 852m
DOWN
BANBRIDGE
Banbridge
River Bann
Dromore
Craigavon
Lisburn
LISBURN
Belfast
Belfast Lough
CASTLEREAGH
Lurgan
CRAIGAVON
M1
Portadown
R. Blackwater
Armagh
ARMAGH
Keady
Newtownhamilton
NEWRY AND MOURNE
Newry
Warrenpoint
Carlingford Lough
Kilkeel
LOUTH
Dundalk
Crossmaglen
Clones
MONAGHAN
Monaghan
Castleblayney
Cavan
Lough Oughter
Upper Lough Erne
Lough Macnean Lower
Lough Macnean Upper
Enniskillen
FERMANAGH
Lower Lough Erne
Lough Melvin
Ballyshannon
Lough Allen
LEITRIM
Shannon
Lough Derg
Donegal
OMAGH
Omagh
DUNGANNON
Dungannon
Coalisland
COOKSTOWN
Cookstown
Lough Neagh
Crumlin
Antrim
ANTRIM
Randalstown
M22
Lough Beg
MAGHERAFELT
Magherafelt
529m
Maghera
Sawel 683m
Dungiven
LIMAVADY
Limavady
Londonderry
LONDONDERRY
River Foyle
Strabane
STRABANE
Newtownstewart
River Derg
River Finn
Ballybofey
DONEGAL
Letterkenny
R. Swilly
Kilmacrenan
Tory Island

Iona
Fionnphort
ROSS OF MULL
Firth of Lorn
Oban
Kerrera
Loch Awe
Inveraray
ARGYLL AND
Furnace
Scarba
Colonsay
Oronsay
Scalasaig
Kilmory
Sound of Jura
JURA
Lochgilphead
Tarbert
Tighnabruai
Bute
Rothesay
Clachan
Claonaig
Sound of Bute
Lochranza
Goat Fell 874 m
Arran
Brodi
NORT AYRSH
Kilbrannan Sound
KINTYRE
Port Askaig
Craighouse
Islay
Gigha
Ardminish
Portnahaven
Port Ellen
Ardbeg
Mull of Oa
Campbeltown
Southend
Ails Cra

© Oxford University Press

Scale 1:1 000 000

One centimetre on the map represents
10 kilometres on the ground.

0 10 20 30 40 50 km

Lockerbie · 3°W · 2°W · C · D

NORTHUMBERLAND

Newcastle u

Cram

M6

Annan · 55°N

River Irthing · Haltwhistle · Hexham · R. Tyne

Gates

Was

Carlisle · Brampton

Che

le-Str

Dur

Newton Stewart · 4°W · Castle Douglas · Kirkbean

Glenluce · Dalbeattie · Kirkcudbright

Wigtown

Whithorn

Luce Bay

Wigtown Bay

Solway Firth

Wigton

River Ellen · Maryport

Cockermouth · 931m Skiddaw · Keswick · Derwent Water

CUMBRIA

Penrith

Cross Fell 893m

PENNINES

River Wear · Consett

DURHAM · Spenny

Bishop Auckland · Newton A

Mickle Fell 790m · Appleby-in-Westmorland · Brough

Barnard Castle · DAR · Darli

River Tees

Workington

Whitehaven

St Bees Head

Helvellyn 950m · Ullswater

LAKE DISTRICT

Ambleside · Windermere · Windermere

Kirkby Stephen

Richmond

River Swale

Mull of Galloway

978m Scafell Pike

Coniston Water

Seascale

Point of Ayre

Ramsey

Kirk Michael · Snaefell 620m

ISLE OF MAN

Peel

South Barrule 483m

Douglas

Castletown

Kendal

River Lune

Whernside 737m

NORTH YORKSH

R. Ure · Leyburn

E

Dalton-in-Furness

Barrow-in-Furness

Morecambe Bay

Carnforth

R. Greta · 723m Ingleborough · Pen-y-Ghent 693m · Great Whernsio 704m

N

I

N

E

S

River Wharfe

54°N

Morecambe · Lancaster

Heysham · 560m Ward's Stone

River Aire · Skipton

Har

Irish Sea

Fleetwood

River Wyre

FOREST OF BOWLAND

M6

Barnoldswick

Clitheroe

Ilkley · Keighley

BLACKPOOL

LANCASHIRE · River Ribble

Colne · Nelson

Bradford

Blackpool · M55

Preston

Burnley

Halifax · WE

Lytham St Anne's

Blackburn

BLACKBURN WITH DARWEN

Brighouse · De

Huddersfield

YORK

Leyland · Chorley

M6

Bolton · Bury

Rochdale

M62

Southport

M61

Oldham

Formby

Skelmersdale

Wigan

GREATER MANCHESTER

Manchester

Kirkby

Salford

Sale

Stockport · The Peak 636m

Bootle · MERSEYSIDE · St Helens

Wallasey

Liverpool · Widnes

Warrington

Cheadle

Birkenhead

WARRINGTON

Runcorn · HALTON

M53

R. Mersey

M6

Macclesfield · Buxton

Ellesmere Port

Northwich

CHESHIRE

Carmel Head · Amlwch

Holyhead

Holy Island

ISLE OF ANGLESEY

Anglesey

Bangor

Llandudno · Conwy · Rhyl

Colwyn Bay

FLINTSHIRE · Flint

Chester

Winsford

Crewe

Kidsgrove · STOKE-ON-TRENT

Newcastle-under-Lyme · Stoke-on-Trent

Caernarfon Bay

Caernarfon

Bethesda

R. Conwy

CONWY

Denbigh

Mold

DENBIGHSHIRE

53°N

Snowdon 1085m

LLEYN PENINSULA

Portmadog

Pwllheli

Blaenau Ffestiniog

Bala

River Clwyd · Llangollen

River Dee

Wrexham

WREXHAM

Whitchurch

ENGLA

M6

Harlech

GWYNEDD

CAMBRIAN MOUNTAINS

Bala Lake

POWYS

Lake Vyrnwy

Oswestry

Market Drayton

Uttoxeter

Burton upo

Tren

Barmouth

Dolgellau · Cader Idris 892m

R. Vyrnwy · Welshpool

Shrewsbury

Stafford

Rugeley

Lichfie

Cardigan Bay

R. Dyfi · Machynlleth

WALES

R. Severn

SHROPSHIRE

4°W · B · 3°W

Newport

TELFORD AND WREKIN

Telford

407m · M54 · The Wrekin

Wolverhampton

STAFFORDSHIRE

Cannock

Tamworth

C · 2°W · D

A   6°W   B   5°W   C   4°W   D

Irish Sea

Formb
MERS
Bo
Wallas
Liver
Birkenhe

Malahide
Howth
Dublin
Dún Laoghaire

3

Bray
Greystones

**REPUBLIC OF
IRELAND**

53°N
Wicklow

Arklow

**Irish
Sea**

Carmel Head   Amlwch
Holyhead   **ISLE OF
ANGLESEY**
Holy
Island   *Anglesey*   Bangor
Bethesda

Caernarfon Bay
Caernarfon
Snowdon
1085m

Llandudno
Conwy   Rhyl
Colwyn
Bay   **FLINTSHIRE**
Flint
Denbigh   River Clwyd
CONWY
DENBIGHSHIRE   Wrex

L
L
E
Y
N
P
E
N
I
N
S
U
L
A   Blaenau
Ffestiniog   River Dee
Porthmadog
Pwllheli   Llangollen
Harlech   Bala   Oswes
GWYNEDD   Bala
Lake   Lake
Vyrnwy
905m
Aran Fawddy   R. Vyrnwy
Barmouth   Dolgellau   Welshpool
Cader Idris
892m   **WALES**
Machynlleth   R. Dyfi
R. Severn   Mo

**Cardigan
Bay**

2

52°N

St George's Channel

Aberystwyth   752m
Plynlimon   Newtown
Llanidloes   **SHR**

CEREDIGION   Rhayader   Knig

Aberaeron   Llandrindod
Wells
New Quay   **P O W Y S**

C
A
M
B
R
I
A
N

M
O
U
N
T
A
I
N
S   Builth Wells

Cemaes Head   River Teifi   **MYNYDD
EPPYNT**
Cardigan   Lampeter
Strumble Head   River Teifi   R. Wye   Ha
Newcastle Emlyn
Llandovery
Fishguard   R. Tywi   River Usk   Brecon   811m
**MYNYDD
PRESELI**   **C A R M A R T H E N S H I R E**   **BRECON**   Mo
St David's Head   886m
St David's   **PEMBROKESHIRE**   Carmarthen   Llandeilo   **BEACONS**   Aberg

Haverfordwest   R. Tywi   Ammanford   BLAENAU
St Brides   **MERTHYR   GWENT**
Bay   Kidwelly   Aberdare   **Tydfil**   Abertille
Milford
Haven   Burry
Port   Pontardulais   **RHONDDA**   **MERTHYR   Pontyp
NEATH   TYDFIL**
Pembroke   Tenby   **SWANSEA   PORT TALBOT**   **CYNON**   Cwmb

1

Llanelli   Neath   Rhondda   **TAFF**   CAERPHILLY
Swansea   **New**
Carmarthen
Bay   *G O W E R*   Port   Pontypridd   Caerphilly
Talbot   M4   **CARDIFF**
Worms Head   BRIDGEND   Car
Bridgend

N O R T H   THE VALE OF
GLAMORGAN   Barry

A T L A N T I C

B r i s t o l   C h a n n e l   Weston-su

O C E A N
Bridgwater
Bay
Lynton
Ilfracombe   **D E V O N**   Minehead
Lundy   Dunkery
Beacon
E X M O O R 519m

Key

- – – – national boundary
- – – – county or unitary authority boundary
- ⎯⎯ motorway and main road
- ⎯⎯ railway
- ✈ main airport
- river
- canal
- lake
- ▲ peak or highest point

towns

- built-up areas
- ■ largest towns
- ● large towns
- · other towns

Land height

measured in metres above sea level

- more than 1000 m
- 500 – 1000 m
- 200 – 500 m
- 100 – 200m
- less than 100 m

Scale

1: 1 000 000

One centimetre on the map represents 10 kilometres on the ground.

0   10   20   30   40   50 km

Transverse Mercator Projection
© Oxford University Press

Map labels

Wigan, GREATER MANCHESTER, Oldham, Barnsley, Doncaster, R. Don, River Trent
Manchester, Salford, SOUTH YORKSHIRE, Rotherham, Gainsborough
Sale, Stockport, The Peak 636m, Sheffield, Worksop
Warrington, Cheadle, M1
Northwich, Macclesfield, Buxton, Chesterfield, NOTTINGHAMSHIRE
Winsford, CHESHIRE, Bakewell, DERBYSHIRE, Mansfield, Newark-on-Trent
Crewe, Kidsgrove, Matlock, Sutton in Ashfield
Newcastle-under-Lyme, STOKE-ON-TRENT, Stoke-on-Trent, Ashbourne, Arnold, 53°N
Whitchurch, Uttoxeter, Ilkeston, NOTTINGHAM CITY, Grantham
Market Drayton, Derby, DERBY CITY, Nottingham
Newport, TELFORD AND WREKIN, Stafford, Burton upon Trent, Long Eaton
Shrewsbury, Telford, STAFFORDSHIRE, Rugeley, R. Trent, Loughborough
The Wrekin 407m, Cannock, Lichfield, Coalville, LEICESTERSHIRE, Melton Mowbray, RUTLAND
SHROPSHIRE, Tamworth, LEICESTER CITY, Leicester, Rutland Water
Wolverhampton, WEST MIDLANDS, Walsall, Hinckley, Wigston
Bridgnorth, Dudley, Sutton Coldfield, West Bromwich, Nuneaton, Market Harborough, Corby
540m Brown Clee Hill, Stourbridge, Warley, Birmingham, Bedworth, Kettering
Ludlow, Bewdley, Halesowen, Solihull, Coventry, Rugby, NORTHAMPTONSHIRE
Kidderminster, Kenilworth, Wellingborough
Stourport-on-Severn, Bromsgrove, Redditch, Royal Leamington Spa
Leominster, Droitwich, Warwick, Daventry, Northampton
River Teme, WORCESTERSHIRE, Worcester, WARWICKSHIRE, MILTON KEYNES
HEREFORDSHIRE, Bromyard, River Avon, Stratford-upon-Avon, Towcester, Milton Keynes
Hereford, Great Malvern, Evesham, Banbury, Buckingham, 52°N
Ledbury, Broadway, ENGLAND
Ross-on-Wye, Tewkesbury, Moreton-in-Marsh, Stow-on-the-Wold, Chipping Norton, Leighton Buzzard, LUTON
Cheltenham, BUCKINGHAMSHIRE, Dunstable
Gloucester, COTSWOLD HILLS, Bicester, Aylesbury, Hemel Hempstead
Stroud, GLOUCESTERSHIRE, Witney, River Thame, High Wycombe
Cirencester, OXFORDSHIRE, Oxford, River Cherwell, CHILTERN HILLS
Dursley, Abingdon, Thame, Marlow, Maidenhead
Chipping Sodbury, Malmesbury, Faringdon, Didcot, Henley-on-Thames, WINDSOR AND MAIDENHEAD, SLOUGH
SOUTH GLOUCESTERSHIRE, Wantage, Swindon, Windsor, Slough
Mangotsfield, Chippenham, SWINDON, WEST BERKSHIRE, Reading, Bracknell, Staines
BRISTOL, Kingswood, R. Lambourn, M4, READING, BRACKNELL FOREST
Keynsham, Calne, Marlborough, River Kennet, Newbury, Wokingham, Camberley
BATH AND NORTH EAST SOMERSET, Bath, Devizes, 297m Walbury Hill, Basingstoke, Farnborough, Woking
SOMERSET, Trowbridge, WILTSHIRE, SALISBURY PLAIN, HAMPSHIRE DOWNS, Aldershot, Guildford
Frome, Westbury, Warminster, Andover, Amesbury, HAMPSHIRE, Alton, Farnham
Shepton Mallet, MENDIP HILLS, Wells

Dublin, Manchester, Liverpool, Birmingham, Cardiff

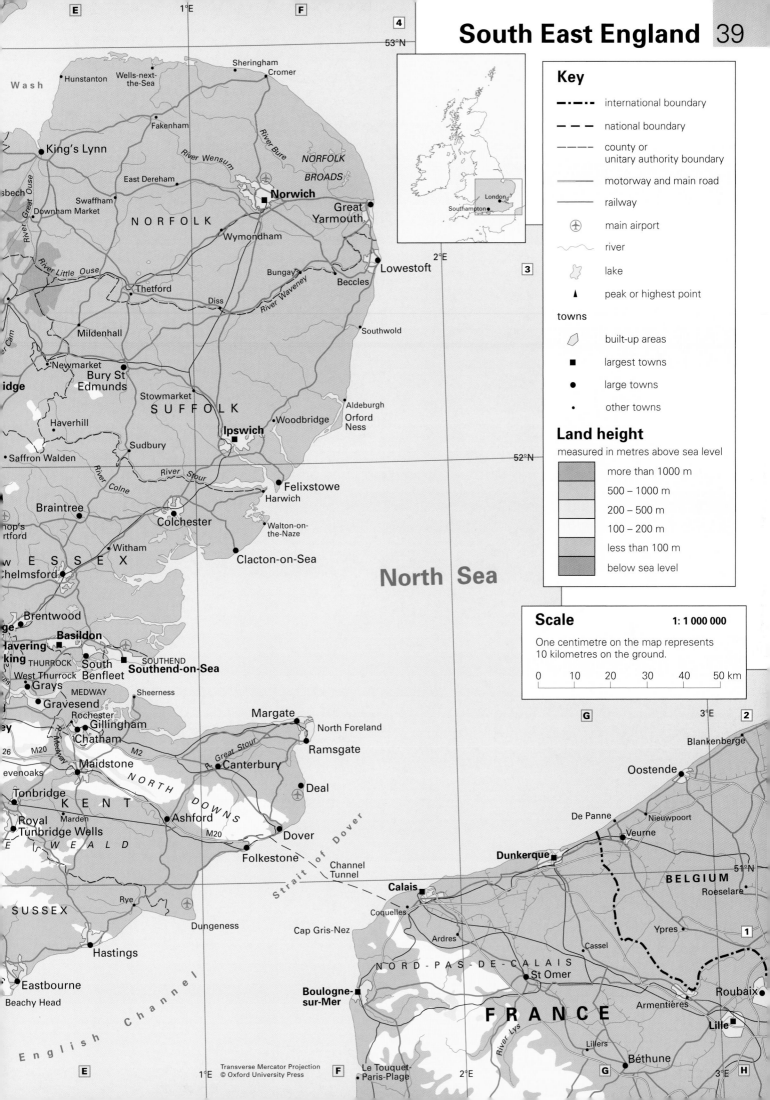

Key

—··—··—	international boundary
—–—–—	county or unitary authority boundary
═══════	motorway and main road
————	railway
✈	main airport
~~	river
⊢⊢⊢	canal
🝝	lake
▲	peak or highest point

towns

⬠	built-up areas
■	largest towns
●	large towns
•	other towns

Land height

measured in metres above sea level

	more than 1000 m
	500 – 1000 m
	200 – 500 m
	100 – 200 m
	less than 100 m

NORTH

ATLANTIC

OCEAN

51°N

NORTH

ATLANTIC

OCEAN

Bristol Chan

Lundy

Lynton

Ilfracombe

Mine
Dunker
▲ 51
River Exe

Braunton
Barnstaple *EXMOOR*
South
Molton

Bideford Bay

● Bideford

Hartland
Point

Great
Torrington

River Torridge

Tiver

D E V O N

River Taw

**B u d e
Bay** ● Bude

Holsworthy

Hatherleigh

Creditor

Boscastle

Okehampton

Exeter

Launceston

Yes Tor
619

River

DARTMOOR

Trevose Head

River Camel

Brown Willy
▲ 420m
*BODMIN
MOOR*

Teign

Bovey Tracey

Teignmou

Padstow

R. Tamar

River Tavy

Tavistock

Newton Abbot

Wadebridge

Bodmin

River Fowey

Liskeard

Buckfastleigh

River Dart

Newquay

CORNWALL

Lostwithiel

Saltash

✈ PLYMOUTH

Totnes

TOR

St Agnes ●

Fal

River

St
Austell

Fowey

Looe

Torpoint

■ **Plymouth**

Dartmouth

Kingsbridge

St Ives ●

Truro ●

Redruth ●
Camborne ●

Penryn ●

Falmouth

**Bigbury
Bay**

Star
Bay

St Just ●

Penzance

Helston

Salcombe

Start

Sennen
Land's
End

Mount's Bay

Mullion

50°N

Bryher

St Martin's
Tresco

St Mary's

Hugh Town

*Isles of
Scilly*

Lizard

Lizard
Point

6°W

5°W

4°W

Scale

1 : 1 000 000

One centimetre on the map represents
10 kilometres on the ground.

0	10	20	30	40	50 km

Cardiff

Southampton

*Isles of
Scilly*

Channel
Islands

49°N

Transverse Mercator Projection
© Oxford University Press

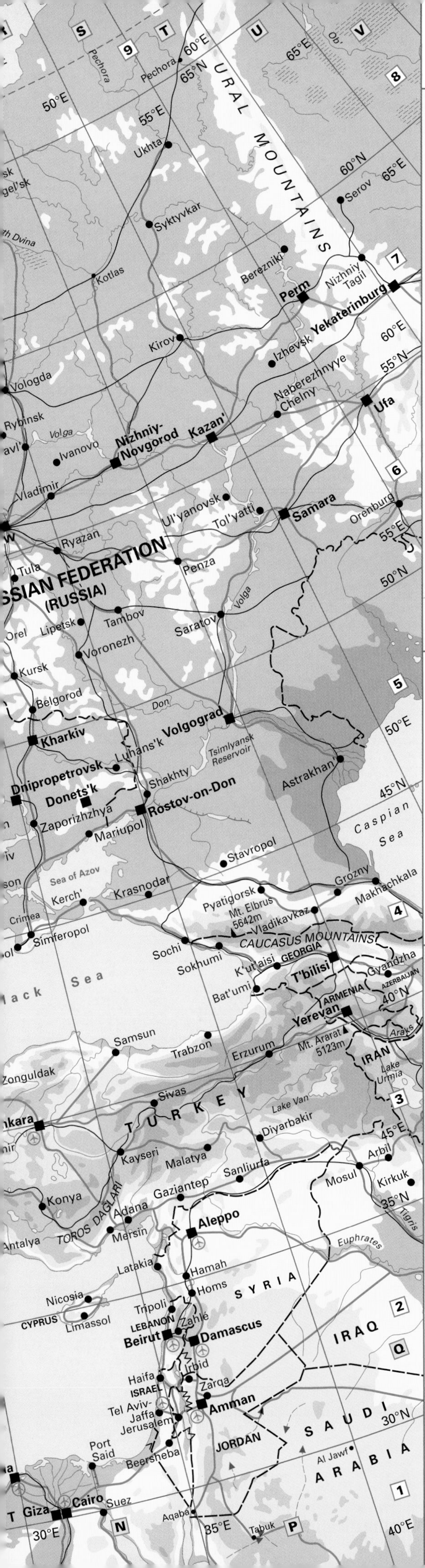

Map labels (left page — Russia/Middle East physical map)

Pechora · S · T · U · 9 · 8 · V

50°E · 60°E · 65°E · Ob'

gel'sk · Pechora · URAL MOUNTAINS · 55°E · 60°N

th Dvina · Ukhta · Serov · 65°N

Kotlas · Syktyvkar · 7

Berezniki · 65°E

Perm · Nizhniy Tagil · 60°E

Kirov · **Yekaterinburg** · 55°N

Izhevsk · 60°E

Naberezhnyye Chelny

Nizhniy- Novgorod · **Kazan'** · **Ufa** · 6

Vologda · Volga

Rybinsk · Ul'yanovsk · Orenburg · 55°N

avl · Ivanovo · Tol'yatti · **Samara** · 50°N

Vladimir · Ryazan · Penza · Volga

RUSSIAN FEDERATION (RUSSIA)

Tula · Tambov · Saratov · 5

Orel · Lipetsk · Voronezh · Don · 50°E

Kursk · Belgorod

Kharkiv · Luhans'k · **Volgograd** · 45°N

Tsimlyansk Reservoir

Dnipropetrovsk · Shakhty · Astrakhan

Donets'k · Zaporizhzhya · **Rostov-on-Don** · 4

Mariupol · Caspian Sea

iv · Sea of Azov · Stavropol

Kerch' · Krasnodar · Grozny · Makhachkala

Crimea · Pyatigorsk · 45°N

ol · Simferopol · Mt. Elbrus 5642m · Vladikavkaz

Black Sea · Sochi · CAUCASUS MOUNTAINS

Sokhumi · K'ut'aisi · **GEORGIA**

Samsun · Bat'umi · **T'bilisi** · Gyandzha

Trabzon · **ARMENIA** · **AZERBAIJAN** · 40°N

Erzurum · **Yerevan** · Araks

Mt. Ararat 5123m · **IRAN**

Zonguldak · Sivas · Lake Van · Urmia · 3

ka · **TURKEY** · Diyarbakir · 45°E

Kayseri · Malatya · Arbil · 35°N

Konya · Gaziantep · Mosul · Kirkuk

TOROS DAĞLARI · Adana · Sanliurfa · Tigris

Antalya · Mersin · **Aleppo** · Euphrates

Latakia · Hamah

Nicosia · Tripoli · **S Y R I A** · 2

CYPRUS · Limassol · Homs · **IRAQ** · Q

LEBANON · Zahlé

Beirut · **Damascus**

Haifa · Irbid · Zarqa

ISRAEL · Tel Aviv- Jaffa · **Amman** · 30°N

Jerusalem · **JORDAN** · **S A U D I**

Port Said · Beersheba

a · **A R A B I A**

Giza · **Cairo** · Suez · Al Jawf · 1

30°E · Aqaba · Tabuk · P

35°E · 40°E · N

The European Union (top-right political map)

SWEDEN · FINLAND

Helsinki · Stockholm · Tallinn · **ESTONIA**

LATVIA · Riga

DENMARK · **LITHUANIA** · Vilnius

REPUBLIC OF IRELAND · Dublin · Copenhagen

UNITED KINGDOM · London

NETHERLANDS · Amsterdam · Berlin · Warsaw

Brussels · BELGIUM · GERMANY · POLAND

Paris · LUXEMBOURG · Luxembourg · Prague · CZECH REP. · SLOVAKIA

FRANCE · Vienna · Bratislava

AUSTRIA · HUNGARY · Budapest · ROMANIA

SLOVENIA · Ljubljana · Zagreb · Bucharest

CROATIA · BULGARIA · Sofia

PORTUGAL · ITALY · Ankara · TURKEY

Lisbon · Madrid · Rome · GREECE

SPAIN · Athens · Nicosia

MALTA · Valletta · CYPRUS

The European Union

— · — international boundary

• national capital

member country of the European Union

countries that have applied to join the European Union

Scale

1: 40 000 000

One centimetre on the map represents 400 kilometres on the ground.

0 · 400 · 800 · 1200 km

Wealth

Gross Domestic Product (GDP) per person, 2002, in $ US

The annual total value of all the goods and services produced in a country divided by the number of people living in that country.

more than 25 000
among the top 20 countries of the world

20 000 – 25 000
among the top 25 countries of the world

15 000 – 20 000
among the top 35 countries of the world

10 000 – 15 000
among the top 50 countries of the world

0 – 10 000
among the top 120 countries of the world

European average
wealth per person:
18 422 US dollars

World average
wealth per person:
7804 US dollars

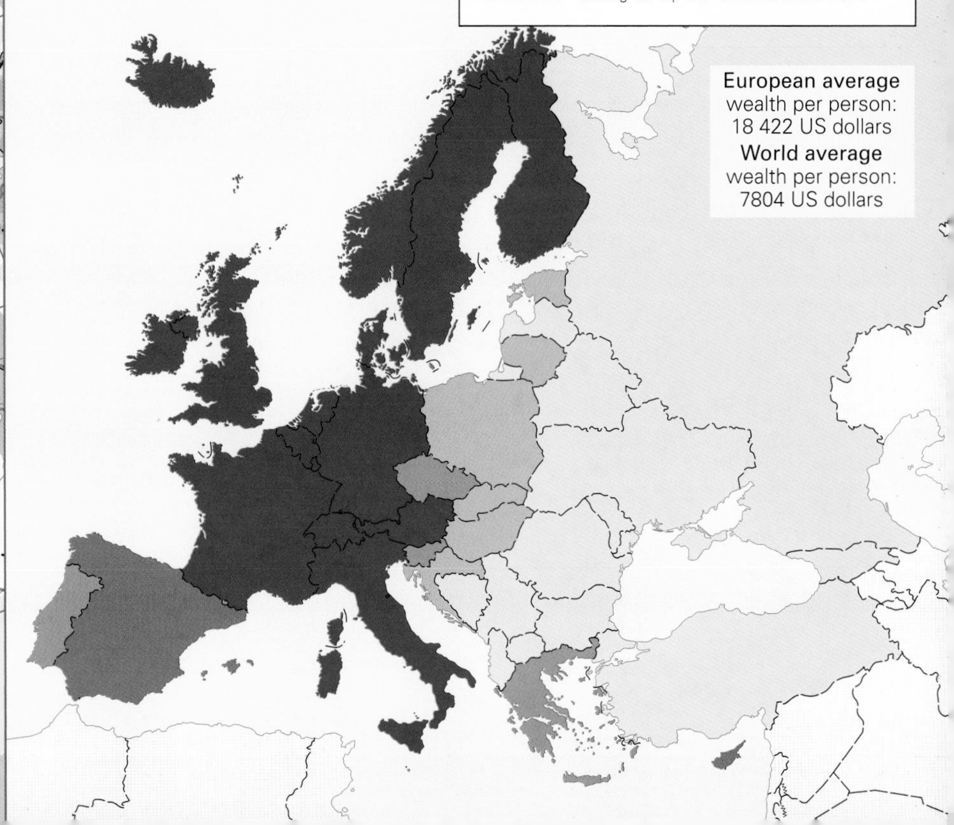

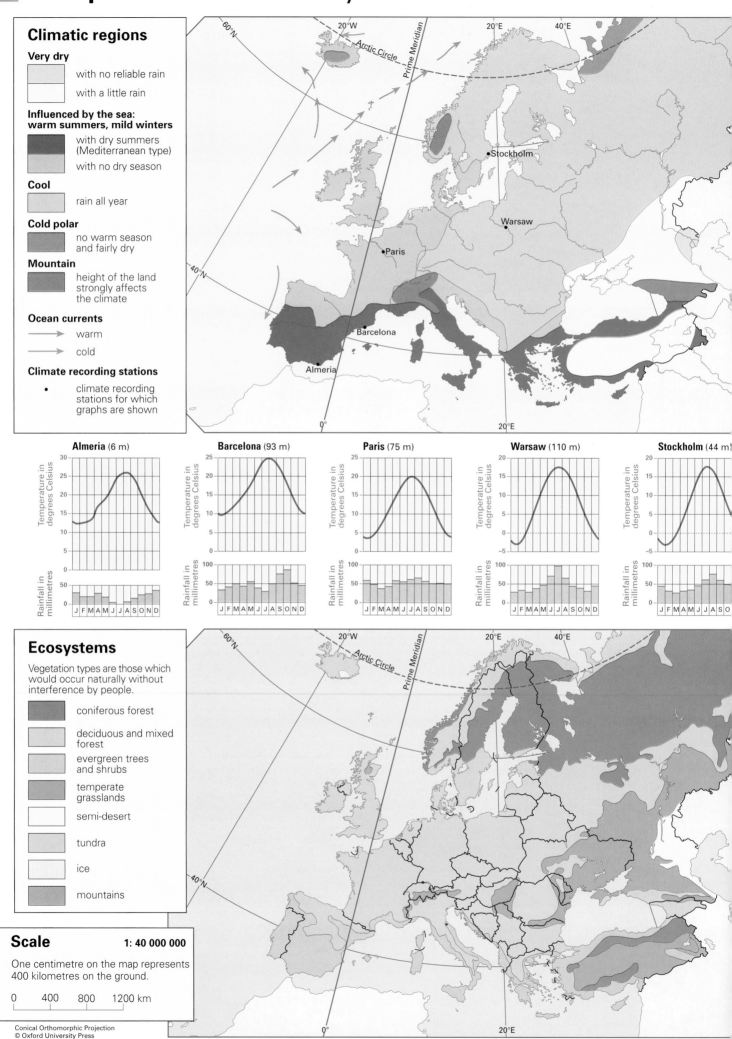

Climatic regions

Very dry

with no reliable rain

with a little rain

Influenced by the sea: warm summers, mild winters

with dry summers (Mediterranean type)

with no dry season

Cool

rain all year

Cold polar

no warm season and fairly dry

Mountain

height of the land strongly affects the climate

Ocean currents

→ warm

→ cold

Climate recording stations

• climate recording stations for which graphs are shown

Almeria (6 m)
Barcelona (93 m)
Paris (75 m)
Warsaw (110 m)
Stockholm (44 m)

Ecosystems

Vegetation types are those which would occur naturally without interference by people.

coniferous forest

deciduous and mixed forest

evergreen trees and shrubs

temperate grasslands

semi-desert

tundra

ice

mountains

Scale

1: 40 000 000

One centimetre on the map represents 400 kilometres on the ground.

0   400   800   1200 km

Conical Orthomorphic Projection
© Oxford University Press

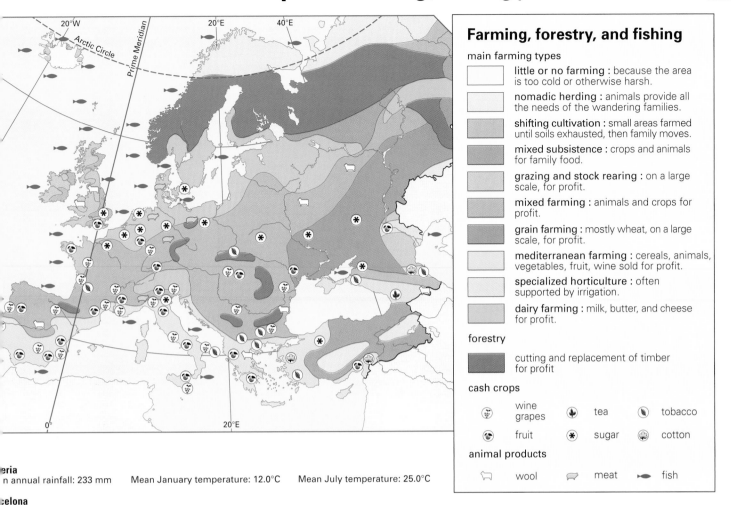

Farming, forestry, and fishing

main farming types

little or no farming : because the area is too cold or otherwise harsh.

nomadic herding : animals provide all the needs of the wandering families.

shifting cultivation : small areas farmed until soils exhausted, then family moves.

mixed subsistence : crops and animals for family food.

grazing and stock rearing : on a large scale, for profit.

mixed farming : animals and crops for profit.

grain farming : mostly wheat, on a large scale, for profit.

mediterranean farming : cereals, animals, vegetables, fruit, wine sold for profit.

specialized horticulture : often supported by irrigation.

dairy farming : milk, butter, and cheese for profit.

forestry

cutting and replacement of timber for profit

cash crops

⊛	wine grapes	♠	tea	◔	tobacco
◍	fruit	✳	sugar	⊕	cotton

animal products

🐑	wool	🐖	meat	⤚	fish

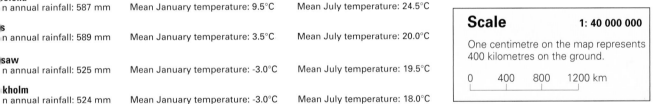

eria
n annual rainfall: 233 mm   Mean January temperature: 12.0°C   Mean July temperature: 25.0°C

celona
n annual rainfall: 587 mm   Mean January temperature: 9.5°C   Mean July temperature: 24.5°C

s
n annual rainfall: 589 mm   Mean January temperature: 3.5°C   Mean July temperature: 20.0°C

saw
n annual rainfall: 525 mm   Mean January temperature: -3.0°C   Mean July temperature: 19.5°C

kholm
n annual rainfall: 524 mm   Mean January temperature: -3.0°C   Mean July temperature: 18.0°C

Scale   1 : 40 000 000

One centimetre on the map represents 400 kilometres on the ground.

0   400   800   1200 km

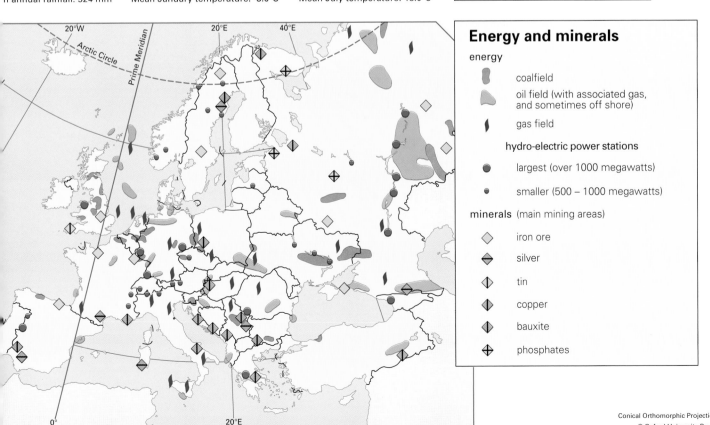

Energy and minerals

energy

◖	coalfield
◗	oil field (with associated gas, and sometimes off shore)
◢	gas field

hydro-electric power stations

●	largest (over 1000 megawatts)
•	smaller (500 – 1000 megawatts)

minerals (main mining areas)

◇	iron ore
⬖	silver
⬔	tin
◈	copper
◉	bauxite
⊕	phosphates

Conical Orthomorphic Projection
© Oxford University Press

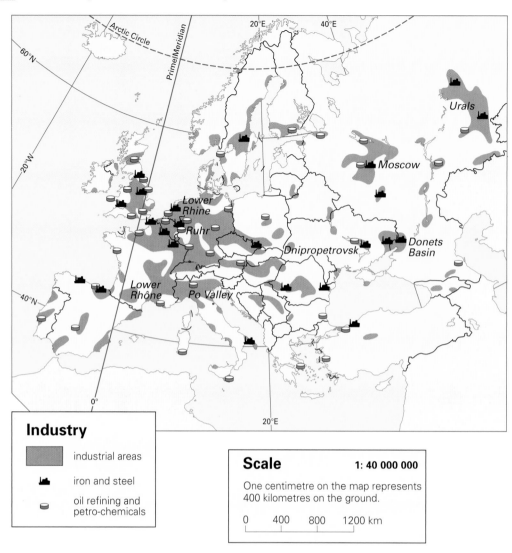

Industry

▨	industrial areas
🏭	iron and steel
⊙	oil refining and petro-chemicals

Scale 1: 40 000 000

One centimetre on the map represents 400 kilometres on the ground.

0   400   800   1200 km

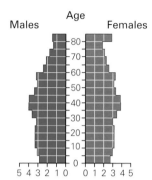

Population structure of the United Kingdom

Age
Males — Females

5 4 3 2 1 0   0 1 2 3 4 5

percent of total population in 2004
Total population : 60.3 million

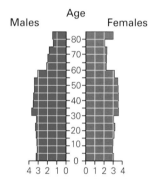

Population structure of France

Age
Males — Females

4 3 2 1 0   0 1 2 3 4

percent of total population in 2004
Total population : 60.4 million

Environmental issues

sea pollution

▨	areas severely polluted for all or part of the year
▨	areas persistently affected by pollution
▼	deep sea dump sites
✱	major oil spills (over 100 000 tonnes)
＊	major oil spills (under 100 000 tonnes)

acid rain

A pH scale measures acidity. Unaffected rain water is slightly acidic with a pH of 5.6

▨	pH less than 4.2 (most acidic)
▨	pH 4.2 – 4.6
▨	pH 4.6 – 5.0

air pollution

◆	cities where sulphur dioxide emissions are recorded and exceed recommended levels

industrial sites emitting the largest amounts of sulphur

◯	over 200 000 tonnes
○	100 000 – 200 000 tonnes
○	50 000 – 100 000 tonnes
○	30 000 – 50 000 tonnes

global warming
addition of greenhouse gases
in tonnes of carbon per person
(look at the world map on page 17)

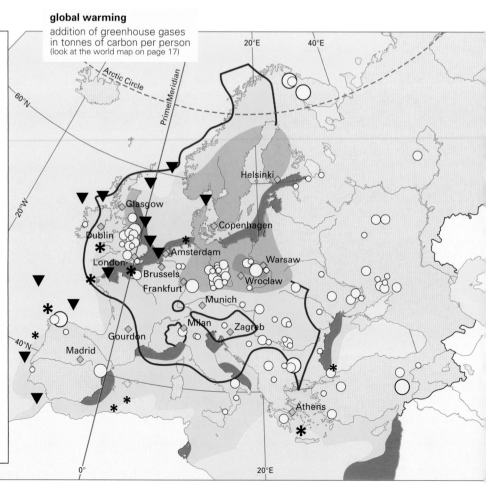

Conical Orthomorphic Projection
© Oxford University Press

Population structure of Germany

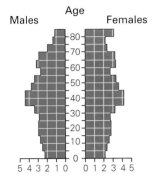

Age

Males — Females

percent of total population in 2004
Total population : 82.4 million

Population structure of Greece

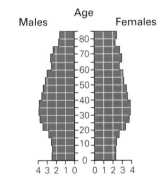

Age

Males — Females

percent of total population in 2004
Total population : 10.6 million

Scale

1: 40 000 000

One centimetre on the map represents
400 kilometres on the ground.

0   400   800   1200 km

Population density

number of people
per square kilometre

high	more than 100
moderate	10 – 100
sparse	1 – 10
very low	less than 1

■ major cities and built
up areas of at least
3 million people

□ cities with
1 – 3 million people

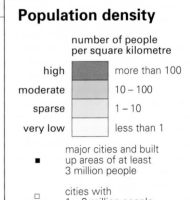

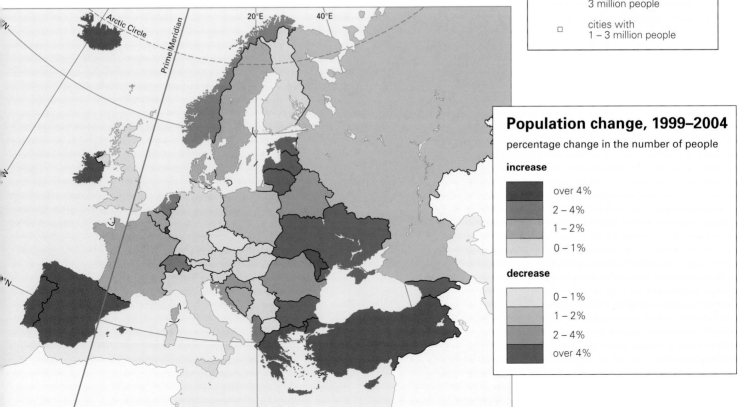

Population change, 1999–2004

percentage change in the number of people

increase

over 4%
2 – 4%
1 – 2%
0 – 1%

decrease

0 – 1%
1 – 2%
2 – 4%
over 4%

Conical Orthomorphic Projection
© Oxford University Press

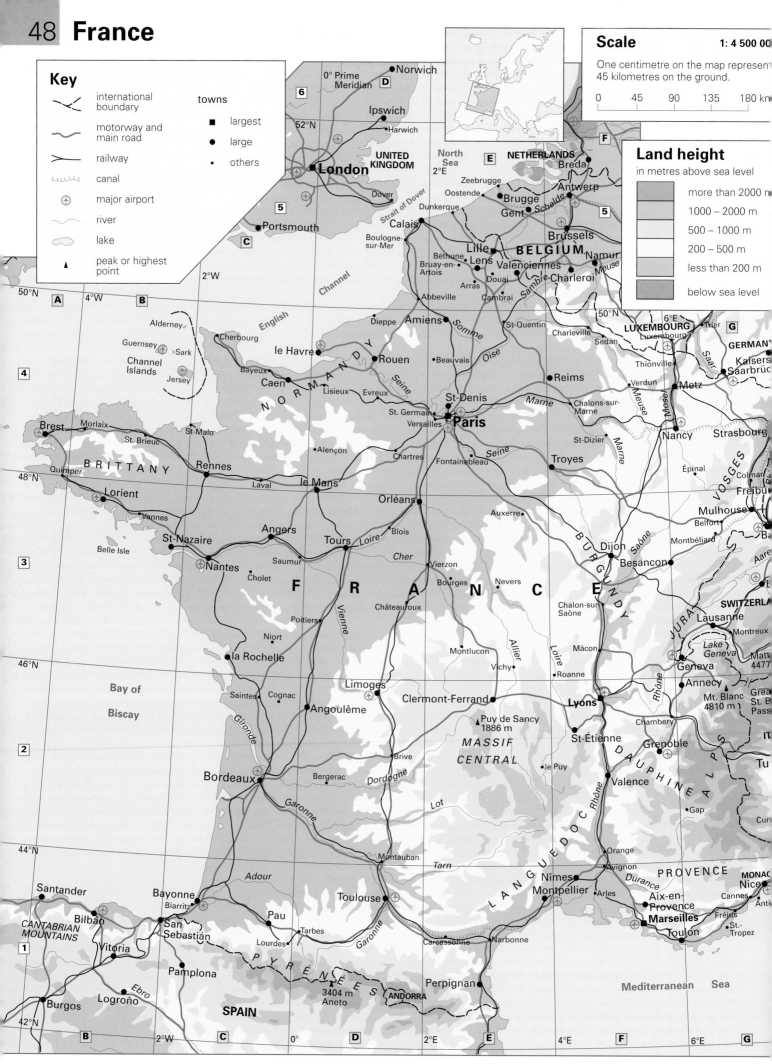

Key

	international boundary
	motorway and main road
	railway
	canal
⊕	major airport
	river
	lake
▲	peak or highest point

towns
- ■ largest
- ● large
- • others

Scale   1: 4 500 00

One centimetre on the map represen
45 kilometres on the ground.

0   45   90   135   180 km

Land height
in metres above sea level

- more than 2000 m
- 1000 – 2000 m
- 500 – 1000 m
- 200 – 500 m
- less than 200 m
- below sea level

Norwich
0° Prime Meridian
Ipswich
Harwich
52°N
UNITED KINGDOM
North Sea 2°E
NETHERLANDS
Breda
London
Zeebrugge
Antwerp
Oostende
Brugge
Gent
Schelde
Dover
Portsmouth
Strait of Dover
Dunkerque
Calais
Brussels
BELGIUM
Boulogne-sur-Mer
Lille
Béthune
Namur
Bruay-en-Artois
Lens
Valenciennes
Meuse
Douai
Charleroi
Arras
Sambre
50°N
Abbeville
Cambrai
LUXEMBOURG 6°E
Channel
Dieppe
Amiens
Somme
St-Quentin
Charleville
Luxembourg
Trier
GERMAN
Alderney
Cherbourg
Oise
Sedan
Kaisers
Guernsey
Sark
le Havre
Rouen
Beauvais
Saarbrüc
Channel Islands
Bayeux
Reims
Thionville
Jersey
Caen
Seine
Verdun
Metz
NORMANDY
Lisieux
Evreux
St-Denis
Marne
Chalons-sur-Marne
Meuse
Nancy
Strasbourg
Brest
Morlaix
Paris
Mosel
St-Malo
St Germain
Versailles
St-Dizier
Marne
Bayeux
BRITTANY
Rennes
Chartres
Fontainebleau
Épinal
VOSGES
Quimper
48°N
Laval
le Mans
Troyes
Freibu
Lorient
Seine
Colmar
Vannes
Orléans
Auxerre
Mulhouse
Angers
Blois
Belfort
B
St-Nazaire
Tours
Loire
Vierzon
Montbéliard
Belle Isle
Saumur
Cher
Dijon
Saône
Besancon
Nantes
Bourges
Nevers
BURGUNDY
Cholet
F   R   A   N   C   E
SWITZERLA
Poitiers
Châteauroux
Chalon-sur-Saône
JURA
Lausanne
Niort
Vienne
Mâcon
Montreux
la Rochelle
Allier
Lake Geneva
Matt
Saintes
Cognac
Montlucon
Loire
Geneva
4477
46°N
Limoges
Vichy
Annecy
Bay of Biscay
Gironde
Angoulême
Clermont-Ferrand
Roanne
Mt. Blanc 4810 m
Grea
St-Étienne
Chambery
St. B
Pass
Brive
Puy de Sancy 1886 m
Lyons
Grenoble
Bergerac
Dordogne
MASSIF CENTRAL
le Puy
DAUPHINÉ ALPS
Bordeaux
Valence
IT
Garonne
Lot
Tu
Rhône
44°N
Montauban
Tarn
Orange
PROVENCE
Adour
Avignon
Santander
Bayonne
Durance
MONAC
Toulouse
Nîmes
Nice
Biarritz
Pau
Garonne
Montpellier
Arles
Aix-en-Provence
Cannes
Bilbao
San Sebastián
Tarbes
LANGUEDOC
Marseilles
Anti
Vitoria
Lourdes
Carcassonne
Narbonne
Toulon
Fréjus
St-Tropez
1
Pamplona
PYRENEES
Perpignan
Mediterranean   Sea
Ebro
ANDORRA
Logroño
3404 Aneto
Burgos
SPAIN

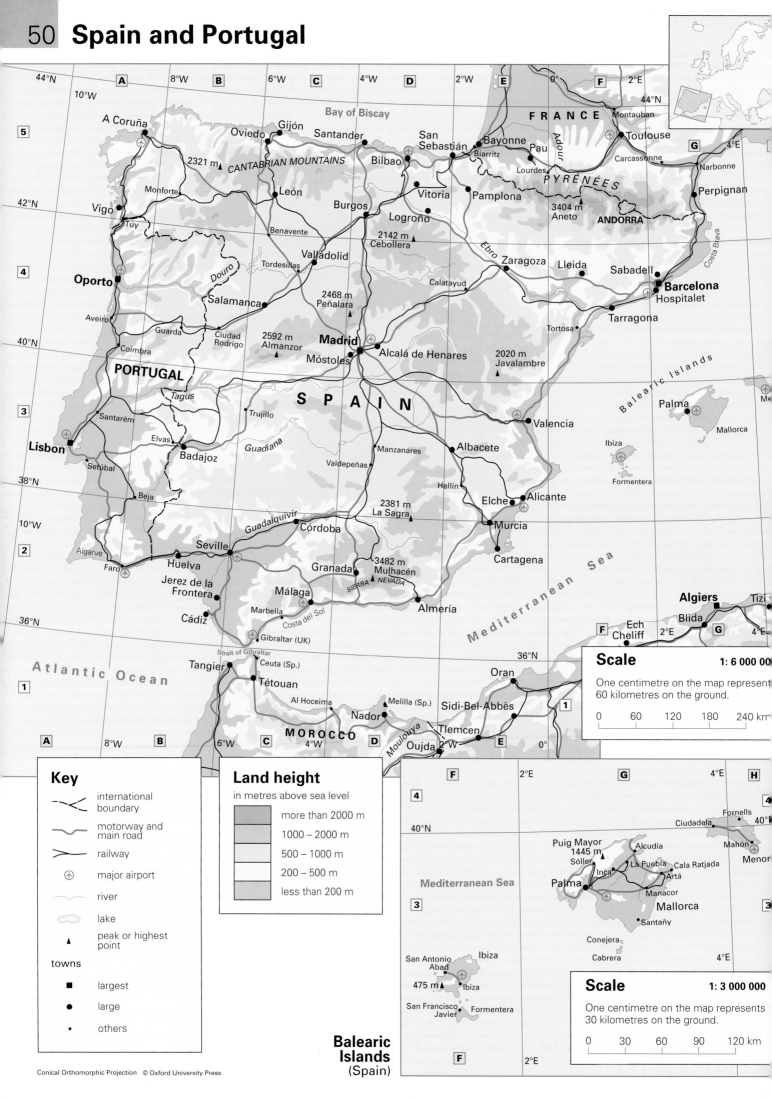

Key

- ![international boundary] international boundary
- ![motorway and main road] motorway and main road
- ![railway] railway
- ⊕ major airport
- ![river] river
- ![lake] lake
- ▲ peak or highest point

towns
- ■ largest
- ● large
- · others

Land height
in metres above sea level

- more than 2000 m
- 1000 – 2000 m
- 500 – 1000 m
- 200 – 500 m
- less than 200 m

Scale
1: 6 000 000

One centimetre on the map represents 60 kilometres on the ground.

0   60   120   180   240 km

Scale
1: 3 000 000

One centimetre on the map represents 30 kilometres on the ground.

0   30   60   90   120 km

Balearic Islands (Spain)

Conical Orthomorphic Projection © Oxford University Press

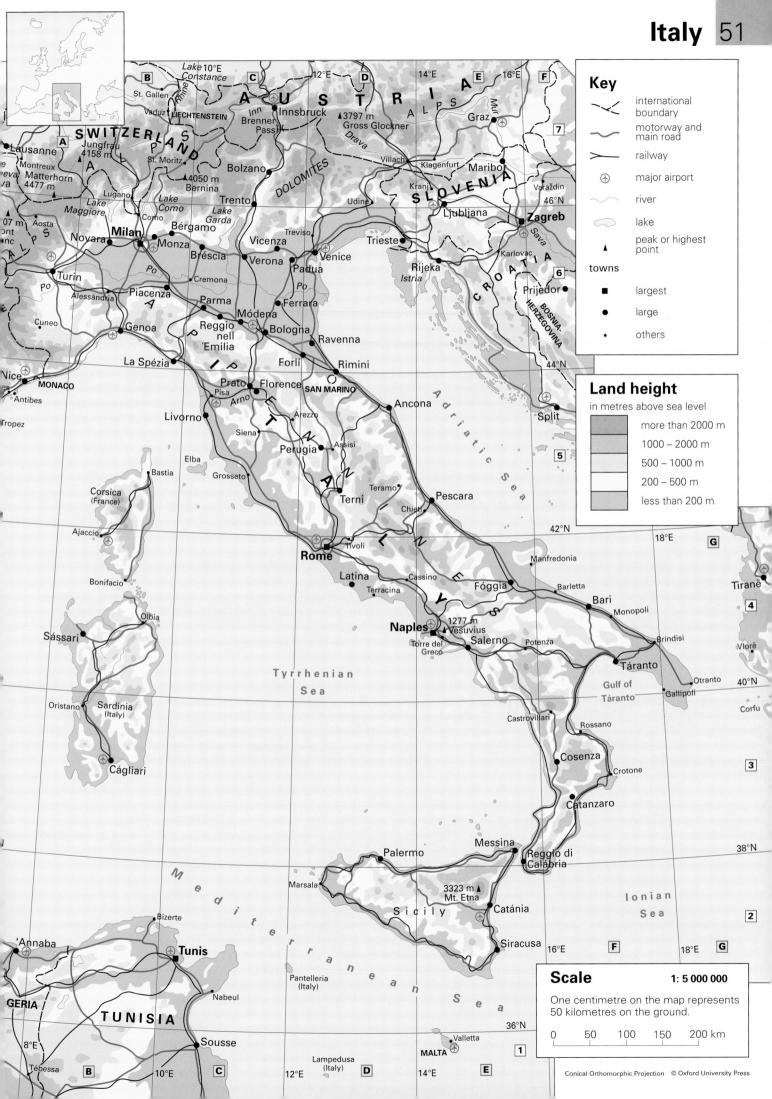

Key

	international boundary
	motorway and main road
	railway
⊕	major airport
	river
	lake
▲	peak or highest point

towns

■	largest
●	large
·	others

Land height
in metres above sea level

	more than 2000 m
	1000 – 2000 m
	500 – 1000 m
	200 – 500 m
	less than 200 m

Scale
1 : 5 000 000

One centimetre on the map represents 50 kilometres on the ground.

0   50   100   150   200 km

Conical Orthomorphic Projection © Oxford University Press

Countries and capitals

— country boundary
--- disputed boundary
• capital city

Kaliningrad (part of Russia)

The British Isles at the same scale

Scale　1 : 80 000 000

One centimetre on the map represents 800 kilometres on the ground.

0　800　1600　2400 km

Countries and capitals map labels

Moscow

RUSSIAN FEDERATION (RUSSIA)

•Ankara
GEORGIA
TURKEY
•Astana
•T'bilisi
KAZAKHSTAN
LEBANON •Yerevan
Beirut **AZERBAIJAN**
SYRIA •Damascus •Baku
ISRAEL **ARMENIA** **UZBEKISTAN**
Jerusalem •Amman •Tashkent
IRAQ **TURKMENISTAN** •Bishkek
•Baghdad Ashgabat **KYRGYZSTAN**
JORDAN Tehran •Dushanbe **TAJIKISTAN**
KUWAIT **IRAN** •
•Kuwait **AFGHANISTAN**
SAUDI **BAHRAIN** •Kabul
ARABIA •Manama **QATAR** •Islamabad
•Riyadh •Doha **PAKISTAN**
UNITED ARAB •New
EMIRATES •Abu Dhabi Delhi
•Sana •Muscat
OMAN
YEMEN REPUBLIC
Socotra (Yemen Rep.)

Ulan Bator•
MONGOLIA
•Beijing
CHINA
Jammu and Kashmir

NORTH KOREA
•Pyongyang •Tokyo
Seoul **JAPAN**
SOUTH KOREA

NEPAL **BHUTAN**
Kathmandu •Thimphu
INDIA Dhaka•
MYANMAR **LAOS** •Hanoi
(BURMA) Vientiane
Yangon **VIETNAM**
BANGLADESH **THAILAND** **CAMBODIA**
Bangkok •Phnom Penh

Lakshadweep (India)
Andaman Islands (India)

MALDIVES •Colombo
•Malé **SRI LANKA**
Nicobar Islands (India)

•Taipei
TAIWAN

•Manila
PHILIPPINES

BRUNEI
•Bandar Seri Begawan
MALAYSIA
Kuala Lumpur•
SINGAPORE•
INDONESIA
•Jakarta
•Dili **EAST TIMOR**

Tropic of Cancer

Kuril Islands (Russia)
Ryukyu Islands (Japan)

Prime Meridian　0° 20°E 40°E 60°N 80°N 60°E 80°E 100°E 120°E 140°E
Arctic Circle
Equator 0°

Land height

in metres above sea level

- more than 5000 m
- 2000 – 5000 m
- 1000 – 2000 m
- 500 – 1000 m
- 200 – 500 m
- sea level – 200 m
- below sea level

▲ highest peaks with heights in metres

lakes

major rivers

marsh

ice cap

Physical map labels

ARCTIC OCEAN
North Pole
Barents Sea
Baltic Sea
Lake Onega
Lake Ladoga
North Dvina
Black Sea
Don
Volga
URAL MOUNTAINS
Ob
S i b e r i a
Yenisey
Irtysh
Lena
Kolyma
Kamchatka Peninsula
Bering Sea
TAURUS MOUNTAINS
CAUCASUS ▲Mt Ararat 5123
Caspian Sea
Aral Sea
Lake Balkhash
ALTAI MOUNTAINS
Gobi Desert
Sea of Okhotsk
Sakhalin
Dead Sea (395m below sea level)
Euphrates
ZAGROS MOUNTAINS
▲Mt Demavand 5671
Tigris
HINDU KUSH
Turpan Depression (154m below sea level)
Tarim Basin
KUNLUN SHAN
Tsaidam Swamps
Hokkaido
Honshu
Sea of Japan
Red Sea
Arabian Peninsula
The Gulf
▲K2 8611
TIBETAN PLATEAU
▲Mt Everest 8848
HIMALAYA
Huang He
Red Basin
Chang Jiang
East China Sea
Indus
Ganges
Brahmaputra
Irrawaddy
Salween
Mekong
Arabian Sea
WESTERN GHATS
DECCAN
Bay of Bengal
Sri Lanka
South China Sea
Taiwan
PACIFIC OCEAN
Philippines
▲Mt Kinabalu 4101
Borneo
Sumatra
New Guinea
▲Jaya Peak 5030
Sulawesi
Java Sea
Arafura Sea
Java
INDIAN OCEAN
Equator 0°
Tropic of Cancer

Prime Meridian 0° 20°E 40°E 60°N 80°N 60°N 40°N 20°N 160°W 180° 160°E 140°E 120°E 100°E 80°E 60°E

Climate data

Verkhoyansk
Mean annual rainfall : 136 m[...]
Mean January temperature[...]
Mean July temperature : 13.[...]

Mumbai
Mean annual rainfall : 1811[...]
Mean January temperature[...]
Mean July temperature : 27.[...]

Jakarta
Mean annual rainfall : 1799[...]
Mean January temperature[...]
Mean July temperature : 27.[...]

Zenithal Equal Area P[...]
© Oxford Univers[...]

Verkhoyansk (100 m)

Mumbai (11 m)

Jakarta (8 m)

Climatic regions

Hot tropical rainy

rain all year

monsoon

dry in winter

Very dry

with no reliable rain

with a little rain

Influenced by the sea: warm summers, mild winters

with dry summers (Mediterranean type)

with dry winters

with no dry season

Cool

with dry winters

rain all year

Cold polar

no warm season and fairly dry

Mountain

height of the land strongly affects the climate

Ocean currents

→ warm

→ cold

Scale

1: 80 000 000

One centimetre on the map represents 800 kilometres on the ground.

0   800   1600   2400 km

Ecosystems

Vegetation types are those which would occur naturally without interference by people.

coniferous forest

deciduous and mixed forest

tropical rain forest

evergreen trees and shrubs

thorn forest

temperate grasslands

semi-desert

desert

tundra

mountains

More information about these ecosystems can be found on page 8.

Verkhoyansk•

Arctic Circle

Prime Meridian

Tropic of Cancer

Mumbai

typhoons

summer monsoon winds

Equator 0°

typhoons

typhoons

Jakarta

Equator 0°

Zenithal Equal Area Projection
© Oxford University Press

Farming, forestry, and fishing

main farming types

little or no farming : because the area is too dry or otherwise harsh.

nomadic herding : animals provide the needs of the wandering families.

shifting cultivation : small areas farmed until soils exhausted, then family moves.

mixed subsistence : crops and animals for family food.

rice subsistence : where heavy rainfall will allow a main crop of rice.

subsistance crops : mostly intensive with the aid of irrigation. Family food only.

grazing and stock rearing : on a large scale, for profit.

mixed farming : animals and crops for profit.

grain farming : mostly wheat, on a large scale, for profit.

plantation : well organized, specializing in one crop for profit, e.g. tea or rubber.

mediterranean farming : cereals, animals, vegetables, fruit, wine, surplus for profit.

specialized horticulture : mostly on oases supported by underground water.

dairy farming : milk, butter, and cheese for profit.

forestry

cutting and replacement of timber for profit

cash crops

coffee	tea	tobacco
fruit	dates	sugar
cotton	rubber	ground-nuts
palm products		

animal products

wool	meat	fish

Energy, Minerals, and Industry

energy

coalfield

oil field (with associated gas, and sometimes off shore)

gas field

hydro-electric power stations

largest (over 3000 megawatts)

smaller (500 – 3000 megawatts)

industry

main centres of industry

minerals (main mining areas)

iron ore	silver	gold
tin	nickel	bauxite
copper	diamonds	
phosphates		

Scale   1: 80 000 000

One centimetre on the map represents 800 kilometres on the ground.

0   800   1600   2400 km

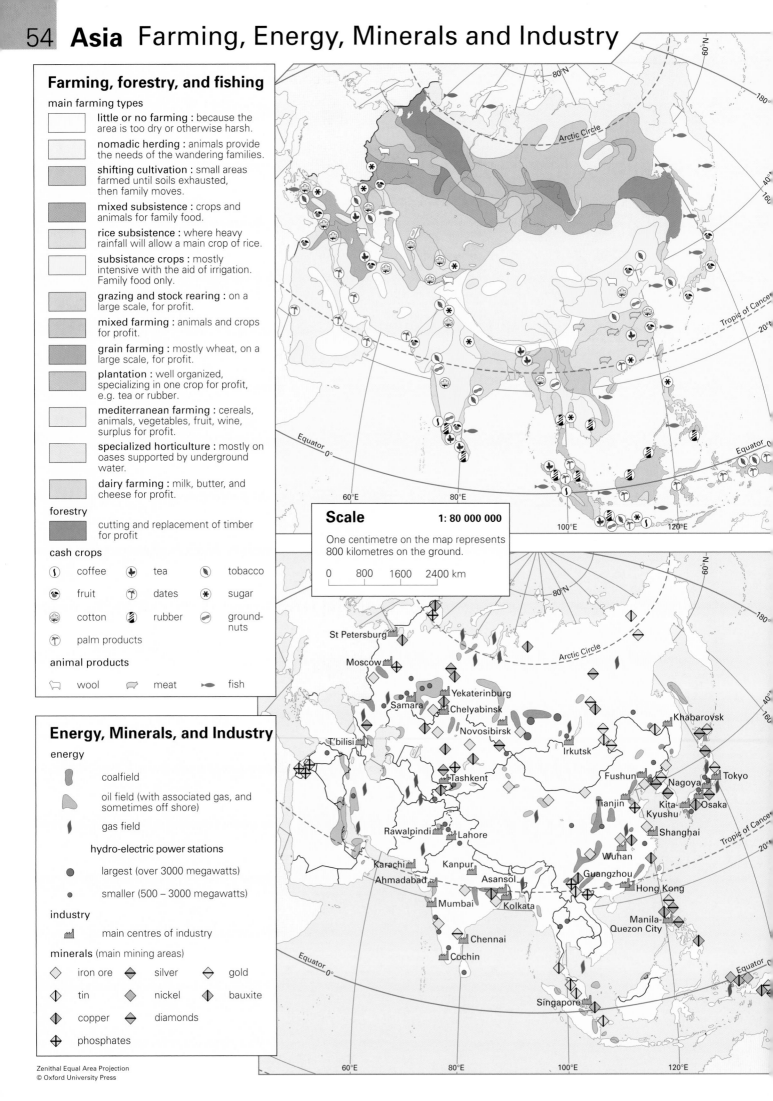

St Petersburg
Moscow
Samara
Yekaterinburg
Chelyabinsk
T'bilisi
Novosibirsk
Irkutsk
Tashkent
Khabarovsk
Fushun
Nagoya
Tokyo
Tianjin
Kita-Kyushu
Osaka
Rawalpindi
Lahore
Shanghai
Karachi
Kanpur
Wuhan
Ahmadabad
Asansol
Guangzhou
Hong Kong
Mumbai
Kolkata
Manila-Quezon City
Chennai
Cochin
Singapore

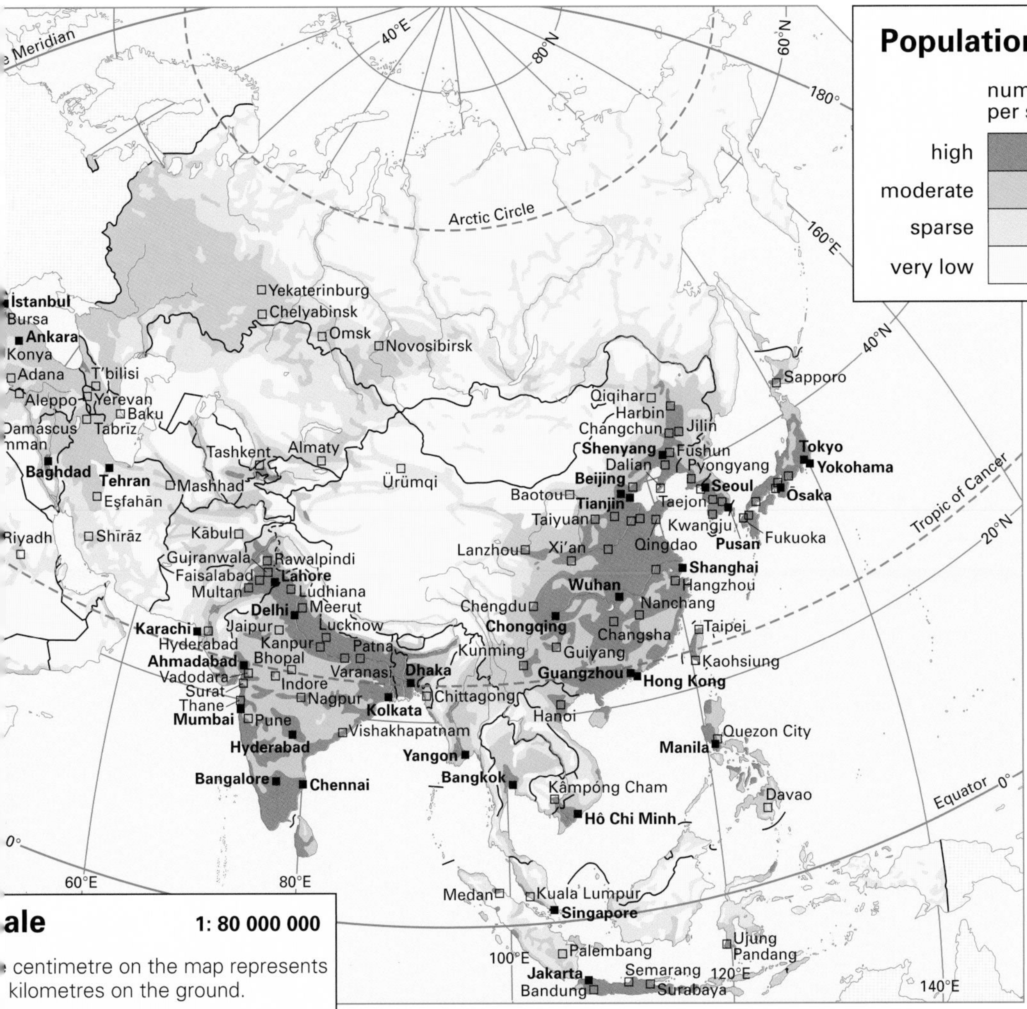

Population density

number of people
per square kilometre

high	more than 100
moderate	10 – 100
sparse	1 – 10
very low	less than 1

■ major cities and built up areas of at least 3 million people

□ cities with 1 – 3 million people

Map labels (top map)

Istanbul, Bursa, Ankara, Konya, Adana, Aleppo, Damascus, nman, Riyadh, T'bilisi, Yerevan, Baku, Tabriz, Baghdad, Tehran, Eşfahān, Mashhad, Shīrāz, Kābul, Gujranwala, Rawalpindi, Faisalabad, Lahore, Multan, Ludhiana, Delhi, Meerut, Jaipur, Kanpur, Lucknow, Patna, Karachi, Hyderabad, Ahmadabad, Bhopal, Vadodara, Varanasi, Surat, Indore, Nagpur, Thane, Mumbai, Pune, Hyderabad, Bangalore, Chennai, Vishakhapatnam, Kolkata, Dhaka, Chittagong, Yangon, Bangkok, Hanoi, Yekaterinburg, Chelyabinsk, Omsk, Novosibirsk, Tashkent, Almaty, Ürümqi, Lanzhou, Chengdu, Chongqing, Kunming, Guiyang, Guangzhou, Hong Kong, Changsha, Wuhan, Nanchang, Hangzhou, Shanghai, Nanjing, Xi'an, Qingdao, Taiyuan, Tianjin, Baotou, Beijing, Shenyang, Dalian, Fushun, Changchun, Harbin, Jilin, Qiqihar, Pyongyang, Taejon, Kwangju, Seoul, Pusan, Fukuoka, Kaohsiung, Taipei, Kāmpóng Cham, Hồ Chi Minh, Kuala Lumpur, Singapore, Medan, Palembang, Jakarta, Bandung, Semarang, Surabaya, Ujung Pandang, Sapporo, Tokyo, Yokohama, Osaka, Manila, Quezon City, Davao, Fukuoka

Population structure of China

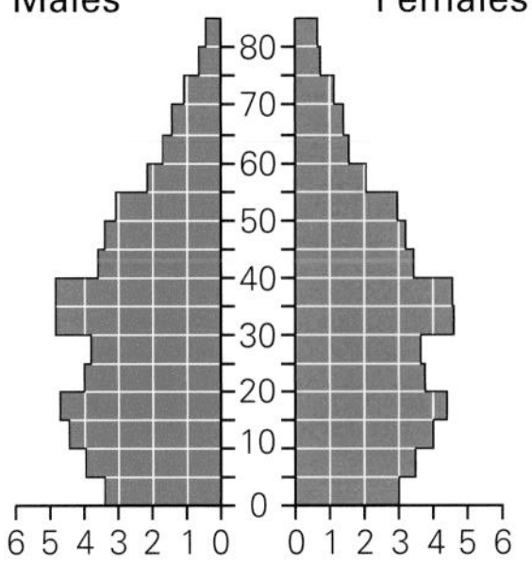

Age
Males — Females

percent of total population in 2004
Total population : 1298.8 million

Population structure of India

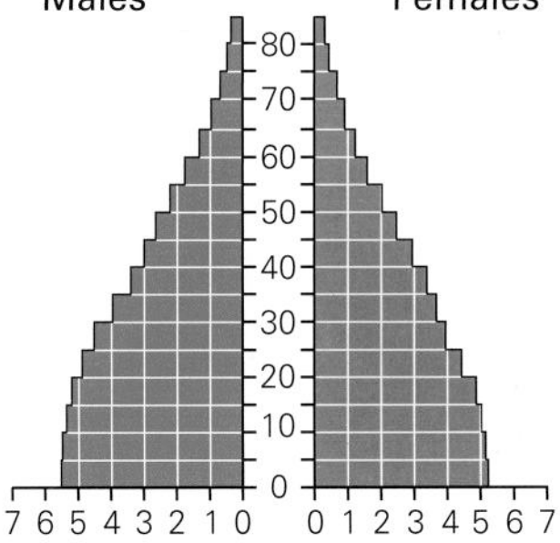

Age
Males — Females

percent of total population in 2004
Total population : 1065.1 million

Scale 1: 80 000 000

centimetre on the map represents
kilometres on the ground.

800   1600   2400 km

global warming

addition of greenhouse gases
in tonnes of carbon per person
(look at the world map on page 17)

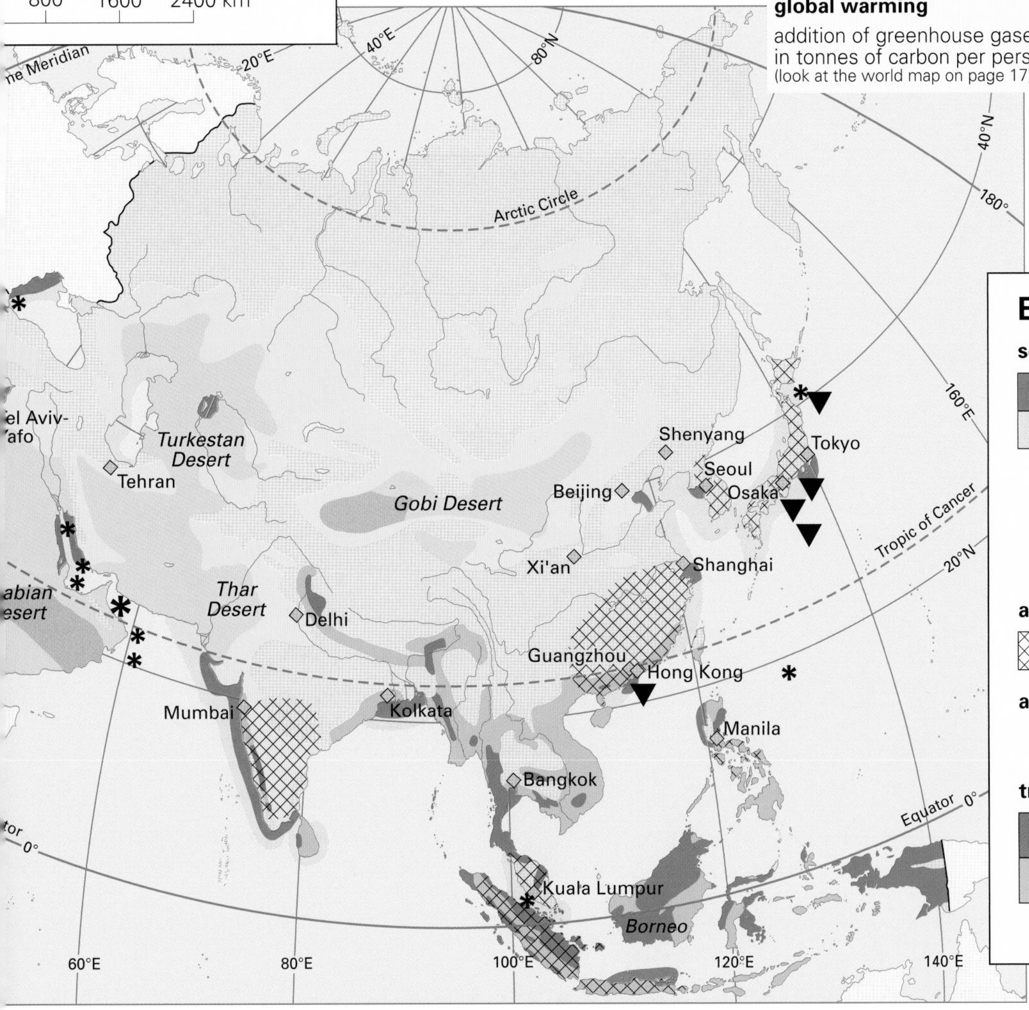

Labels (bottom map)

el Aviv-afo, Tehran, Turkestan Desert, Gobi Desert, Beijing, Shenyang, Seoul, Osaka, Tokyo, Xi'an, Shanghai, Thar Desert, Delhi, Guangzhou, Hong Kong, Manila, Mumbai, Kolkata, Bangkok, Kuala Lumpur, Borneo, abian esert

Environmental issues

sea pollution

▓	areas severely polluted for all or part of the year
░	areas persistently affected by pollution

▼ deep sea dump sites

✱ major oil spills (over 100 000 tonnes)

∗ major oil spills (under 100 000 tonnes)

acid rain

▨ areas where acid rain is becoming a problem

air pollution

◇ cities where sulphur dioxide emissions are recorded and exceed recommended levels

tropical deforestation

existing areas of rainforest

former areas of rainforest

desertification

existing areas of desert

high risk areas

moderate risk areas

Zenithal Equal Area Projection
© Oxford University Press

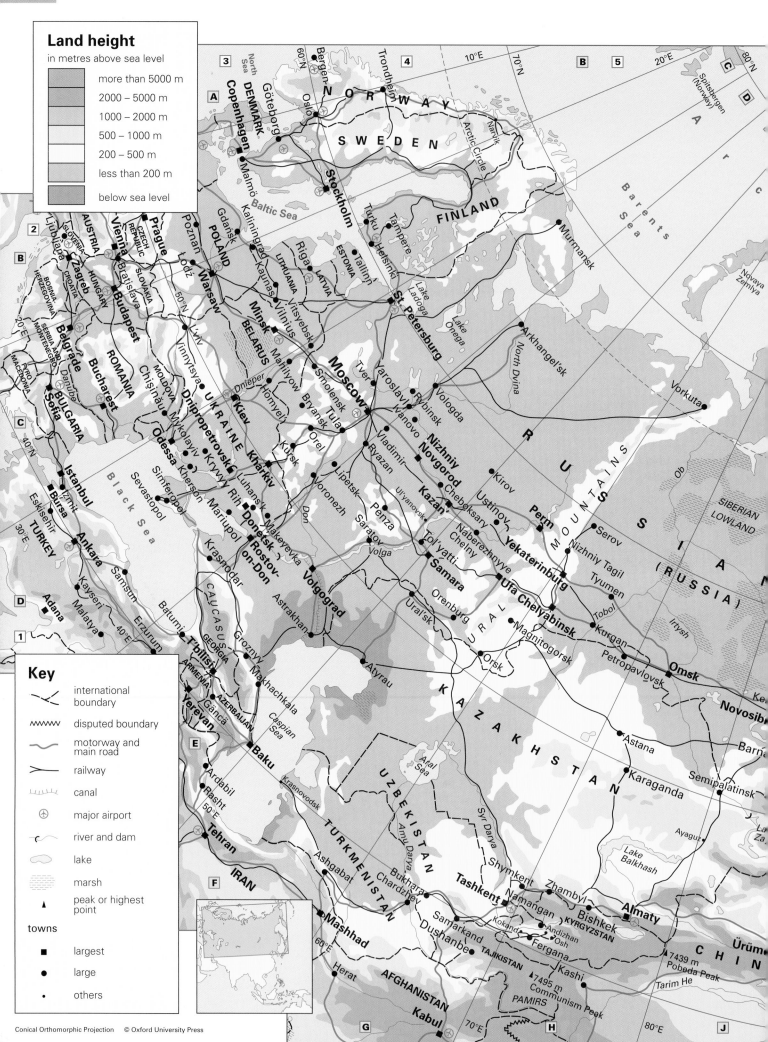

Land height
in metres above sea level

more than 5000 m
2000 – 5000 m
1000 – 2000 m
500 – 1000 m
200 – 500 m
less than 200 m
below sea level

Key

international boundary
disputed boundary
motorway and main road
railway
canal
major airport
river and dam
lake
marsh
peak or highest point

towns

■ largest
● large
· others

Conical Orthomorphic Projection   © Oxford University Press

Scale 1: 20 000 000

One centimetre on the map represents 200 kilometres on the ground.

0 200 400 600 800 km

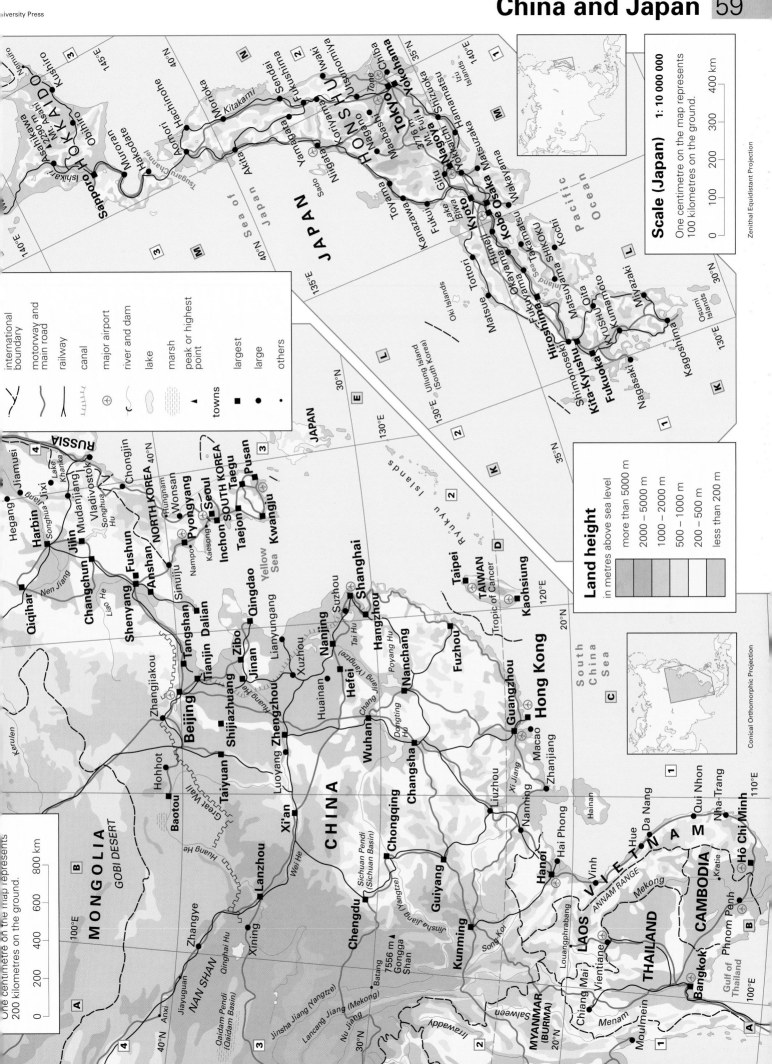

...iversity Press

Scale (Japan) 1: 10 000 000

One centimetre on the map represents
100 kilometres on the ground.

0 100 200 300 400 km

Zenithal Equidistant Projection

Legend

international boundary

motorway and main road

railway

canal

major airport

river and dam

lake

marsh

peak or highest point

towns
- largest
- large
- others

Land height
in metres above sea level

- more than 5000 m
- 2000 – 5000 m
- 1000 – 2000 m
- 500 – 1000 m
- 200 – 500 m
- less than 200 m

Conical Orthomorphic Projection

One centimetre on the map represents
200 kilometres on the ground.

0 200 400 600 800 km

Japan (HOKKAIDO, HONSHU, SHIKOKU, KYUSHU)

Nemuro, Kushiro, Abashiri, Mt. Asahi 2290 m, Asahikawa, Wakkanai, Obihiro, Muroran, Hakodate, Sapporo, Ishikari, Tsugaru Channel, Aomori, Hachinohe, Morioka, Kitakami, Akita, Sendai, Yamagata, Fukushima, Iwaki, Niigata, Utsunomiya, Sado, Toyama, Nagano, Maebashi, Kanazawa, Fukui, Gifu, Nagoya, Shizuoka, Hamamatsu, Mt. Fuji 3776 m, Chiba, TOKYO, Yokohama, Toyohashi, Yokkaichi, KYOTO, Himeji, Kobe, Osaka, Wakayama, Matsuzaka, Tottori, Matsue, Okayama, Takamatsu, Kochi, Matsuyama, Hiroshima, Shimonoseki, Kita-Kyushu, Fukuoka, Oita, Kumamoto, Miyazaki, Nagasaki, Kagoshima, Osumi Islands, Oki Islands, Izu Islands, Lake Biwa, Tone, Koriyama, Ryukyu Islands, Pacific Ocean, Sea of Japan, Ullung Island (South Korea)

China and mainland

Anxi, Jiayuguan, Qinghai Hu, Xining, Zhangye, Lanzhou, Qaidam Pendi (Qaidam Basin), NAN SHAN, MONGOLIA, GOBI DESERT, Kerulen, Hohhot, Baotou, Great Wall, Huang He, Taiyuan, Xi'an, Wei He, CHINA, Chengdu, Sichuan Pendi (Sichuan Basin), Gongga Shan 7556 m, Batang, Jinsha Jiang (Yangtze), Lancang Jiang (Mekong), Nu Jiang, Chongqing, Guiyang, Kunming, Song Koi, Guilin, Liuzhou, Nanning, Xi Jiang, Zhanjiang, Hainan, Changsha, Nanchang, Dongting Hu, Poyang Hu, Chang Jiang (Yangtze), Wuhan, Hefei, Tai Hu, Huaian, Nanjing, Suzhou, Shanghai, Hangzhou, Fuzhou, Guangzhou, Macao, Hong Kong, Taipei, TAIWAN, Kaohsiung, Tropic of Cancer, South China Sea

Zhengzhou, Luoyang, Jinan, Zibo, Qingdao, Lianyungang, Xuzhou, Shijiazhuang, Tangshan, Beijing, Tianjin, Dalian, Zhangjiakou, Yellow Sea, Huang He (Yellow River)

Qiqihar, Hegang, Jiamusi, Jixi, Harbin, Changchun, Jilin, Mudanjiang, Nen Jiang, Songhua, Liao He, Shenyang, Fushun, Anshan, Lake Khanka, Songhua Hu, RUSSIA, Vladivostok, Chongjin, Hungnam, Wonsan, NORTH KOREA, Sinuiju, Nampo, Kaesong, Pyongyang, Seoul, Inchon, SOUTH KOREA, Taejon, Taegu, Pusan, Kwangju

Southeast Asia

MYANMAR (BURMA), Irrawaddy, Salween, Chiang Mai, Mekong, LAOS, Louangphrabang, Vientiane, Menam, THAILAND, Bangkok, Gulf of Thailand, Hanoi, Hai Phong, Vinh, Hue, Da Nang, ANNAM RANGE, VIETNAM, Qui Nhon, Nha Trang, Hồ Chí Minh, Kratie, Phnom Penh, CAMBODIA, Moulmein

Key

towns
- peak or highest point
- marsh
- largest
- large
- others

- international boundary
- motorway and main road
- railway
- major airport
- river
- lake

Land height
in metres above sea level
- more than 2000 m
- 1000 – 2000 m
- 500 – 1000 m
- 200 – 500 m
- less than 200 m

Scale
1 : 20 000 000

One centimetre on the map represents 200 kilometres on the ground.

Conical Orthomorphic Projection   © Oxford University Press

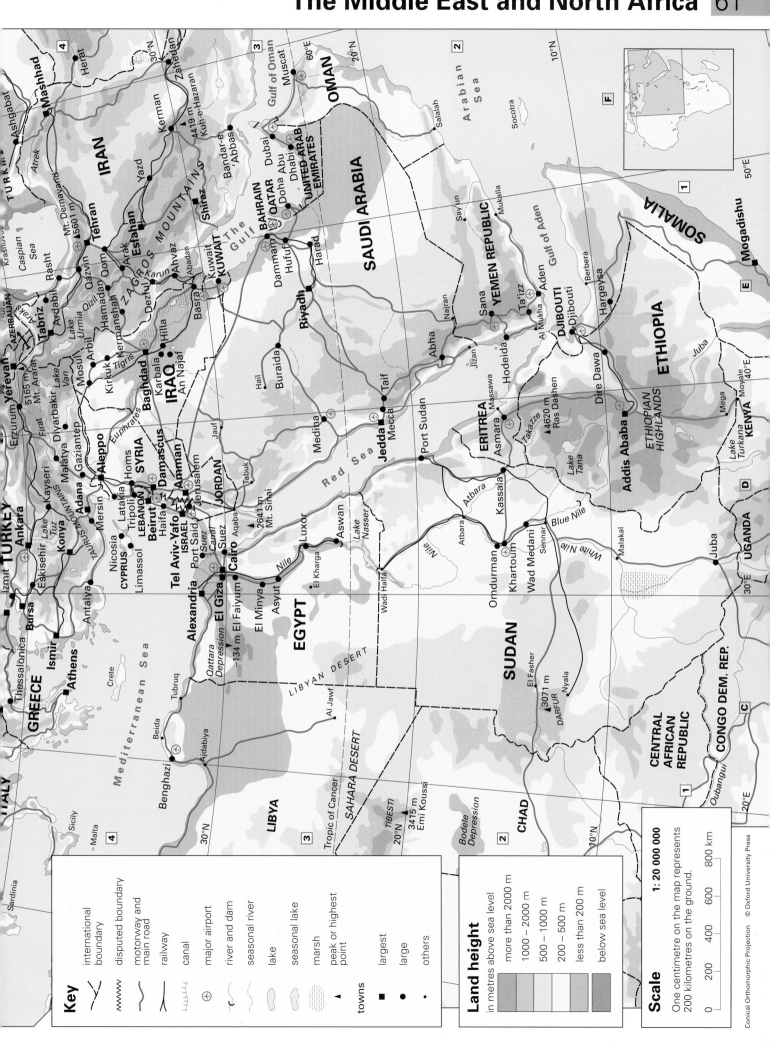

Key

— — —	international boundary
— · — · —	disputed boundary
wwww	motorway and main road
———	railway
———	canal
⊕	major airport
✈	river and dam
	seasonal river
	lake
	seasonal lake
	marsh
▲	peak or highest point

towns
■	largest
●	large
·	others

Land height

in metres above sea level

	more than 2000 m
	1000 – 2000 m
	500 – 1000 m
	200 – 500 m
	less than 200 m
	below sea level

Scale

1: 20 000 000

One centimetre on the map represents 200 kilometres on the ground.

0 200 400 600 800 km

Conical Orthomorphic Projection   © Oxford University Press

Countries and capitals

— country boundary

• capital city

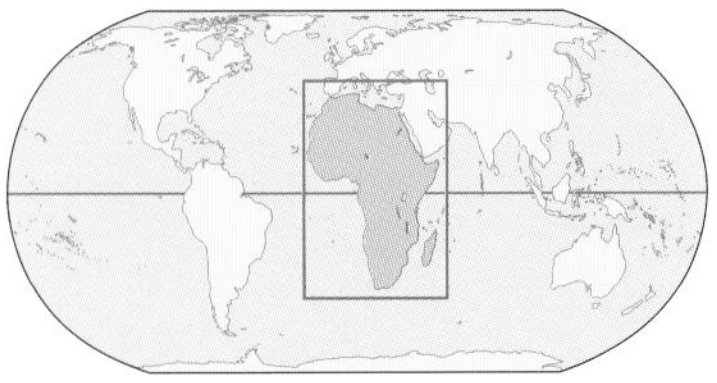

The British Isles at the same scale

Map 1 — Countries and capitals

Madeira (Portugal)
Rabat-Salé
Canary Islands (Spain)
Laâyoune
MOROCCO
Algiers
Tunis
TUNISIA
Tripoli
ALGERIA
LIBYA
Cairo
EGYPT
Tropic of Cancer
20°N
WESTERN SAHARA
CAPE VERDE
Nouakchott
MAURITANIA
MALI
NIGER
CHAD
Khartoum
ERITREA
Asmara
SENEGAL
Dakar
THE GAMBIA
Banjul
Bissau
Bamako
Niamey
SUDAN
Djibouti
DJIBOUTI
GUINEA BISSAU
BURKINA
Ouagadougou
Ndjamena
Addis Ababa
GUINEA
Conakry
Freetown
SIERRA LEONE
COTE D'IVOIRE
GHANA
BENIN
TOGO
NIGERIA
Abuja
Porto Novo
CENTRAL AFRICAN REPUBLIC
ETHIOPIA
SOMALIA
Monrovia
Yamoussoukro
Accra
Lomé
CAMEROON
Bangui
LIBERIA
Malabo
Yaoundé
EQUATORIAL GUINEA
SÃO TOME AND PRINCIPE
Libreville
GABON
CONGO
DEMOCRATIC REPUBLIC OF CONGO
Kampala
UGANDA
KENYA
Mogadishu
Equator
0°
Brazzaville
Kinshasa
Kigali
RWANDA
BURUNDI
Bujumbura
Nairobi
Cabinda (Angola)
TANZANIA
Dodoma
Luanda
COMOROS
ANGOLA
ZAMBIA
MALAWI
Lilongwe
MOZAMBIQUE
Antananarivo
MADAGASCAR
Lusaka
Harare
20°S
Tropic of Capricorn
Windhoek
ZIMBABWE
BOTSWANA
NAMIBIA
Gaborone
Pretoria
Maputo
Mbabane
SWAZILAND
REPUBLIC OF SOUTH AFRICA
Maseru
LESOTHO
Ascension Island (U.K.)
St Helena (U.K.)
Prime Meridian
0°
20°E
40°E

Map 2 — Land and Water

NORTH ATLANTIC OCEAN
Madeira Islands
Mediterranean Sea
ATLAS MOUNTAINS
Nile Delta
Canary Islands
Tropic of Cancer
20°N
Qattara Depression (133m below sea level)
Cape Verde Islands
Sahara Desert
Lake Nasser
Red Sea
Senegal
Gambia
Niger
Nile
Lake Chad
Chari
Lake Asal (155m below sea level)
Benue
ETHIOPIAN HIGHLANDS
Lake Volta
Mt. Cameroun ▲4095
Oubangui
Lake Turkana
INDIAN OCEAN
Equator 0°
Gulf of Guinea
Niger Delta
Principe
São Tomé
Congo
Kasai
Rift Valley
Lake Victoria
Mt. Kenya ▲5200
▲5895 Mt. Kilimanjaro
0°
Ascension Island
Lake Tanganyika
Seychelles
SOUTH ATLANTIC OCEAN
ANGOLA PLATEAU
Lake Nyasa (Lake Malawi)
Comoro Archipelago
St Helena
Cubango
Victoria Falls
Zambezi
Madagascar
Mauritius
20°S
Tropic of Capricorn
Namib Desert
Okavango Swamp
Mozambique Channel
Réunion
Kalahari Desert
Vaal
Orange
DRAKENSBERG
Cape of Good Hope
Prime Meridian
0°
20°E
40°E
60°E
20°N

Scale

1: 60 00

One centimetre on the map repr 600 kilometres on the ground.

0   600   1200   1800 km

Land height

in metres above sea level

more than 5000 r
2000 – 5000 m
1000 – 2000 m
500 – 1000 m
200 – 500 m
sea level – 200 m
below sea level
▲ highest peaks wi heights in metres
lakes
major rivers
marsh

Zenithal Equal Area
© Oxford Unive

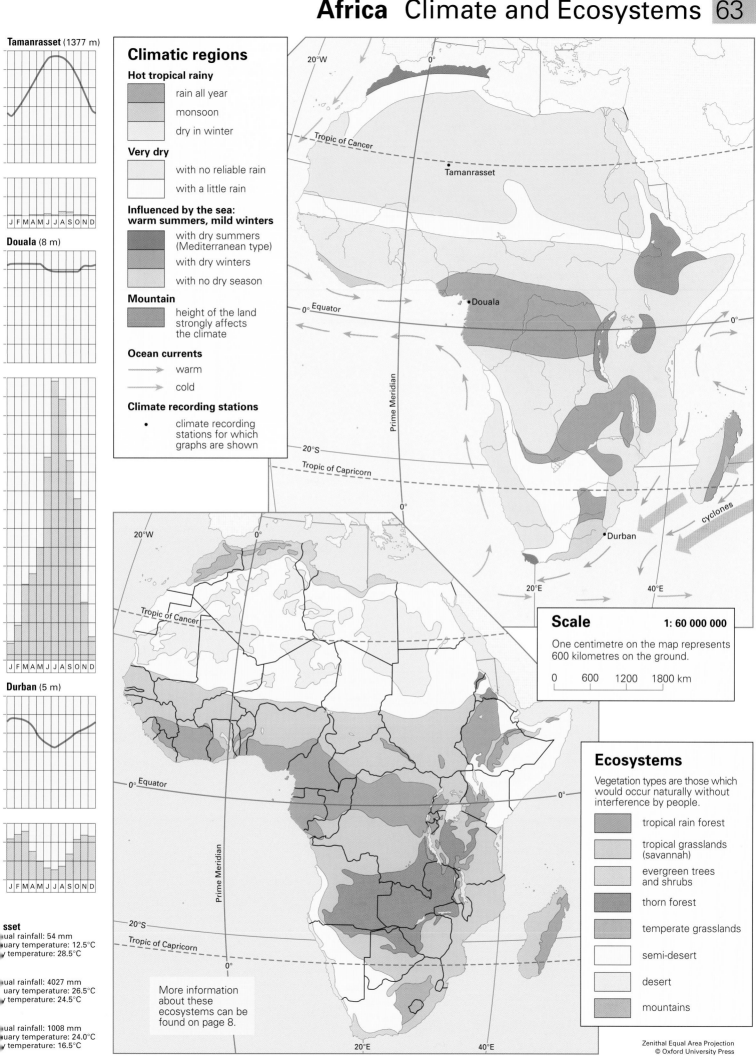

Tamanrasset (1377 m)

J F M A M J J A S O N D

Douala (8 m)

J F M A M J J A S O N D

Durban (5 m)

J F M A M J J A S O N D

Climatic regions

Hot tropical rainy

- rain all year
- monsoon
- dry in winter

Very dry

- with no reliable rain
- with a little rain

**Influenced by the sea:
warm summers, mild winters**

- with dry summers
(Mediterranean type)
- with dry winters
- with no dry season

Mountain

- height of the land
strongly affects
the climate

Ocean currents

- → warm
- → cold

Climate recording stations

- • climate recording
stations for which
graphs are shown

20°W
0°
Tropic of Cancer
Tamanrasset
0° Equator
Douala
Prime Meridian
20°S
Tropic of Capricorn
0°
Durban
cyclones
20°E
40°E
0°

Scale   1: 60 000 000

One centimetre on the map represents
600 kilometres on the ground.

0   600   1200   1800 km

sset

- ual rainfall: 54 mm
- uary temperature: 12.5°C
- y temperature: 28.5°C

- ual rainfall: 4027 mm
- uary temperature: 26.5°C
- temperature: 24.5°C

- ual rainfall: 1008 mm
- uary temperature: 24.0°C
- temperature: 16.5°C

20°W
0°
Tropic of Cancer
0° Equator
Prime Meridian
20°S
Tropic of Capricorn
0°
20°E
40°E

More information
about these
ecosystems can be
found on page 8.

Ecosystems

Vegetation types are those which
would occur naturally without
interference by people.

- tropical rain forest
- tropical grasslands
(savannah)
- evergreen trees
and shrubs
- thorn forest
- temperate grasslands
- semi-desert
- desert
- mountains

Zenithal Equal Area Projection
© Oxford University Press

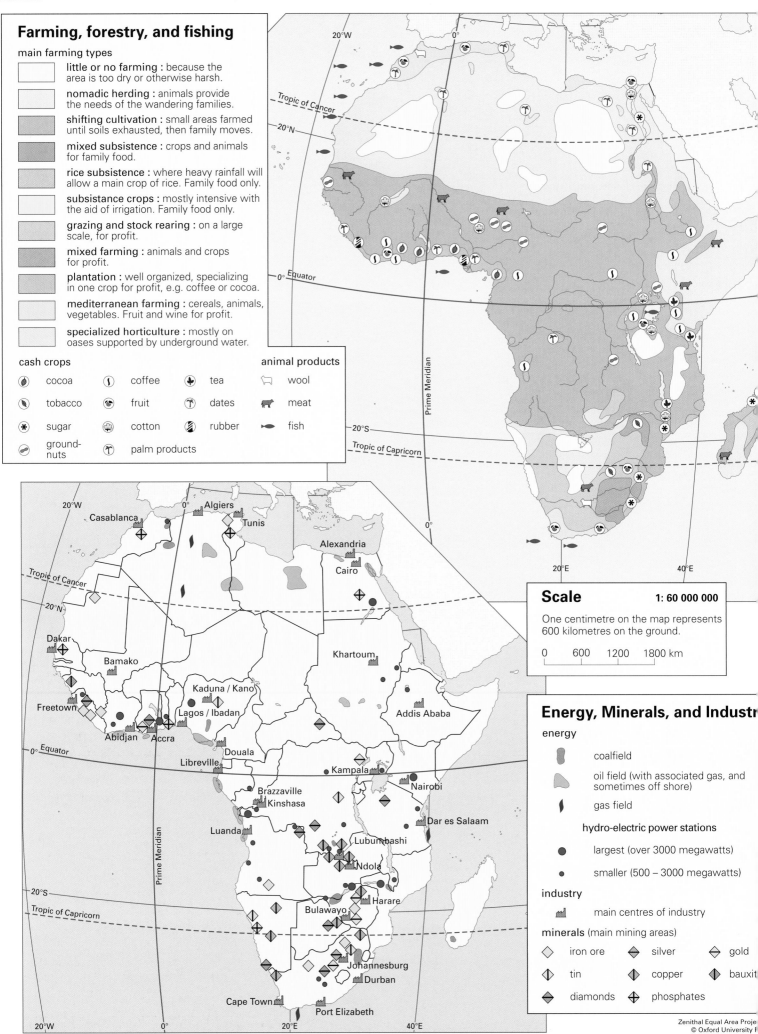

Farming, forestry, and fishing

main farming types

	little or no farming : because the area is too dry or otherwise harsh.
	nomadic herding : animals provide the needs of the wandering families.
	shifting cultivation : small areas farmed until soils exhausted, then family moves.
	mixed subsistence : crops and animals for family food.
	rice subsistence : where heavy rainfall will allow a main crop of rice. Family food only.
	subsistance crops : mostly intensive with the aid of irrigation. Family food only.
	grazing and stock rearing : on a large scale, for profit.
	mixed farming : animals and crops for profit.
	plantation : well organized, specializing in one crop for profit, e.g. coffee or cocoa.
	mediterranean farming : cereals, animals, vegetables. Fruit and wine for profit.
	specialized horticulture : mostly on oases supported by underground water.

cash crops

- cocoa
- tobacco
- sugar
- ground-nuts
- coffee
- fruit
- cotton
- palm products
- tea
- dates
- rubber

animal products

- wool
- meat
- fish

Scale   1: 60 000 000

One centimetre on the map represents 600 kilometres on the ground.

0   600   1200   1800 km

Energy, Minerals, and Industry

energy

- coalfield
- oil field (with associated gas, and sometimes off shore)
- gas field

hydro-electric power stations

- largest (over 3000 megawatts)
- smaller (500 – 3000 megawatts)

industry

- main centres of industry

minerals (main mining areas)

- iron ore
- tin
- diamonds
- silver
- copper
- phosphates
- gold
- bauxite

pulation density

number of people
per square kilometre

high	more than 100
derate	10 – 100
sparse	1 – 10
ry low	less than 1

■ major cities and
built up areas of
at least 3 million
people

□ cities with
1 – 3 million
people

opulation structure of Kenya

Age

Males   Females

80
70
60
50
40
30
20
10
0

5 4 3 2 1 0 0 1 2 3 4 5 6 7 8 9

nt of total population in 2004
otal population : 33.0 million

Population structure of Egypt

Age

Males   Females

80
70
60
50
40
30
20
10
0

7 6 5 4 3 2 1 0 0 1 2 3 4 5 6 7

percent of total population in 2004
Total population : 76.1 million

global warming

addition of greenhouse gases
in tonnes of carbon per person
(look at the world map on page 17)

Scale   1: 60 000 000

One centimetre on the map represents
600 kilometres on the ground.

0   600   1200   1800 km

Environmental issues

sea pollution

areas severely polluted for all or part of
the year

areas persistently affected by pollution

▼ deep sea dump sites

✱ major oil spills (over 100 000 tonnes)

✳ major oil spills (under 100 000 tonnes)

acid rain

areas where acid rain is becoming
a problem

tsetse fly

areas affected by the tsetse fly

tropical deforestation

existing areas
of rainforest

former areas
of rainforest

desertification

existing areas
of desert

high risk areas

moderate risk
areas

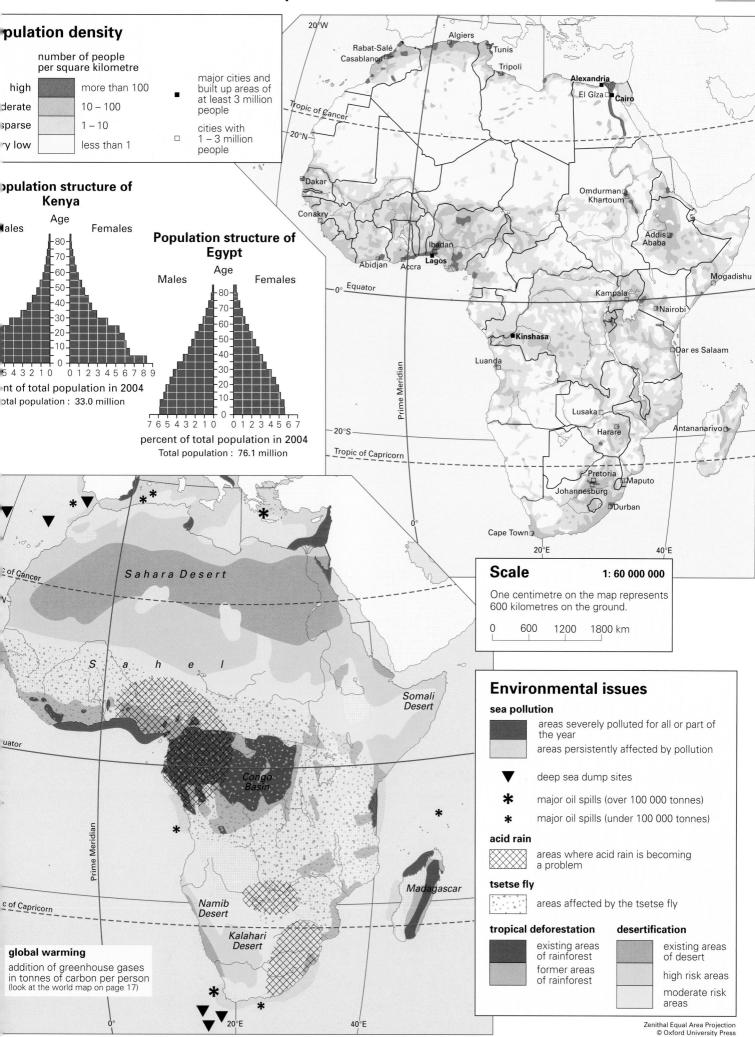

Zenithal Equal Area Projection
© Oxford University Press

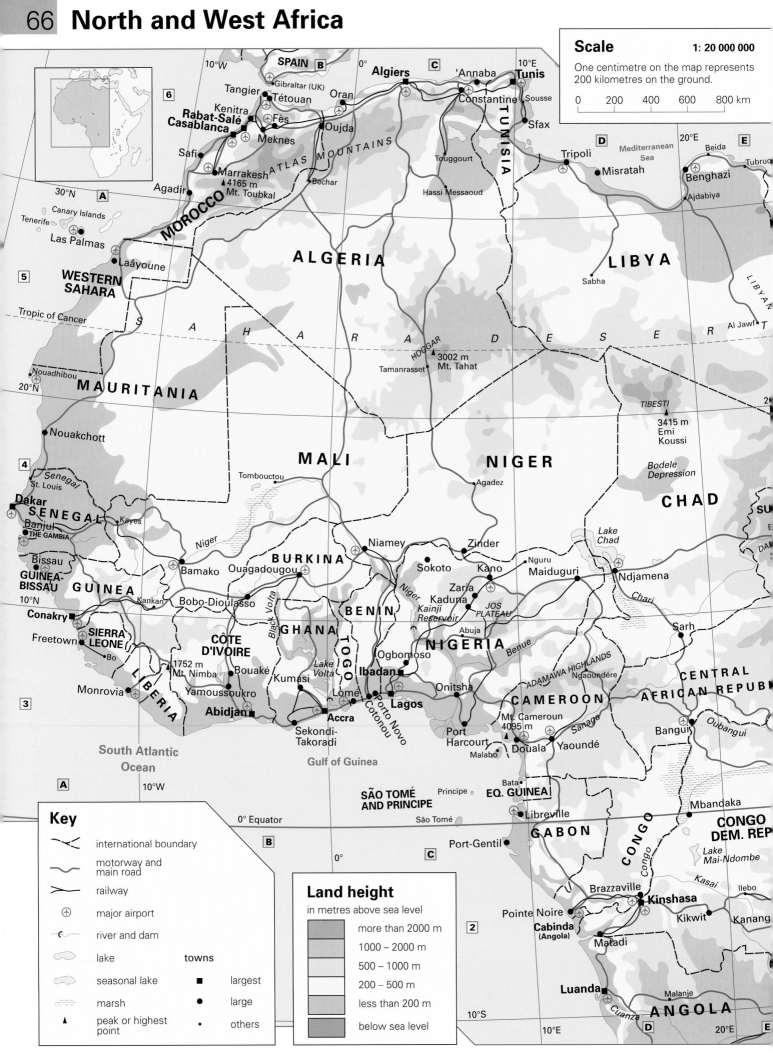

Scale 1: 20 000 000
One centimetre on the map represents 200 kilometres on the ground.

0 200 400 600 800 km

Key

- international boundary
- motorway and main road
- railway
- ⊕ major airport
- river and dam
- lake
- seasonal lake
- marsh
- ▲ peak or highest point

towns
- ■ largest
- ● large
- · others

Land height
in metres above sea level

- more than 2000 m
- 1000 – 2000 m
- 500 – 1000 m
- 200 – 500 m
- less than 200 m
- below sea level

Zenithal Equal Area Projection   © Oxford University Press

B 20°E C 30°E D 40°E E 50°E

CHAD

El Fasher
▲ 3071 m
DARFUR
Nyala

Wad Medani
Sennar
Malakal

ERITREA
▲4620 m
Ras Dashen
Lake Tana
DJIBOUTI
Djibouti
Gulf of Aden
Berbera
Hargeysa

SUDAN

ETHIOPIA
Addis Ababa
Dire Dawa

ERIA
Chari
Ngaoundéré
ADAMAWA HIGHLANDS
MEROON
Sanaga
Yaoundé

CENTRAL AFRICAN REPUBLIC

Sarh

Bangui
Oubangui
Uele

Juba

ETHIOPIAN HIGHLANDS

SOMALIA

Mega
Moyale

Lake Turkana

Mogadishu

JINEA

Kisangani
Boyoma Falls

Lake Albert
Lake Kyoga
UGANDA
Kampala
Entebbe
Kisumu

KENYA

5200 m
Mt. Kenya
Nairobi

Equator 0°

ABON

CONGO

Mbandaka
Lake Mai-Ndombe
Lualaba

CONGO DEM. REP.

Mt. Ruwenzori 5118 m
Lake Edward
Lake Kivu
Bukavu
RWANDA
Kigali
Lake Victoria
Mwanza

5895 m
Mt. Kilimanjaro

Brazzaville
Congo
Kasai
Ilebo
Kinshasa
Kikwit
Kananga
Mbuji-Mayi

Bujumbura
BURUNDI
Kigoma
Kalemie

Tabora

Mombasa

Indian Ocean

nda
Matadi
ola

Kalemie
Lake Tanganyika

Tanga
TANZANIA
Dodoma

Zanzibar
Dar es Salaam

uanda
Malanje
Cuanza
Kasai

Lake Mweru

Lake Rukwa

Lake Bangweulu

WESTERN RIFT VALLEY

Ruvuma

Aldabra Islands

10°S

Lobito
Benguela
Huambo
Cuango
Likasi
Lubumbashi

Lake Nyasa (Lake Malawi)

Moroni
COMOROS

ANGOLA

Kitwe
Ndola
Kabwe

Lilongwe

Nampula

Mahajanga

Lubango
Cubango

ZAMBIA

Lusaka

Lake Cabora Bassa
Blantyre

Moçambique

Toamasina

Cunene
Etosha Pan
Zambezi

Lake Kariba
Harare

Zambezi

Beira

Antananarivo

20°S

Victoria Falls
ZIMBABWE

MOZAMBIQUE

Mozambique Channel

MADAGASCAR

NAMIBIA
NAMIB DESERT

Okavango Swamp

Bulawayo

Europa

Tropic of Capricorn

Walvis Bay
Windhoek

BOTSWANA

KALAHARI DESERT

Limpopo

Toliara

Lüderitz

Gaborone

Pretoria
Johannesburg
Mbabane
Maputo

SWAZILAND

40°E 50°E

Atlantic Ocean

Orange
Kimberley
Vaal
Maseru
▲3482 m
Pietermaritzburg

HIGH VELD
DRAKENSBERG

30°S

Bloomfontein
LESOTHO
Durban

REPUBLIC OF SOUTH AFRICA

Cape Town
Cape of Good Hope

GREAT KARROO

East London

Port Elizabeth

10°E 20°E 30°E

Scale

1: 20 000 000

One centimetre on the map represents 200 kilometres on the ground.

0 200 400 600 800 km

For explanations of the symbols and colours used on this map look at the opposite page.

Zenithal Equal Area Projection © Oxford University Press

Countries and capitals

— country boundary

• capital city

The British Isles at the same scale

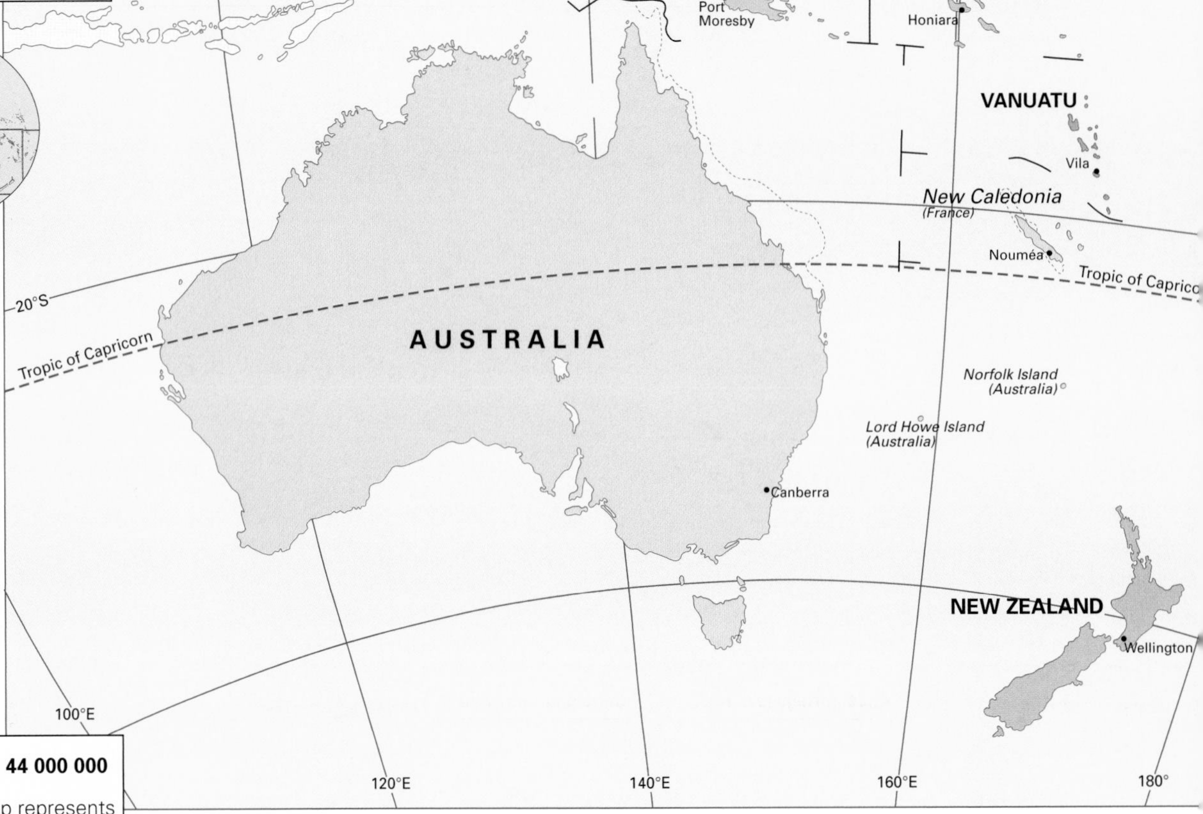

Scale
1: 44 000 000

One centimetre on the map represents 440 kilometres on the ground.

0   440   880   1320 km

Land height
in metres above sea level

more than 2000 m

1000 – 2000 m

500 – 1000 m

200 – 500 m

sea level – 200 m

below sea level

▲ highest peaks with heights in metres

lakes

major rivers

major seasonal rivers

coral reef

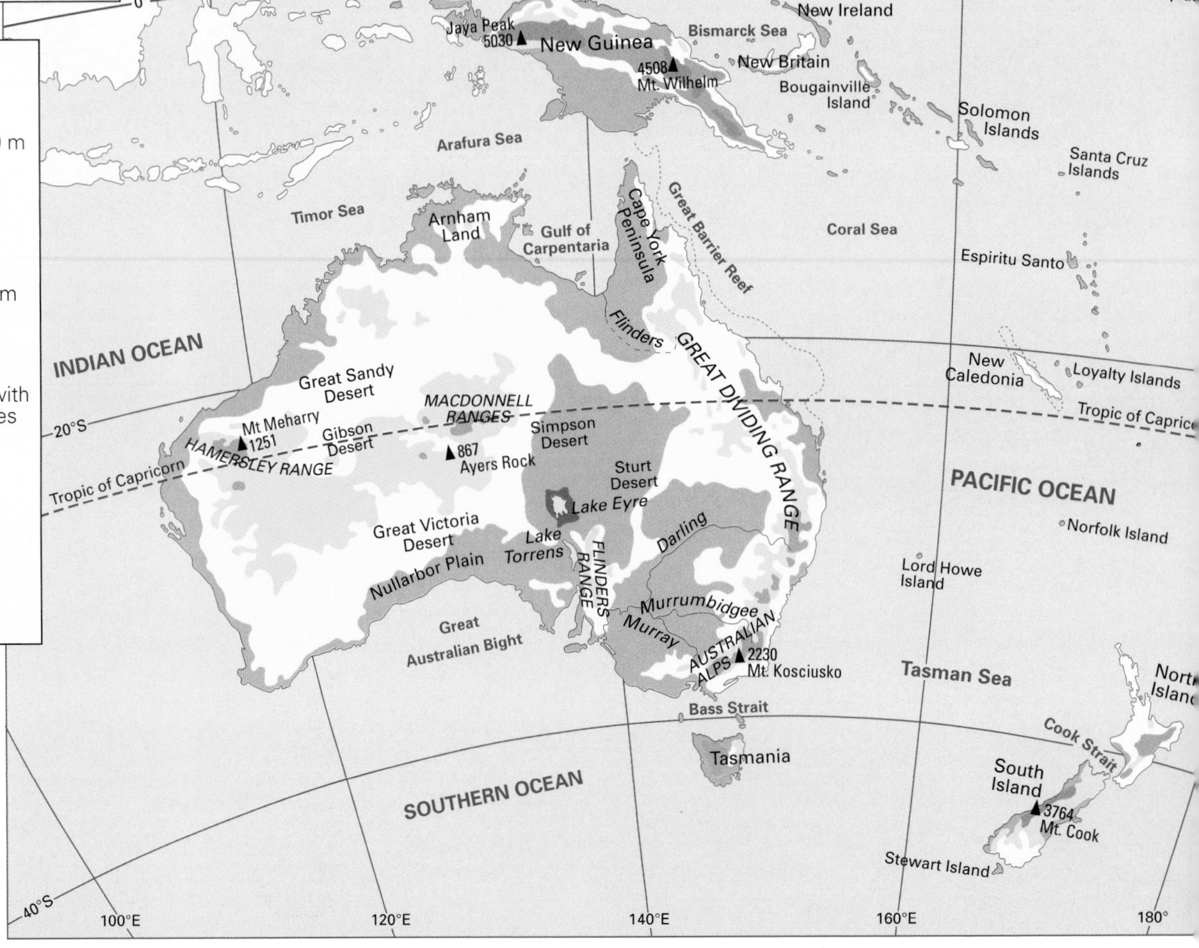

Modified Zenithal Equidistant Projection
© Oxford University Press

Top map labels

0° Equator   140°E   160°E   Equat

PAPUA NEW GUINEA   SOLOMON ISLANDS

Port Moresby   Honiara

VANUATU

Vila

New Caledonia (France)

Nouméa   Tropic of Caprico

20°S

Tropic of Capricorn

AUSTRALIA

Norfolk Island (Australia)

Lord Howe Island (Australia)

• Canberra

NEW ZEALAND

• Wellington

100°E   120°E   140°E   160°E   180°

Bottom map labels

0° Equator   140°E   160°E   Equa

New Ireland

Jaya Peak 5030 ▲   New Guinea   Bismarck Sea   New Britain

4508 ▲ Mt. Wilhelm   Bougainville Island

Arafura Sea   Solomon Islands   Santa Cruz Islands

Timor Sea   Arnham Land   Gulf of Carpentaria   Cape York Peninsula   Great Barrier Reef   Coral Sea

Espiritu Santo

INDIAN OCEAN   Flinders   GREAT DIVIDING RANGE   New Caledonia   Loyalty Islands

Great Sandy Desert   MACDONNELL RANGES   Tropic of Capric

20°S   Mt Meharry ▲ 1251   Gibson Desert   Simpson Desert   PACIFIC OCEAN

Tropic of Capricorn   HAMERSLEY RANGE   867 ▲ Ayers Rock   Sturt Desert

Great Victoria Desert   Lake Eyre   Darling

Nullarbor Plain   Lake Torrens   FLINDERS RANGE   Murrumbidgee   Norfolk Island

Great Australian Bight   Murray   Lord Howe Island

AUSTRALIAN ALPS ▲ 2230 Mt. Kosciusko

Bass Strait   Tasman Sea   Nort Island

Tasmania   Cook Strait

South Island

SOUTHERN OCEAN   3764 ▲ Mt. Cook

Stewart Island

100°E   120°E   140°E   160°E   180°

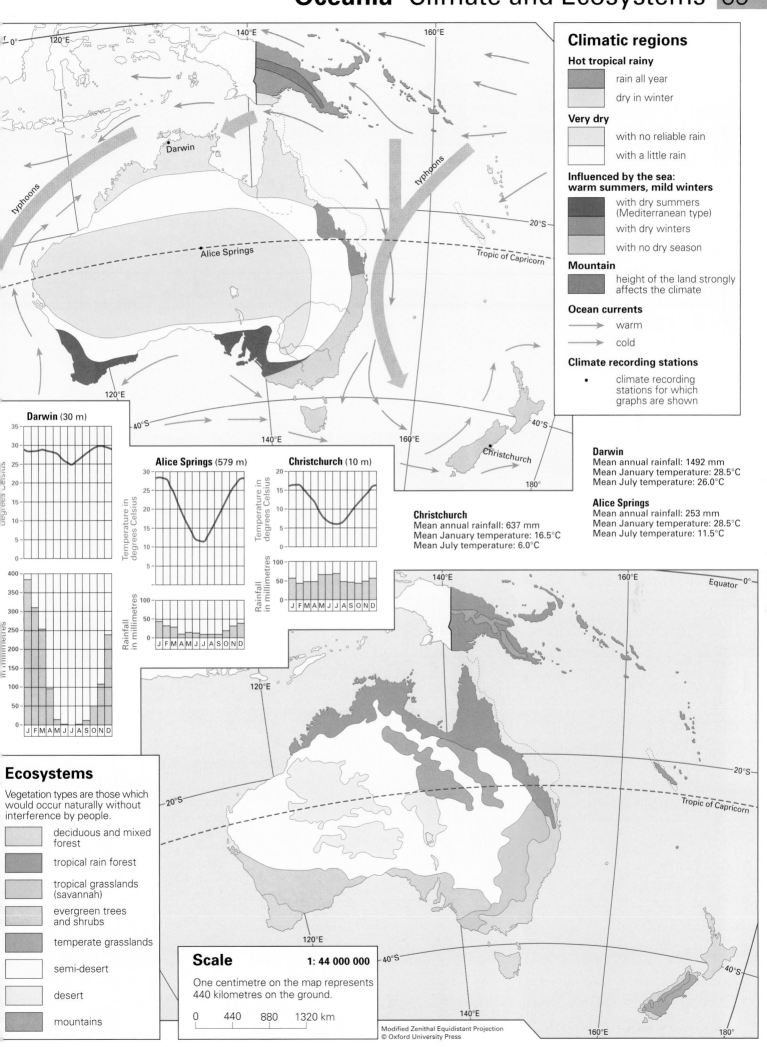

Climatic regions

Hot tropical rainy

- rain all year
- dry in winter

Very dry

- with no reliable rain
- with a little rain

Influenced by the sea: warm summers, mild winters

- with dry summers (Mediterranean type)
- with dry winters
- with no dry season

Mountain

- height of the land strongly affects the climate

Ocean currents

- → warm
- → cold

Climate recording stations

- • climate recording stations for which graphs are shown

Darwin (30 m)

Alice Springs (579 m)

Christchurch (10 m)

Darwin
Mean annual rainfall: 1492 mm
Mean January temperature: 28.5°C
Mean July temperature: 26.0°C

Alice Springs
Mean annual rainfall: 253 mm
Mean January temperature: 28.5°C
Mean July temperature: 11.5°C

Christchurch
Mean annual rainfall: 637 mm
Mean January temperature: 16.5°C
Mean July temperature: 6.0°C

Ecosystems

Vegetation types are those which would occur naturally without interference by people.

- deciduous and mixed forest
- tropical rain forest
- tropical grasslands (savannah)
- evergreen trees and shrubs
- temperate grasslands
- semi-desert
- desert
- mountains

Scale   1: 44 000 000

One centimetre on the map represents 440 kilometres on the ground.

0   440   880   1320 km

Modified Zenithal Equidistant Projection
© Oxford University Press

Farming, forestry, and fishing

main farming types

little or no farming : because the area is too dry or otherwise harsh.

shifting cultivation : small areas farmed until soils exhausted, then family moves.

mixed subsistence : crops and animals for family food.

grazing and stock rearing : on a large scale, for profit.

intensive grazing : fattening of lambs, mainly for meat, and of beef cattle. All for profit.

mixed farming : animals and crops for profit.

grain farming : mostly wheat but also other cereals, for profit.

plantation : well organized, specializing in one crop for profit, e.g. sugar or cocoa.

specialized horticulture : mostly supported by irrigation.

dairy farming : milk, butter, and cheese for profit. Also lamb fattening in New Zealand.

forestry

forestry for profit

cash crops

cocoa		coffee		fruit	
sugar		cotton		rice	
palm products					

animal products

wool   meat   fish

area irrigated by the River Murray Scheme

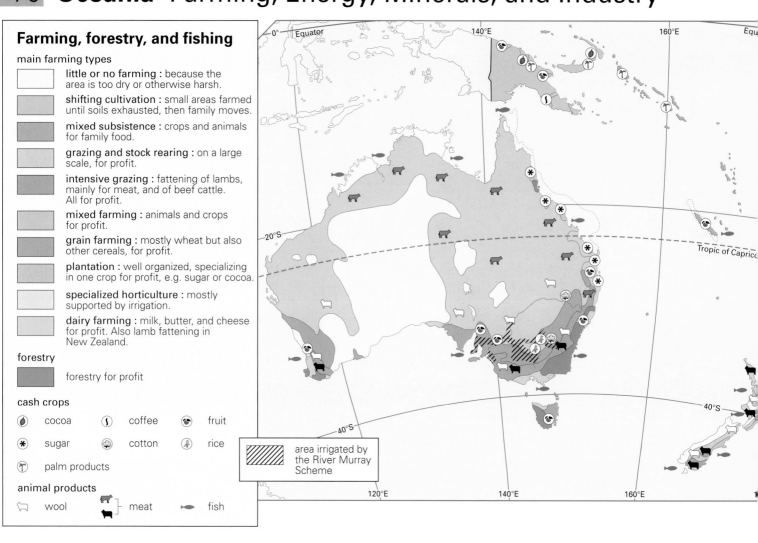

Energy, Minerals, and Industry

energy

coalfield

oil field (with associated gas, and sometimes off shore)

gas field

hydro-electric power stations

largest (over 3000 megawatts)

smaller (500 – 3000 megawatts)

industry

main centres of industry

minerals (main mining areas)

silver		gold		tin	
copper		bauxite		nickel	
zinc		lead		uranium	
diamonds		iron ore (iron sands in New Zealand)			

Australian underground water supplies

areas where artesian water is generally available

areas where artesian water is available in places

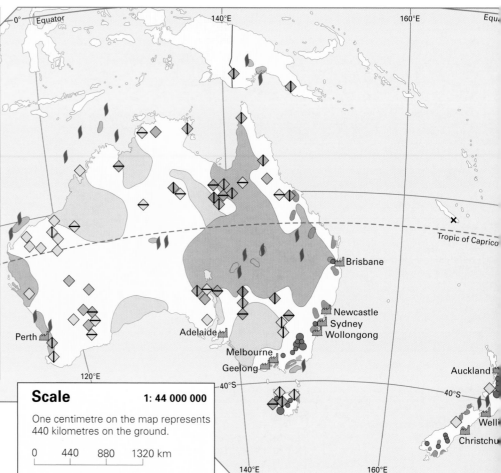

Scale   1: 44 000 000

One centimetre on the map represents 440 kilometres on the ground.

0   440   880   1320 km

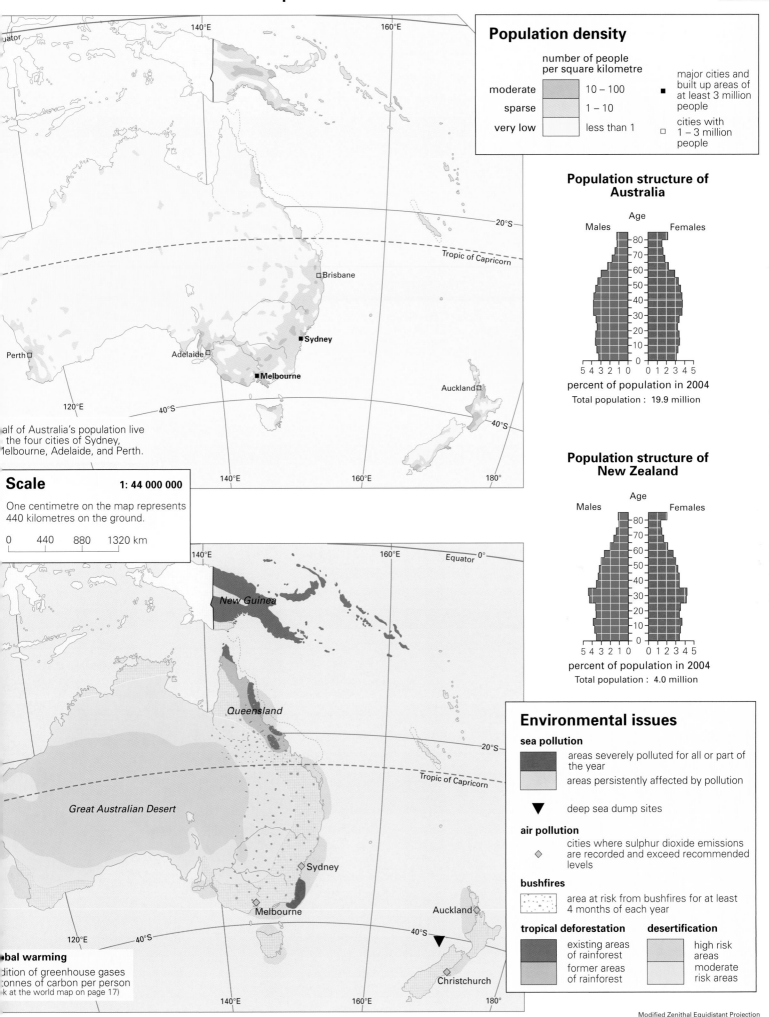

Population density

number of people per square kilometre

moderate	10 – 100
sparse	1 – 10
very low	less than 1

■ major cities and built up areas of at least 3 million people

□ cities with 1 – 3 million people

Population structure of Australia

Age

Males   Females

80
70
60
50
40
30
20
10
0

5 4 3 2 1 0   0 1 2 3 4 5

percent of population in 2004

Total population : 19.9 million

Population structure of New Zealand

Age

Males   Females

80
70
60
50
40
30
20
10
0

5 4 3 2 1 0   0 1 2 3 4 5

percent of population in 2004

Total population : 4.0 million

...alf of Australia's population live
...the four cities of Sydney,
...lelbourne, Adelaide, and Perth.

Scale   1: 44 000 000

One centimetre on the map represents 440 kilometres on the ground.

0   440   880   1320 km

Environmental issues

sea pollution

areas severely polluted for all or part of the year

areas persistently affected by pollution

▼ deep sea dump sites

air pollution

◇ cities where sulphur dioxide emissions are recorded and exceed recommended levels

bushfires

area at risk from bushfires for at least 4 months of each year

tropical deforestation

existing areas of rainforest

former areas of rainforest

desertification

high risk areas

moderate risk areas

...bal warming
...dition of greenhouse gases
...onnes of carbon per person
...k at the world map on page 17)

New Guinea

Queensland

Great Australian Desert

Brisbane

Sydney

Adelaide

Melbourne

Perth

Auckland

Christchurch

Tropic of Capricorn

Equator

Modified Zenithal Equidistant Projection
© Oxford University Press

Land height
in metres above sea level

- more than 2000 m
- 1000 – 2000 m
- 500 – 1000 m
- 200 – 500 m
- less than 200 m
- below sea level

Key

international boundary	
state boundary	
motorway and main road	
railway	
major airport	⊕
river	
seasonal river	
lake	
seasonal lake	
marsh	
coral reef	
peak or highest point	▲
towns	largest ■ large ● others ·

Scale   1: 21 000 000

One centimetre on the map represents 210 kilometres on the ground.

Zenithal Equidistant Projection   © Oxford University

SOLOMON ISLANDS
Honiara

Bougainville
New Ireland
New Britain
PAPUA NEW GUINEA
Madang
Lae
Wau
Goroka
Mendi
Mount Hagen
Port Moresby
Kerema
5030 m Java Peak
IRIAN JAYA
Fly

Coral Sea
Great Barrier Reef
Townsville
Cairns
Cooktown
Charters Towers
Cape York
Torres Strait

GREAT DIVIDING RANGE
QUEENSLAND
Rockhampton
Bundaberg
Maryborough
Brisbane
Gold Coast
Grafton
Toowoomba
Charleville
Cunnamulla
Bourke
Longreach
Cooper Creek
Mount Isa

Gulf of Carpentaria
NORTHERN TERRITORY
Tennant Creek
Birdum
Katherine
Darwin
Daly
Victoria
Ord
Wyndham
Derby
Fitzroy
Broome

MACDONNELL RANGES
Alice Springs
Mt. Ziel 1510 m
Finke
SIMPSON DESERT
STURT DESERT
867 m Ayers Rock

SOUTH AUSTRALIA
Lake Eyre
Lake Torrens
FLINDERS RANGE
Port Augusta
Port Pirie
Whyalla
Port Lincoln
Adelaide
Spencer Gulf

NEW SOUTH WALES
Darling
Murrumbidgee
Murray
Dubbo
Broken Hill
Mildura
Newcastle
Sydney
Wollongong
Canberra
Mt Kosciusko 2230 m
SNOWY MTNS.
Cape Howe

VICTORIA
Ballarat
Geelong
Melbourne
Bass Strait

TASMANIA
Launceston
Burnie

Tasman Sea

WESTERN AUSTRALIA
GREAT SANDY DESERT
GIBSON DESERT
GREAT VICTORIA DESERT
NULLARBOR PLAIN
Lake Mackay
1251 m Mt. Meharry
HAMERSLEY RANGE
Marble Bar
Newman
Port Hedland
Roebourne
Carnarvon
Meekatharra
Mount Magnet
Murchison
Kalgoorlie
Esperance
Geraldton
Perth
Fremantle
Bunbury
Cape Leeuwin
Albany
Great Australian Bight
Tropic of Capricorn

INDONESIA
Ujung Pandang
Ambon
Buru
Seram
Aru Islands
Tanimbar Islands
EAST TIMOR
Dili
Timor
Kupang
Sumba
Sumbawa
Flores
Lombok
Bali
Java
Madura
Sulawesi
Borneo

Banda Sea
Arafura Sea
Timor Sea
Indian Ocean
Southern Ocean
Tasman Sea

10°S   20°S   30°S   40°S
110°E   120°E   130°E   140°E   150°E   160°E

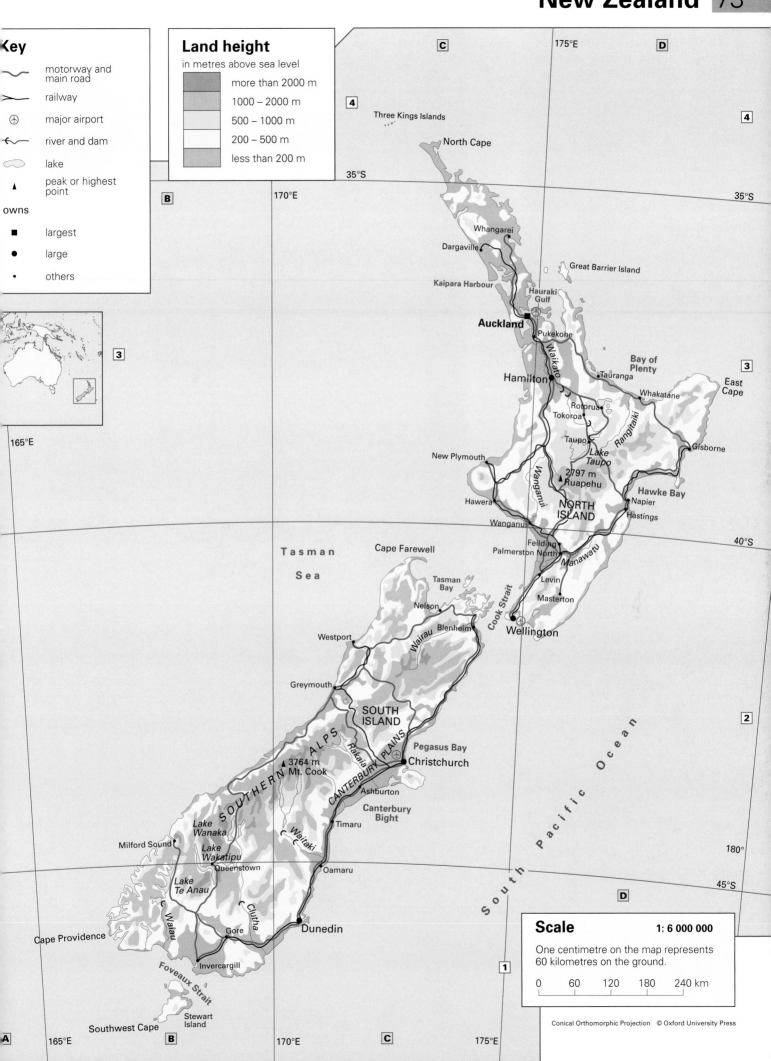

Key

- ～ motorway and main road
- ～ railway
- ⊕ major airport
- ～ river and dam
- ⬭ lake
- ▲ peak or highest point

Towns

- ■ largest
- ● large
- · others

Land height

in metres above sea level

- more than 2000 m
- 1000 – 2000 m
- 500 – 1000 m
- 200 – 500 m
- less than 200 m

Three Kings Islands

North Cape

North Cape

Whangarei

Dargaville

Kaipara Harbour

Great Barrier Island

Hauraki Gulf

Auckland

Pukekohe

Waikato

Hamilton

Bay of Plenty

Tauranga

Whakatāne

East Cape

Rotorua

Tokoroa

Rangitaiki

Taupo

Gisborne

New Plymouth

Lake Taupo

▲ 2797 m Ruapehu

Wanganui

Hawke Bay

Hawera

NORTH ISLAND

Napier

Hastings

Wanganui

Feilding

Palmerston North

Manawatu

Levin

Masterton

Tasman Sea

Cape Farewell

Tasman Bay

Nelson

Cook Strait

Wellington

Westport

Wairau

Blenheim

Greymouth

SOUTH ISLAND

Pegasus Bay

Christchurch

SOUTHERN ALPS

▲ 3764 m Mt. Cook

Rakaia

CANTERBURY PLAINS

Ashburton

Canterbury Bight

Lake Wanaka

Milford Sound

Lake Wakatipu

Waitaki

Timaru

Queenstown

Oamaru

Lake Te Anau

Clutha

Waiau

Gore

Dunedin

Cape Providence

Invercargill

Foveaux Strait

Southwest Cape

Stewart Island

South Pacific Ocean

Tasman Sea

165°E

170°E

175°E

180°

35°S

40°S

45°S

Scale 1: 6 000 000

One centimetre on the map represents 60 kilometres on the ground.

0   60   120   180   240 km

Conical Orthomorphic Projection   © Oxford University Press

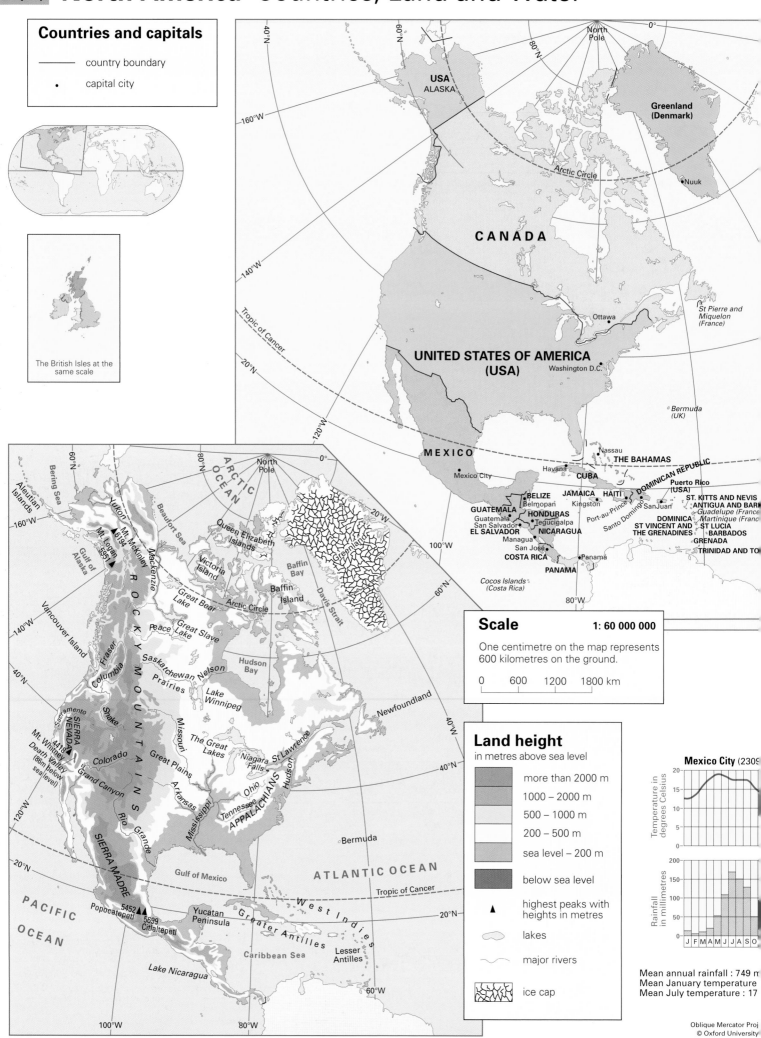

Countries and capitals

— country boundary
• capital city

The British Isles at the same scale

USA
ALASKA

CANADA

Greenland
(Denmark)

Arctic Circle

North Pole

Nuuk

Ottawa

UNITED STATES OF AMERICA
(USA)

Washington D.C.

St Pierre and
Miquelon
(France)

Bermuda
(UK)

MEXICO

Mexico City

Nassau
Havana
THE BAHAMAS

BELIZE   CUBA
Belmopan   JAMAICA   HAITI
GUATEMALA   Kingston   Port-au-Prince
Guatemala   HONDURAS
San Salvador   Tegucigalpa
EL SALVADOR   NICARAGUA
Managua
San José
COSTA RICA   Panamá
PANAMA

DOMINICAN REPUBLIC
San Juan   Puerto Rico
(USA)
ST. KITTS AND NEVIS
Santo Domingo   ANTIGUA AND BARB
Guadelupe (France
DOMINICA   Martinique (Franc
ST VINCENT AND   ST LUCIA
THE GRENADINES   BARBADOS
GRENADA
TRINIDAD AND TO

Cocos Islands
(Costa Rica)

Scale   1: 60 000 000

One centimetre on the map represents
600 kilometres on the ground.

0   600   1200   1800 km

Aleutian
Islands
Bering Sea
Gulf of
Alaska
Yukon
Mt McKinley 6194
Mt Logan 5951
ARCTIC OCEAN
North Pole
Beaufort Sea
Mackenzie
Queen Elizabeth
Islands
Victoria
Island
Greenland
Baffin
Bay
Baffin
Island
Davis Strait
Vancouver Island
ROCKY MOUNTAINS
Fraser
Columbia
Great Bear
Lake
Great Slave
Lake
Peace
Arctic Circle
Saskatchewan
Nelson
Prairies
Hudson
Bay
Lake
Winnipeg
Newfoundland
Sacramento
SIERRA
NEVADA 4418
Snake
Mt Whitney
Death Valley
(86m below
sea level)
Colorado
Grand Canyon
Missouri
Great Plains
Arkansas
The Great
Lakes
Niagara
Falls
St Lawrence
Hudson
APPALACHIANS
Ohio
Tennessee
Mississippi
Rio Grande
SIERRA MADRE
Popocatepetl 5452
Citlaltepetl 5699
Yucatan
Peninsula
Greater Antilles
Gulf of Mexico
Bermuda
ATLANTIC OCEAN
Tropic of Cancer
West Indies
Lesser
Antilles
Caribbean Sea
Lake Nicaragua
PACIFIC OCEAN

Land height
in metres above sea level

more than 2000 m
1000 – 2000 m
500 – 1000 m
200 – 500 m
sea level – 200 m
below sea level

▲ highest peaks with heights in metres
lakes
major rivers
ice cap

Mexico City (2309

Temperature in degrees Celsius
20
15
10
5
0

Rainfall in millimetres
200
150
100
50
0
J F M A M J J A S O

Mean annual rainfall : 749 m
Mean January temperature :
Mean July temperature : 17

Oblique Mercator Proj
© Oxford University

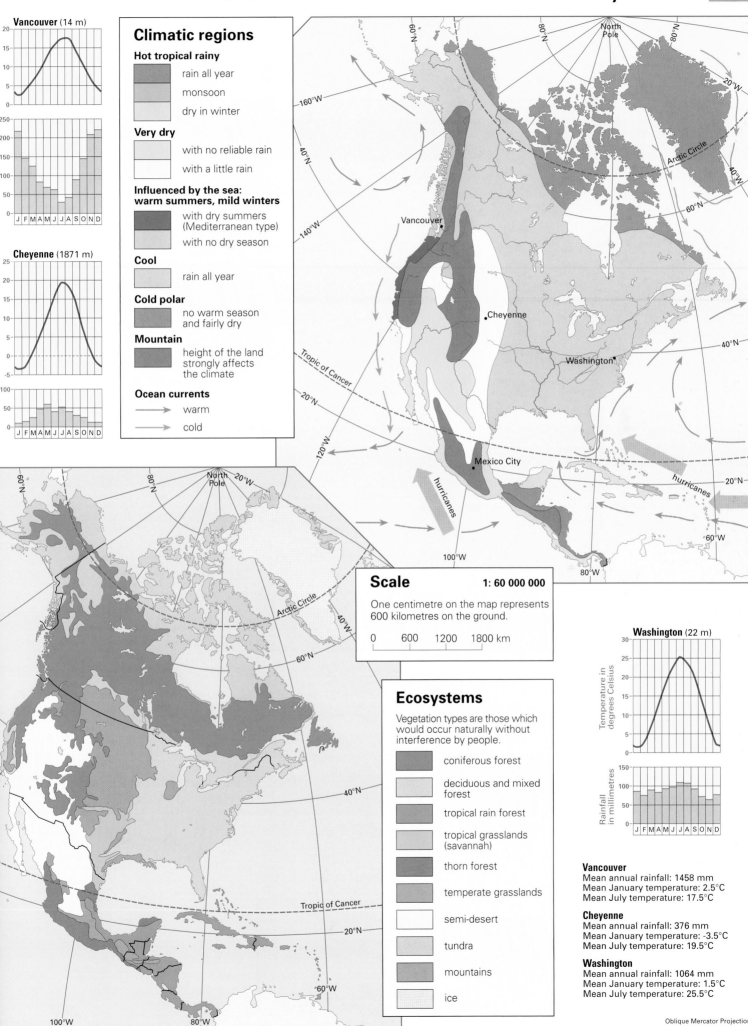

Vancouver (14 m)

Cheyenne (1871 m)

Climatic regions

Hot tropical rainy

- rain all year
- monsoon
- dry in winter

Very dry

- with no reliable rain
- with a little rain

Influenced by the sea: warm summers, mild winters

- with dry summers (Mediterranean type)
- with no dry season

Cool

- rain all year

Cold polar

- no warm season and fairly dry

Mountain

- height of the land strongly affects the climate

Ocean currents

- → warm
- → cold

Scale

1: 60 000 000

One centimetre on the map represents 600 kilometres on the ground.

0   600   1200   1800 km

Ecosystems

Vegetation types are those which would occur naturally without interference by people.

- coniferous forest
- deciduous and mixed forest
- tropical rain forest
- tropical grasslands (savannah)
- thorn forest
- temperate grasslands
- semi-desert
- tundra
- mountains
- ice

Washington (22 m)

Temperature in degrees Celsius

Rainfall in millimetres

Vancouver
Mean annual rainfall: 1458 mm
Mean January temperature: 2.5°C
Mean July temperature: 17.5°C

Cheyenne
Mean annual rainfall: 376 mm
Mean January temperature: -3.5°C
Mean July temperature: 19.5°C

Washington
Mean annual rainfall: 1064 mm
Mean January temperature: 1.5°C
Mean July temperature: 25.5°C

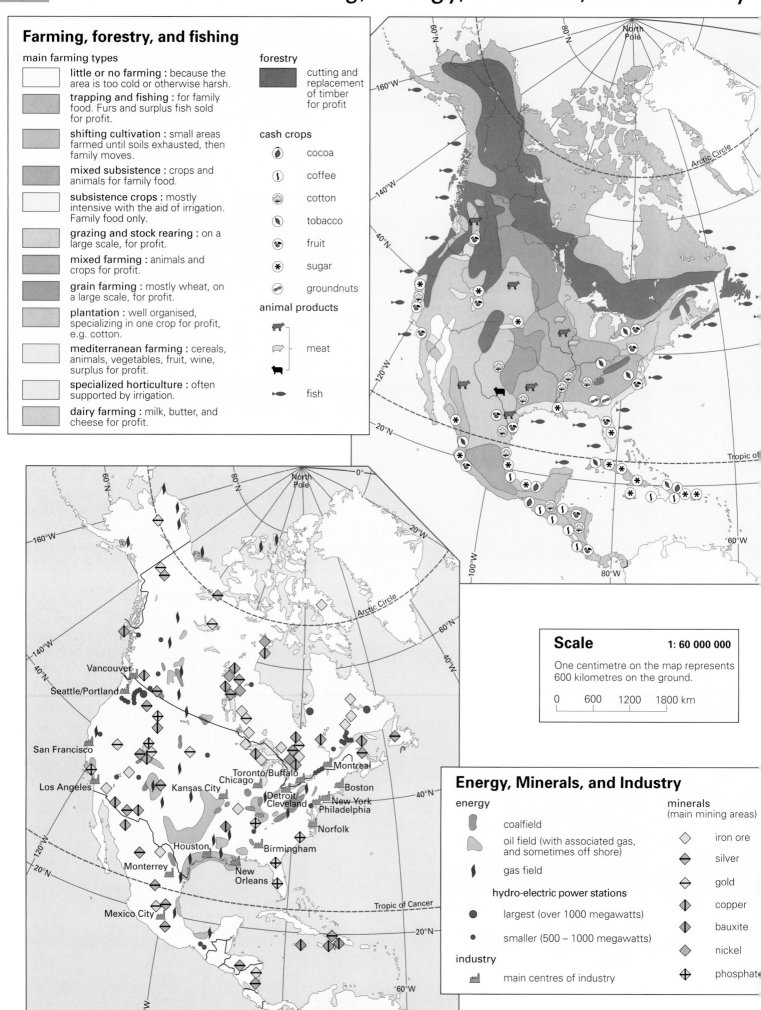

Farming, forestry, and fishing

main farming types

little or no farming : because the area is too cold or otherwise harsh.

trapping and fishing : for family food. Furs and surplus fish sold for profit.

shifting cultivation : small areas farmed until soils exhausted, then family moves.

mixed subsistence : crops and animals for family food.

subsistence crops : mostly intensive with the aid of irrigation. Family food only.

grazing and stock rearing : on a large scale, for profit.

mixed farming : animals and crops for profit.

grain farming : mostly wheat, on a large scale, for profit.

plantation : well organised, specializing in one crop for profit, e.g. cotton.

mediterranean farming : cereals, animals, vegetables, fruit, wine, surplus for profit.

specialized horticulture : often supported by irrigation.

dairy farming : milk, butter, and cheese for profit.

forestry

cutting and replacement of timber for profit

cash crops

- cocoa
- coffee
- cotton
- tobacco
- fruit
- sugar
- groundnuts

animal products

- meat
- fish

Scale   1 : 60 000 000

One centimetre on the map represents 600 kilometres on the ground.

0   600   1200   1800 km

Energy, Minerals, and Industry

energy

- coalfield
- oil field (with associated gas, and sometimes off shore)
- gas field

hydro-electric power stations

- largest (over 1000 megawatts)
- smaller (500 – 1000 megawatts)

industry

- main centres of industry

minerals
(main mining areas)

- iron ore
- silver
- gold
- copper
- bauxite
- nickel
- phosphate

Oblique Mercator Proje
© Oxford University

pulation density

number of people
per square kilometre

high		more than 100
erate		10 – 100
parse		1 – 10
y low		less than 1

■ major cities and built up areas of at least 3 million people

□ cities with 1 – 3 million people

ation structure of United States

Age

Females

3 2 1 0 0 1 2 3 4 5

of the population in 2004

opulation : 293.0 million

Population structure of Mexico

Males   Age   Females

80
70
60
50
40
30
20
10
0

7 6 5 4 3 2 1 0 0 1 2 3 4 5 6 7

percent of the population in 2004

Total population : 105.0 million

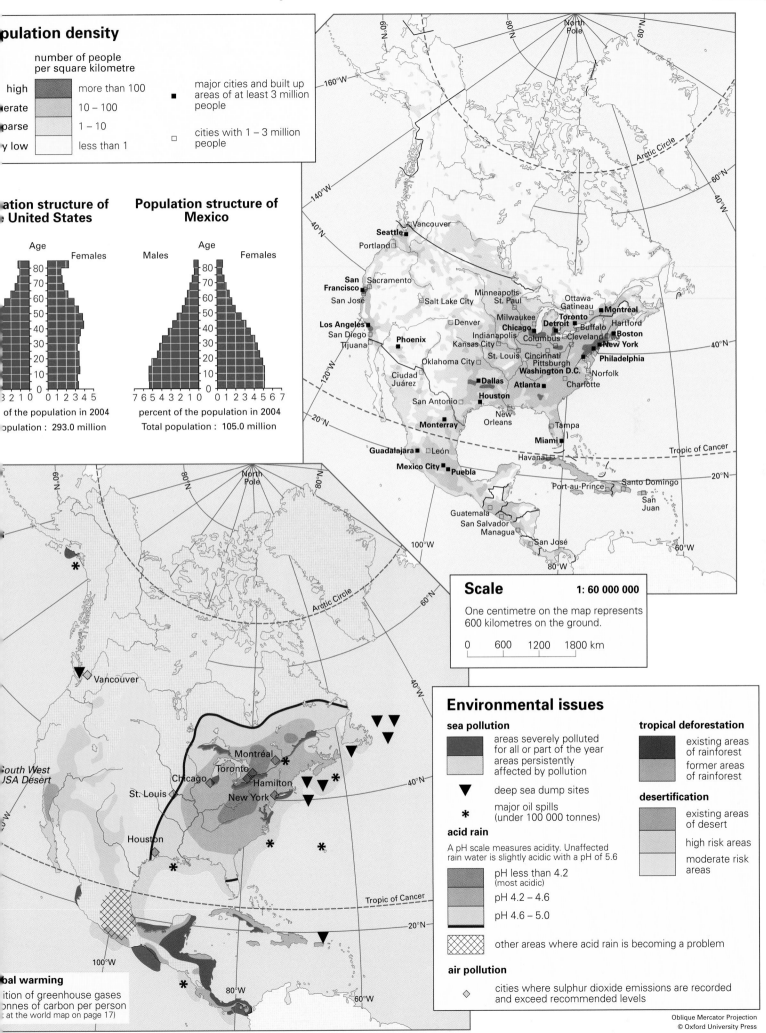

Scale

1 : 60 000 000

One centimetre on the map represents 600 kilometres on the ground.

0   600   1200   1800 km

Environmental issues

sea pollution

areas severely polluted for all or part of the year

areas persistently affected by pollution

▼ deep sea dump sites

✳ major oil spills (under 100 000 tonnes)

acid rain

A pH scale measures acidity. Unaffected rain water is slightly acidic with a pH of 5.6

pH less than 4.2 (most acidic)

pH 4.2 – 4.6

pH 4.6 – 5.0

other areas where acid rain is becoming a problem

air pollution

◇ cities where sulphur dioxide emissions are recorded and exceed recommended levels

tropical deforestation

existing areas of rainforest

former areas of rainforest

desertification

existing areas of desert

high risk areas

moderate risk areas

bal warming

ition of greenhouse gases
nnes of carbon per person
at the world map on page 17)

South West USA Desert

Oblique Mercator Projection
© Oxford University Press

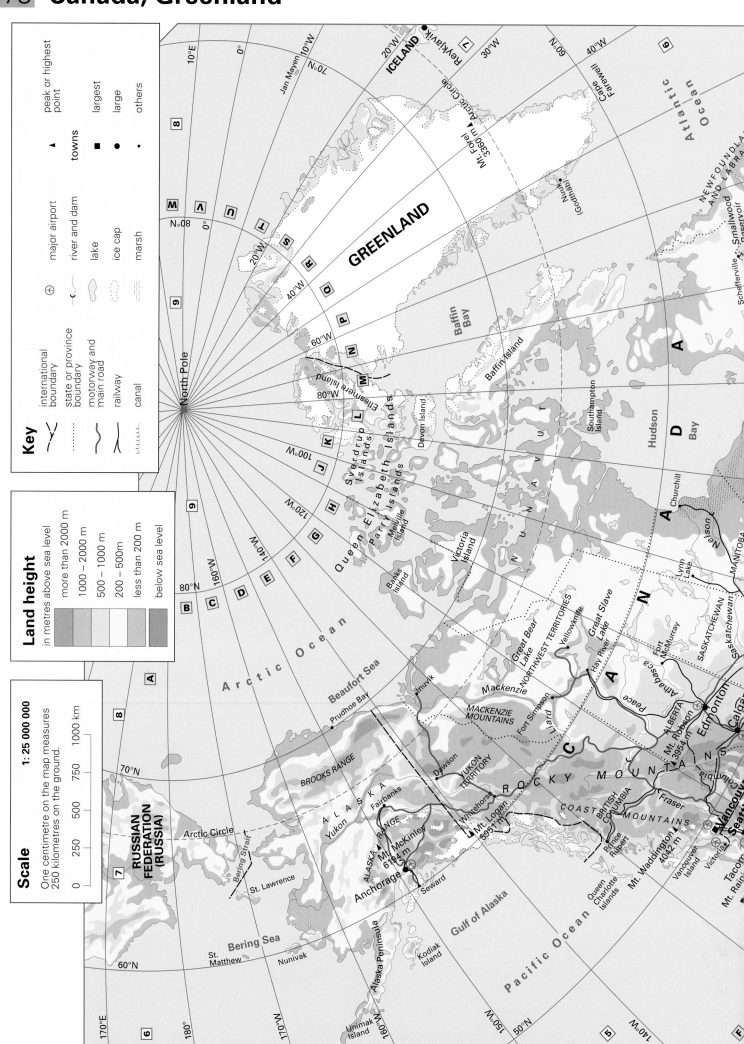

Key

international boundary

state or province boundary

motorway and main road

railway

canal

major airport

river and dam

lake

ice cap

marsh

peak or highest point

towns

largest

large

others

Land height

in metres above sea level

more than 2000 m

1000 – 2000 m

500 – 1000 m

200 – 500m

less than 200 m

below sea level

Scale

1: 25 000 000

One centimetre on the map measures 250 kilometres on the ground.

0   250   500   750   1000 km

GREENLAND

ICELAND

Reykjavik

Mt. Forel ▲ 3360 m

Nuuk (Godthåb)

Jan Mayen

Baffin Bay

Baffin Island

Ellesmere Island

Devon Island

Southampton Island

Hudson Bay

Victoria Island

Banks Island

Melville Island

Parry Islands

Queen Elizabeth Islands

Sverdrup Islands

NUNAVUT

NEWFOUNDLAND AND LABRADOR

Smallwood Reservoir

Schefferville

Churchill

Nelson

Lynn Lake

MANITOBA

SASKATCHEWAN

Great Bear Lake

Great Slave Lake

Yellowknife

NORTHWEST TERRITORIES

Hay River

Fort McMurray

Athabasca

Fort Simpson

Liard

Peace

Mackenzie

Inuvik

MACKENZIE MOUNTAINS

Dawson

YUKON TERRITORY

Whitehorse

Fort Nelson

ALBERTA

Edmonton

Calgary

Mt. Robson 3954 m

BRITISH COLUMBIA

ROCKY MOUNTAINS

Fraser

Columbia

Mt. Waddington 4042 m

Prince Rupert

Queen Charlotte Islands

COAST MOUNTAINS

Mt. Logan 5951 m

Vancouver Island

Victoria

Vancouver

Seattle

Tacoma

Mt. Rainier

Arctic Ocean

Beaufort Sea

Prudhoe Bay

BROOKS RANGE

ALASKA

Yukon

Fairbanks

ALASKA RANGE

Mt. McKinley 6194 m

Anchorage

Seward

Kodiak Island

Gulf of Alaska

Pacific Ocean

RUSSIAN FEDERATION (RUSSIA)

Bering Strait

St. Lawrence

St. Matthew

Nunivak

Unimak Island

Bering Sea

Alaska Peninsula

Arctic Circle

North Pole

Atlantic Ocean

CANADA

C   A   N   A   D   A

170°E

180°

170°W

160°W

150°W

140°W

60°N

70°N

Arctic Circle

50°N

10°E

0°

10°W

20°W

30°W

40°W

60°W

Arctic Circle

Cape Farewell

80°N

80°N

80°W

60°W

40°W

100°W

120°W

140°W

160°W

180°

70°N

60°N

A   B   C   D   E   F   G   H   J   K   L   M   N   P   Q   R   S   T   U   V   M

5   6   7   8   9

Abbreviations

CONN.	CONNECTICUT
DEL.	DELAWARE
MARY.	MARYLAND
MASS.	MASSACHUSETTS
MISS.	MISSISSIPPI
N.H.	NEW HAMPSHIRE
N.J.	NEW JERSEY
PENN.	PENNSYLVANIA
R.I.	RHODE ISLAND
VER.	VERMONT
W.VA.	WEST VIRGINIA

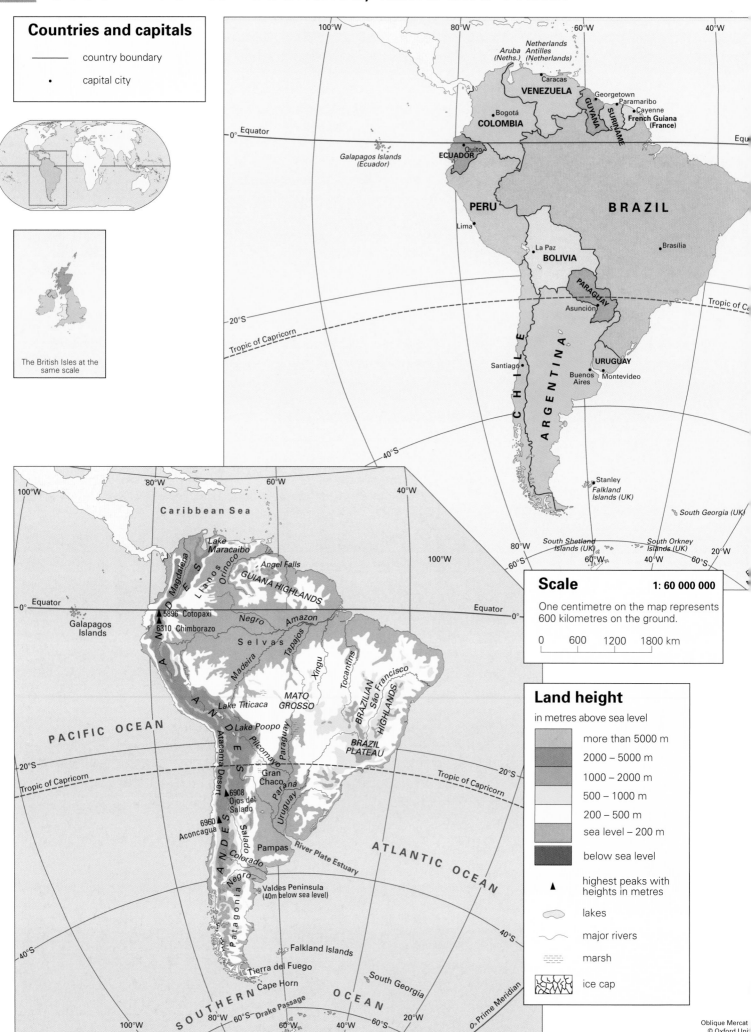

Countries and capitals

——— country boundary

• capital city

The British Isles at the same scale

Caribbean Sea

Lake Maracaibo

Magdalena

Llanos

Orinoco

Angel Falls

GUIANA HIGHLANDS

▲5896 Cotopaxi

6310 Chimborazo

Negro

Amazon

Madeira

Tapajós

S e l v a s

Xingu

Tocantins

São Francisco

BRAZILIAN HIGHLANDS

Lake Titicaca

MATO GROSSO

Lake Poopo

Pilcomayo

Paraguay

BRAZIL PLATEAU

PACIFIC OCEAN

Galapagos Islands

A N D E S

Atacama Desert

▲6908 Ojos del Salado

6960 ▲ Aconcagua

Salado

Colorado

Gran Chaco

Paraná

Uruguay

Pampas

River Plate Estuary

ATLANTIC OCEAN

Negro

Patagonia

Valdés Peninsula (40m below sea level)

Tierra del Fuego

Cape Horn

Falkland Islands

South Georgia

SOUTHERN OCEAN

Drake Passage

Equator

Tropic of Capricorn

Equator

Tropic of Capricorn

Netherlands Antilles (Netherlands)

Aruba (Neths.)

Caracas

VENEZUELA

Georgetown

Paramaribo

GUYANA

SURINAME

Cayenne

French Guiana (France)

• Bogotá

COLOMBIA

Quito

ECUADOR

PERU

• Lima

• La Paz

BOLIVIA

• Brasília

PARAGUAY

Asunción

URUGUAY

Santiago •

C H I L E

A R G E N T I N A

Buenos Aires

• Montevideo

• Stanley

Falkland Islands (UK)

South Georgia (UK)

South Shetland Islands (UK)

South Orkney Islands (UK)

B R A Z I L

Galapagos Islands (Ecuador)

Equator

Tropic of Capricorn

Scale

1: 60 000 000

One centimetre on the map represents 600 kilometres on the ground.

| 0 | 600 | 1200 | 1800 km |

Land height

in metres above sea level

- more than 5000 m
- 2000 – 5000 m
- 1000 – 2000 m
- 500 – 1000 m
- 200 – 500 m
- sea level – 200 m
- below sea level

▲ highest peaks with heights in metres

lakes

major rivers

marsh

ice cap

Oblique Mercat
© Oxford Uni

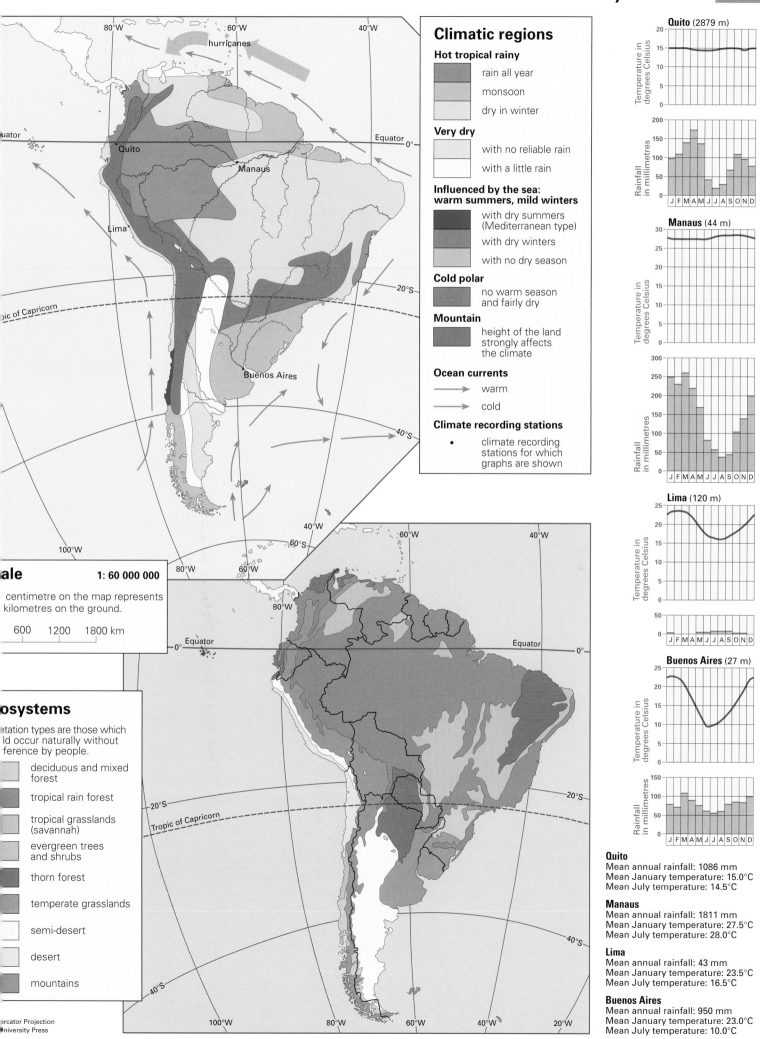

Climatic regions

Hot tropical rainy
- rain all year
- monsoon
- dry in winter

Very dry
- with no reliable rain
- with a little rain

Influenced by the sea: warm summers, mild winters
- with dry summers (Mediterranean type)
- with dry winters
- with no dry season

Cold polar
- no warm season and fairly dry

Mountain
- height of the land strongly affects the climate

Ocean currents
- → warm
- → cold

Climate recording stations
- • climate recording stations for which graphs are shown

Scale
1: 60 000 000

1 centimetre on the map represents 600 kilometres on the ground.

600   1200   1800 km

Ecosystems

Vegetation types are those which would occur naturally without interference by people.

- deciduous and mixed forest
- tropical rain forest
- tropical grasslands (savannah)
- evergreen trees and shrubs
- thorn forest
- temperate grasslands
- semi-desert
- desert
- mountains

Mercator Projection
University Press

Quito (2879 m)

Manaus (44 m)

Lima (120 m)

Buenos Aires (27 m)

Quito
Mean annual rainfall: 1086 mm
Mean January temperature: 15.0°C
Mean July temperature: 14.5°C

Manaus
Mean annual rainfall: 1811 mm
Mean January temperature: 27.5°C
Mean July temperature: 28.0°C

Lima
Mean annual rainfall: 43 mm
Mean January temperature: 23.5°C
Mean July temperature: 16.5°C

Buenos Aires
Mean annual rainfall: 950 mm
Mean January temperature: 23.0°C
Mean July temperature: 10.0°C

Farming, forestry, and fishing

main farming types

little or no farming : because the area is too dry or otherwise harsh.

shifting and marginal cultivation : small areas of forest cleared and farmed until soils exhausted, then family moves. Some hunting and gathering. Some timber cutting, no replacement. In mountains, families try to grow food on the same soil for many years.

mixed subsistence : crops and animals for family food.

subsistence crops : mostly intensive. Family food only.

grazing and stock rearing : on a large scale, for profit.

mixed farming : animals and cereal crops for profit.

grain farming : mostly wheat and maize, on a large scale, for profit.

plantation : well organised, specializing in one crop for profit, e.g. coffee or sugar.

mediterranean farming : cereals, animals, vegetables, fruit, wine, surplus for profit.

specialized horticulture : often supported by irrigation.

dairy farming : milk, butter, and cheese for profit.

forestry

cutting and replacement of timber for profit

cash crops

◐ cocoa

Ⓢ coffee

cotton

tobacco

fruit

✳ sugar

groundnuts

animal products

wool

meat

fish

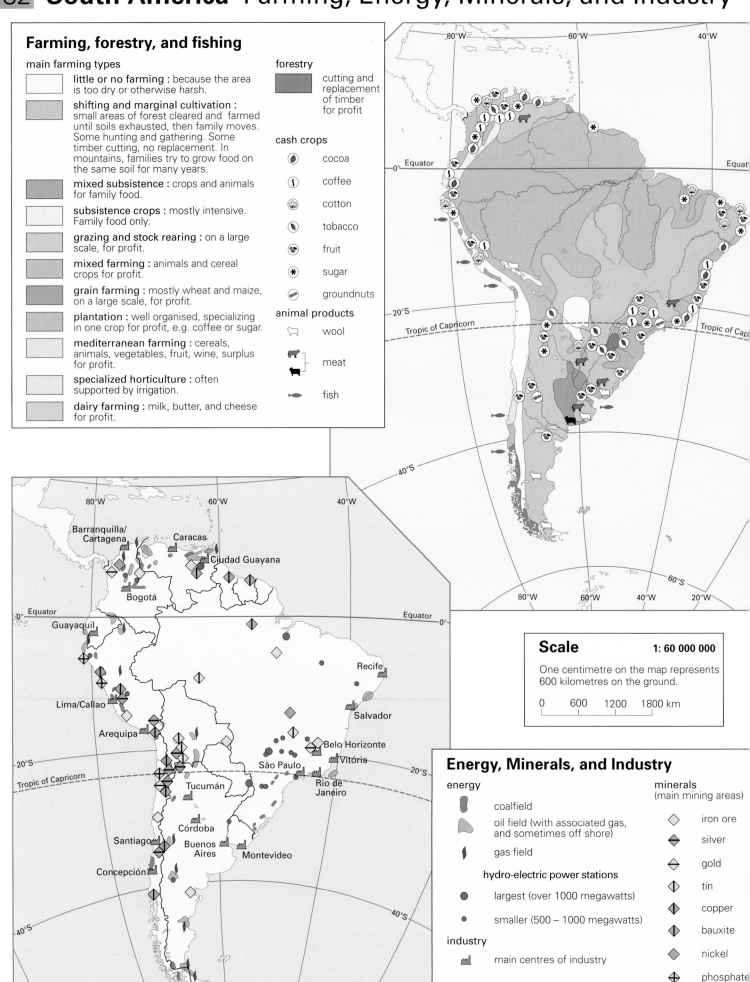

Scale

1: 60 000 000

One centimetre on the map represents 600 kilometres on the ground.

0   600   1200   1800 km

Energy, Minerals, and Industry

energy

coalfield

oil field (with associated gas, and sometimes off shore)

gas field

hydro-electric power stations

● largest (over 1000 megawatts)

• smaller (500 – 1000 megawatts)

industry

main centres of industry

minerals
(main mining areas)

◇ iron ore

silver

gold

tin

copper

bauxite

◇ nickel

phosphate and nitrate (including guano)

Oblique Mercator Proje

© Oxford University P

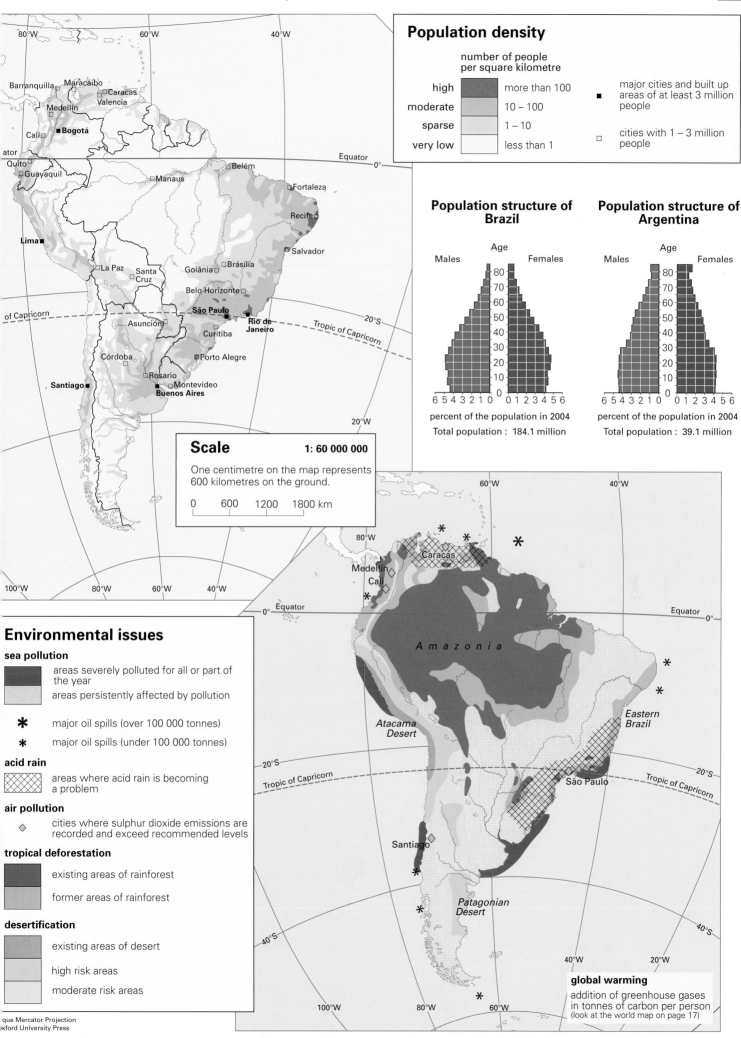

Population density

number of people
per square kilometre

high	more than 100
moderate	10 – 100
sparse	1 – 10
very low	less than 1

■ major cities and built up areas of at least 3 million people

□ cities with 1 – 3 million people

Population structure of Brazil

Age

Males   Females

percent of the population in 2004
Total population : 184.1 million

Population structure of Argentina

Age

Males   Females

percent of the population in 2004
Total population : 39.1 million

Scale   1: 60 000 000

One centimetre on the map represents
600 kilometres on the ground.

0   600   1200   1800 km

Environmental issues

sea pollution

areas severely polluted for all or part of the year

areas persistently affected by pollution

✳ major oil spills (over 100 000 tonnes)

✳ major oil spills (under 100 000 tonnes)

acid rain

areas where acid rain is becoming a problem

air pollution

◇ cities where sulphur dioxide emissions are recorded and exceed recommended levels

tropical deforestation

existing areas of rainforest

former areas of rainforest

desertification

existing areas of desert

high risk areas

moderate risk areas

global warming

addition of greenhouse gases
in tonnes of carbon per person
(look at the world map on page 17)

que Mercator Projection
xford University Press

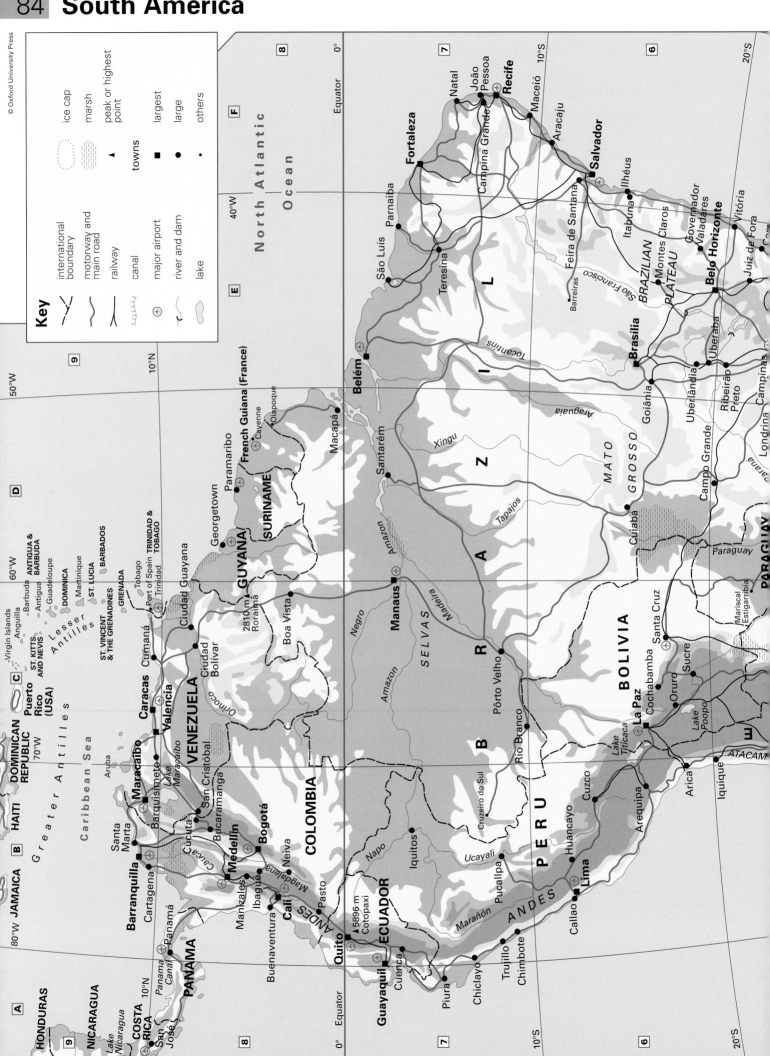

Key

international boundary		ice cap	
motorway and main road		marsh	
railway		peak or highest point	
canal			
major airport	towns	largest	
river and dam		large	
lake		others	

Land height
in metres above sea level

more than 5000 m
2000 – 5000 m
1000 – 2000 m
500 – 1000 m
200 – 500 m
less than 200 m

Scale
1: 21 000 000

One centimetre on the map represents
210 kilometres on the ground.

0   210   420   630   840 km

Transverse Mercator Projection   © Oxford University Press

South Atlantic
Ocean

Southern Ocean

Pacific
Ocean

South Georgia
(UK)

South Orkney
Islands (UK)

South Shetland
Islands (UK)

Antarctic Circle

Antarctic
Peninsula

ANTARCTICA

Stanley
Falkland
Islands (UK)

Cape Horn
Tierra
del Fuego

Punta Arenas

Chiloé
Island

Puerto Montt
Osorno
Valdivia
Temuco
Concepción
Talcahuano
Chillán
Talca
Santiago
Valparaíso
Viña del Mar
Aconcagua
6960 m
San Juan
Mendoza

Esquel

Comodoro
Rivadavia

PATAGONIA

Negro
Colorado

Bahía Blanca

ARGENTINA

Mar del Plata

La Plata
Buenos Aires
Rosario
Santa Fé
Córdoba
Santiago
del Estero
Resistencia
Corrientes

Paraná
Salado
Paraná

Uruguay

URUGUAY
Montevideo
River Plate
Estuary

Pelotas
Rio Grande
Porto Alegre
Caxias do Sul
Florianópolis

ANDES
CHILE

Juan
Fernández
Islands

F
E
D 50°W
C 60°W
B 70°W
A 80°W

30°S
40°S
50°S
60°S

30°W
40°W

90°W

60°S
50°S
40°S
30°S

60°W
100°W

5 4 3 2 1

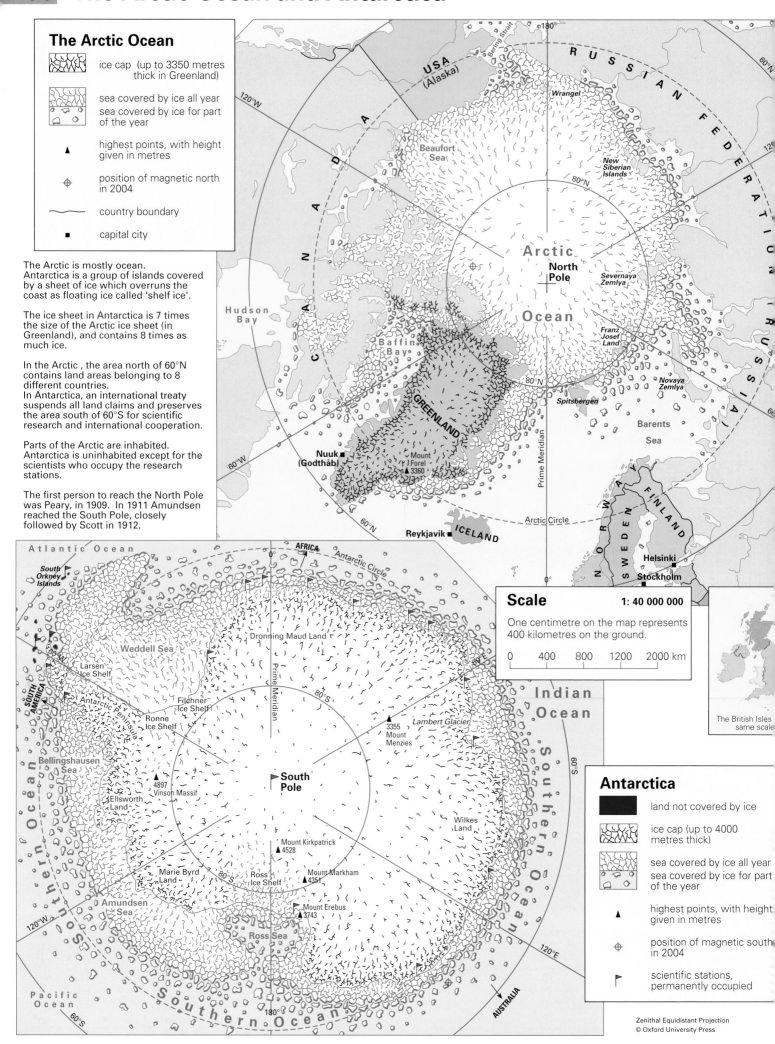

The Arctic Ocean

ice cap (up to 3350 metres thick in Greenland)

sea covered by ice all year
sea covered by ice for part of the year

▲ highest points, with height given in metres

⊕ position of magnetic north in 2004

country boundary

■ capital city

The Arctic is mostly ocean. Antarctica is a group of islands covered by a sheet of ice which overruns the coast as floating ice called 'shelf ice'.

The ice sheet in Antarctica is 7 times the size of the Arctic ice sheet (in Greenland), and contains 8 times as much ice.

In the Arctic, the area north of 60°N contains land areas belonging to 8 different countries.
In Antarctica, an international treaty suspends all land claims and preserves the area south of 60°S for scientific research and international cooperation.

Parts of the Arctic are inhabited. Antarctica is uninhabited except for the scientists who occupy the research stations.

The first person to reach the North Pole was Peary, in 1909. In 1911 Amundsen reached the South Pole, closely followed by Scott in 1912.

Scale
1: 40 000 000

One centimetre on the map represents 400 kilometres on the ground.

| 0 | 400 | 800 | 1200 | 2000 km |

The British Isles same scale

Antarctica

land not covered by ice

ice cap (up to 4000 metres thick)

sea covered by ice all year
sea covered by ice for part of the year

▲ highest points, with height given in metres

⊕ position of magnetic south in 2004

⚑ scientific stations, permanently occupied

Zenithal Equidistant Projection
© Oxford University Press

How to use the index

To find a place on an atlas map use either the grid code or latitude and longitude.

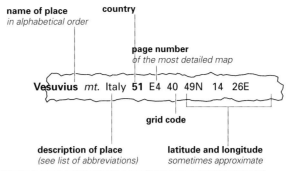

name of place
in alphabetical order

country

page number
of the most detailed map

Vesuvius *mt.* Italy **51** E4 40 49N 14 26E

grid code

description of place
(see list of abbreviations)

latitude and longitude
sometimes approximate

Grid code

Vesuvius is in grid square E4

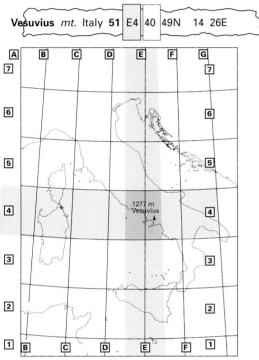

Latitude and longitude

Vesuvius is at latitude 40 49N longitude 14 26E

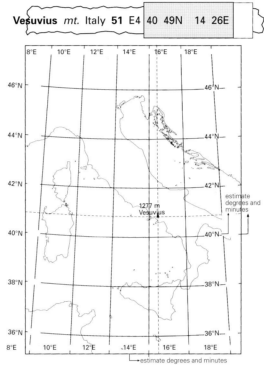

Abbreviations used in the index

admin.	administrative area
b.	bay or harbour
bor.	borough
c.	cape, point or headland
co.	county
est.	estuary
geog.reg.	geographical region
i.	island
is.	islands
l.	lake, lakes, lagoon
mt.	mountain
mts.	mountains
p.	peninsula
pk.	peak
plat.	plateau
pt.	point
r.	river
res.	reservoir
sd.	sound, strait or channel
sum.	summit
tn.	town
u.a.	unitary authority
vol.	volcano

A

Aachen Germany **49** D4 50 46N 6 06E
Aare *r.* Switzerland **49** D2 47 15N 7 30E
Abadan Iran **61** E4 30 20N 48 15E
Abbeville France **48** D5 50 06N 1 51E
Aberaeron Wales **36** C2 52 49N 44 43W
Aberdare Wales **36** D1 51 43N 3 27W
Aberchirder Scotland **31** G2 57 33N 2 38W
Aberdeen Scotland **31** G2 57 10N 2 04W
Aberdeen City *u.a.* Scotland **31** G2 57 10N 2 00W
Aberdeenshire *u.a.* Scotland **31** G2 57 10N 2 50W
Aberfeldy Scotland **31** F1 56 37N 3 54W
Abergavenny Wales **36** D1 51 50N 3 00W
Abertillery Wales **36** D1 51 45N 3 09W
Aberystwyth Wales **36** C2 52 25N 4 05W
Abha Saudi Arabia **61** E2 18 14N 42 31E
Abidjan Côte d'Ivoire **66** B3 5 19N 4 01W
Abingdon England **38** C2 51 41N 1 17W
Aboyne Scotland **31** G2 57 05N 2 50W
Abu Dhabi United Arab Emirates **61** F3 24 28N 54 25E
Abuja Nigeria **66** C3 9 10N 7 11E
Acapulco Mexico **79** K2 16 51N 99 56W
Accra Ghana **66** B3 5 33N 0 15W
Acklins Island The Bahamas **79** M3 22 30N 74 30W
Aconcagua *mt.* Argentina **85** B4 32 40S 70 02W
A Coruña Spain **50** A5 43 22N 8 24W
Adamawa Highlands Africa **66** D3 7 00N 13 00E
Adana Turkey **43** P3 37 00N 35 19E
Addis Ababa Ethiopia **61** D1 9 03N 38 42E
Adelaide Australia **72** D2 34 55S 138 36E
Aden Yemen Republic **61** E2 12 50N 45 03E
Aden, Gulf of Indian Ocean **61** E2 12 30N 47 30E
Adour *r.* France **48** C1 43 45N 0 30W
Adriatic Sea Mediterranean Sea **51** E5 43 00N 15 00E
Aegean Sea Mediterranean Sea **42** L3 39 00N 24 00E
AFGHANISTAN **58** B4
Agadez Niger **66** C4 17 00N 7 56E
Agadir Morocco **66** B6 30 30N 9 40W
Agra India **58** C3 27 09N 78 00E
Aguascalientes Mexico **79** J3 21 51N 102 18W
Ahmadabad India **58** C3 23 03N 72 40E
Ahvaz Iran **61** E4 31 17N 48 43E

Ailsa Craig *i.* Scotland **32** D3 55 16N 5 07W
Aïn Sefra Algeria **42** F2 32 45N 0 35W
Airdrie Scotland **33** F3 55 52N 3 59W
Aire *r.* England **34** C2 54 00N 2 05W
Aix-en-Provence France **48** F1 43 31N 5 27E
Ajaccio Corsica **51** B4 41 55N 8 43E
Ajdabiya Libya **66** E6 30 46N 20 14E
Akita Japan **59** N2 39 44N 140 05E
Akureyri Iceland **42** C9 65 41N 18 04W
Alabama *state* USA **79** L4 32 00N 87 00W
Alaska *state* USA **78** D7 63 00N 150 00W
Alaska, Gulf of USA **78** E6 58 00N 147 00W
Alaska Peninsula USA **78** D6 56 30N 159 00W
Alaska Range *mts.* USA **78** D7/E7 62 30N 152 30W
Albacete Spain **50** E3 39 00N 1 52W
ALBANIA **42** L4
Albany Australia **72** B2 35 00S 117 53E
Alberta *province* Canada **78** H6 55 00N 115 00W
Albert, Lake Congo Dem. Rep./Uganda **67** D5 2 00N 31 00E
Ålborg Denmark **42** H7 57 05N 9 50E
Albuquerque USA **79** J4 35 05N 106 38W
Alcalá de Henares Spain **50** D4 40 28N 3 22W
Alcudia Balearic Islands **50** G3 39 51N 3 06E
Aldabra Islands Indian Ocean **67** E4 9 00S 46 00E
Aldeburgh England **39** F3 52 09N 1 35E
Alderney *i.* Channel Islands British Isles **41** E2 49 43N 2 12W
Aldershot England **38** D2 51 15N 0 47W
Aleppo Syria **61** D4 36 14N 37 10E
Alessándria Italy **51** B6 44 55N 8 37E
Alexandria Egypt **61** C4 31 13N 29 55E
Alexandria Scotland **33** E3 55 59N 4 36W
Algarve *geog. reg.* Portugal **50** A2 37 30N 8 00W
ALGERIA **66** C5
Algiers Algeria **66** C6 36 50N 3 00E
Al Hoceima Morocco **50** D1 35 14N 3 56W
Alicante Spain **50** E3 38 21N 0 29W
Alice Springs Australia **72** D3 23 41S 133 52E
Al Jawf Libya **66** E5 24 12N 23 18E
Allahabad India **58** D3 25 27N 81 50E
Allier *r.* France **48** E3 46 15N 3 15E
Alloa Scotland **33** F4 56 07N 3 49W
Almanzor *mt.* Spain **50** C4 40 15N 5 18W

Almaty Kazakhstan **56** H2 43 19N 76 55E
Almería Spain **50** D2 36 50N 2 26W
Al Mukha Yemen Republic **61** E2 13 20N 43 16E
Aln *r.* England **33** H3 55 30N 1 50W
Alnwick England **33** H3 55 25N 1 42W
Alps *mts.* Europe **49** D2/G2 46 00N 7 30E
Altai Mountains Mongolia **57** K2 47 00N 92 30E
Alton England **38** D2 51 09N 0 59W
Alyth Scotland **31** F1 56 37N 3 13W
Amazon *r.* Brazil **84** D7 2 30S 65 30W
Amble England **33** H3 55 20N 1 34W
Ambleside England **34** C3 54 26N 2 58W
Ambon Indonesia **60** D2 3 41S 128 10E
Amesbury England **38** C2 51 10N 1 47W
Amiens France **48** E4 49 54N 2 18E
Amlwch Wales **36** C3 53 25N 4 20W
Amman Jordan **61** D4 31 04N 46 17E
Ammanford Wales **36** D1 51 48N 3 58W
Amritsar India **58** C4 31 35N 74 56E
Amsterdam Netherlands **49** C5 52 22N 4 54E
Amu Darya *r.* Asia **56** G2 41 00N 61 00E
Amundsen Sea Southern Ocean **86** 72 00S 130 00W
Amur *r.* Asia **57** N3 54 00N 122 00E
Anchorage USA **78** E7 61 10N 150 00W
Ancona Italy **51** D5 43 37N 13 31E
Andaman Islands India **58** E2 12 00N 94 00E
Andaman Sea Indian Ocean **58** E2 13 00N 95 00E
Andes *mts.* South America **84/85** B8/C5 10 00S 77 00W
Andizhan Uzbekistan **56** H2 40 40N 72 12E
ANDORRA **50** F5
Andover England **38** C2 51 13N 1 28W
Andros *i.* The Bahamas **79** M3 24 00N 78 00W
Aneto *mt.* Spain **50** F5 42 37N 0 40E
Angara *r.* Russia **57** K3 59 00N 97 00E
Angeles The Philippines **60** D4 15 09N 120 33E
Angers France **48** C3 47 29N 0 32W
Anglesey *i.* Wales **36** C3 53 13N 4 23W
ANGOLA **67** B3
Angoulême France **48** D2 45 40N 0 10E
Anguilla *i.* Leeward Islands **79** N2 18 14N 63 05W
Angus *u.a.* Scotland **31** F1/G1 56 45N 3 00W
Ankara Turkey **43** N3 39 55N 32 50E
'Annaba Algeria **66** C6 36 55N 7 47E

An Najaf Iraq **61** E4 31 59N 44 19E
Annam Range *mts.* Laos/Vietnam **60** B4 19 00N 104 00E
Annan Scotland **33** F2 54 59N 3 16W
Annan *r.* Scotland **33** F3 55 05N 3 20W
Annapurna *mt.* Nepal **58** D3 28 34N 83 50E
Annecy France **48** G2 45 54N 6 07E
Anshan China **59** D4 41 05N 122 58E
Anstruther Scotland **33** G4 56 14N 2 42W
Antalya Turkey **43** N3 36 53N 30 42E
Antananarivo Madagascar **67** E3 18 52S 47 30E
Antarctic Peninsula Antarctica **86** 68 00S 65 00W
Antibes France **48** G1 43 35N 7 07E
Antigua *i.* Antigua & Barbuda **84** C9 17 09N 61 49W
ANTIGUA AND BARBUDA **79** N2
Antofagasta Chile **84** B5 23 40S 70 23W
Antrim Northern Ireland **32** C2 54 43N 6 13W
Antrim *district* Northern Ireland **32** C2 54 45N 6 25W
Antrim Mountains Northern Ireland **32** C3/D2 55 00N 6 10W
Antwerp Belgium **49** C4 51 13N 4 25E
Anxi China **59** A5 40 32N 95 57E
Aomori Japan **59** N3 40 50N 140 43E
Aosta Italy **51** A6 45 43N 7 19E
Aparri The Philippines **60** D4 18 22N 121 40E
Apeldoorn Netherlands **49** C5 52 13N 5 57E
Appalachians *mts.* USA **79** L4 37 00N 82 00W
Appennines *mts.* Italy **51** C6/F4 44 30N 10 00E
Appleby-in-Westmorland England **34** C3 53 36N 2 29W
Aqaba Jordan **61** D3 29 32N 35 00E
Arabian Sea Indian Ocean **7** 17 00N 60 00E
Aracaju Brazil **84** F6 10 54S 37 07W
Arafura Sea Australia **72** D5 9 00S 133 00E
Araguaia *r.* Brazil **84** D6 12 30S 51 00W
Arak Iran **61** E4 34 05N 49 42E
Araks *r.* Asia **61** E4 39 30N 48 00E
Aral Sea Asia **56** G2 45 00N 60 00E
Aran Fawddy *mt.* Wales **36** D2 52 47N 3 41W
Ararat, Mount Turkey **43** Q3 39 44N 44 15E
Arbil Iraq **61** E4 36 12N 44 01E
Arbroath Scotland **31** G1 56 34N 2 35W
Arctic Ocean **86**
Ardabil Iran **61** E4 38 15N 48 18E

Ardbeg Scotland **32** C3 55 39N 6 05W
Ardennes *mts.* Belgium **49** C4 50 10N 5 45E
Ardminish Scotland **32** D3 55 42N 5 44W
Ardres France **39** F1 50 51N 1 59E
Ards *district* Northern Ireland **32** D2 54 30N 5 30W
Ards Peninsula Northern Ireland **32** D2 54 25N 5 30W
Arequipa Peru **84** B6 16 25S 71 32W
Arezzo Italy **51** C5 43 28N 11 53E
ARGENTINA 85 C4
Argyll and Bute *u.a.* Scotland **32/33** D4/E4 56 10N 5 00W
Århus Denmark **42** J7 56 15N 10 10E
Arica Chile **84** B6 18 30S 70 20W
Arisaig Scotland **30** D1 56 51N 5 51W
Arisaig, Sound of Scotland **30** D1 56 50N 5 50W
Arizona *state* USA **79** H4 34 00N 112 00W
Arkansas *r.* USA **79** K4 35 00N 93 00W
Arkansas *state* USA **79** K4 34 00N 93 00W
Arkhangel'sk Russia **56** E4 64 32N 40 40E
Arklow Republic of Ireland **36** A2 52 48N 6 09W
Arles France **48** F1 43 41N 4 38E
Armagh Northern Ireland **32** C2 54 21N 6 39W
Armagh *district* Northern Ireland **32** C2 54 20N 6 40W
ARMENIA 43 Q4
Armentières France **39** G1 50 41N 2 53E
Arnhem Netherlands **49** C4 52 00N 5 53E
Arno *r.* Italy **51** C5 43 46N 11 00E
Arnold England **37** F2 53 00N 1 09W
Arran *i.* Scotland **32** D3 55 35N 5 15W
Arras France **48** E5 50 17N 2 46E
Artá Balearic Islands **50** G3 39 42N 3 20E
Aru Islands Indonesia **60** E2 6 00S 134 30E
Arun *r.* England **38** D2 51 05N 0 30W
Arundel England **38** D2 51 05N 0 34W
Asahikawa Japan **59** N3 43 46N 142 23E
Asahi, Mount Japan **59** N3 42 42N 142 54E
Asansol India **58** D3 23 40N 86 59E
Ascension Island Atlantic Ocean **5** 7 57S 14 22W
Ashbourne England **37** F3 53 01N 1 43W
Ashburton New Zealand **73** C2 43 54S 171 45E
Ashford England **39** E2 51 09N 0 53E
Ashgabat Turkmenistan **56** F1 37 58N 58 24E
Ashington England **33** H3 55 11N 1 34W
Asmara Eritrea **61** D2 15 20N 38 58E
Assisi Italy **51** D5 43 04N 12 37E
Astana Kazakhstan **56** H3 51 10N 71 28E
Astrakhan Russia **56** E2 46 22N 48 04E
Asunción Paraguay **85** D5 25 15S 57 40W
Aswan Egypt **61** D3 24 05N 32 56E
Asyut Egypt **61** D3 27 14N 31 07E
Atacama Desert Chile **84/85** B5 22 30S 70 00W
Atbara Sudan **61** D2 17 42N 34 00E
Atbara *r.* Sudan **61** D2 17 00N 35 00E
Athabasca *r.* Canada **78** H6 57 30N 112 00W
Athens Greece **42** L3 38 00N 23 44E
Atlanta USA **79** L4 33 45N 84 23W
Atlantic Ocean **79** N4
Atlas Mountains Morocco **66** B6 32 00N 2 00W
Atrek *r.* Iran/Turkmenistan **61** F4 38 00N 57 00E
Atyrau Kazakhstan **56** F2 47 08N 51 59E
Auchterarder Scotland **33** F4 56 18N 3 43W
Auchtermuchty Scotland **33** F4 56 17N 3 15W
Auckland New Zealand **73** C3 36 51S 174 46E
Auderville France **41** F2 49 43N 1 56W
Augsburg Germany **49** F3 48 21N 10 54E
Austin USA **79** K4 30 18N 97 47W
AUSTRALIA 72
AUSTRIA 42 J5
Auxerre France **48** E3 47 48N 3 35E
Aveiro Portugal **50** A4 40 38N 8 40W
Aviemore Scotland **31** F2 57 12N 3 50W
Avignon France **48** F1 43 56N 4 48E
Avon *r.* Warwickshire/Worcestershire England **37** F2 52 15N 1 55W
Avon *r.* Wiltshire/Bath and North East Somerset/ North Somerset England **38** B2 51 20N 2 05W
Avon *r.* Wiltshire/Hampshire/Dorset England **38** C1 50 55N 1 50W
Axe *r.* England **41** E3 50 50N 2 50W
Axminster England **41** E3 50 47N 3 00W
Ayaguz Kazakhstan **56** J2 47 59N 80 27E
Ayers Rock *mt.* Australia **72** D3 25 20S 131 01E
Aylesbury England **38** D2 51 50N 0 50W
Ayr Scotland **33** E3 55 28N 4 38W
Ayr *r.* Scotland **33** E3 55 30N 4 20W
Ayre, Point of *c.* Isle of Man British Isles **33** E2 54 25N 4 22W
AZERBAIJAN 56 E2
Azores *is.* Atlantic Ocean **4** 38 30N 28 00W
Azov, Sea of Asia **43** P5 46 00N 36 00E

B

Bacolod The Philippines **60** D4 10 38N 122 58E
Badajoz Spain **50** B3 38 53N 6 58W
Baden-Baden Germany **49** E3 48 45N 8 15E
Baffin Bay Canada **78** N8 72 00N 64 00W
Baffin Island Canada **78** M8 70 00N 75 00W
Baghdad Iraq **61** E4 33 20N 44 26E
BAHAMAS, THE 79 M3
Bahía Blanca Argentina **85** C4 38 45S 62 15W
BAHRAIN 61 F3
Baie de la Seine *b.* France **41** G2 49 40N 0 30W
Bakewell England **37** F3 53 13N 1 40W
Baku Azerbaijan **56** E2 40 22N 49 53E
Bala Wales **36** D2 52 54N 3 36W
Bala Lake Wales **36** D2 52 53N 3 38W
Balearic Islands Spain **50** F3/H4 40 00N 2 00E
Bali *i.* Indonesia **60** C2 8 30S 115 00E
Balikesir Turkey **42** M3 39 37N 27 51E
Balikpapan Indonesia **60** C2 1 15S 116 50E
Balkhash, Lake Kazakhstan **56** H2 46 00N 75 00E
Ballantrae Scotland **32** D3 55 06N 5 00W
Ballarat Australia **72** E2 37 33S 143 56E
Ballater Scotland **31** F2 57 03N 3 03W
Ballybofey Republic of Ireland **32** A2 54 48N 7 47W
Ballycastle Northern Ireland **32** C3 55 12N 6 15W
Ballymena Northern Ireland **32** C2 54 52N 6 17W

Ballymena *district* Northern Ireland **32** C2 54 55N 6 20W
Ballymoney Northern Ireland **32** C3 55 04N 6 31W
Ballymoney *district* Northern Ireland **32** C3 55 00N 6 30W
Ballyshannon Republic of Ireland **32** A2 54 30N 8 11W
Baltic Sea Europe **42** K7 55 15N 17 00E
Baltimore USA **79** M4 39 18N 76 38W
Bamako Mali **66** B4 12 40N 7 59W
Bamberg Germany **49** F3 49 54N 10 54E
Bamburgh England **33** H3 55 36N 1 42W
Banbridge Northern Ireland **32** C2 54 21N 6 16W
Banbridge *district* Northern Ireland **32** C2 54 20N 6 20W
Banbury England **38** C3 52 04N 1 20W
Banchory Scotland **31** G2 57 30N 2 30W
Banda Aceh Indonesia **60** A3 5 30N 95 20E
Bandar-e 'Abbas Iran **61** F3 27 12N 56 15E
Bandar Seri Begawan Brunei **60** C3 4 53N 114 57E
Banda Sea Indonesia **60** D2 5 50S 126 00E
Bandung Indonesia **60** B2 6 57S 107 34E
Banff Scotland **31** G2 57 40N 2 33W
Bangalore India **58** C2 12 58N 77 35E
Bangka *i.* Indonesia **60** B2 2 30S 107 00E
Bangkok Thailand **60** B4 13 44N 100 30E
BANGLADESH 58 D3/E3
Bangor Northern Ireland **32** D2 54 40N 5 40W
Bangor Wales **36** C3 53 13N 4 08W
Bangui Central African Republic **67** B5 4 23N 18 37E
Bangweulu, Lake Zambia **67** C3 11 15S 29 45E
Banjul The Gambia **66** A4 13 28N 16 39W
Banjarmasin Indonesia **60** C2 3 22S 114 33E
Banks Island Canada **78** G8 73 15N 121 30W
Bann *r.* Northern Ireland **32** C2 54 55N 6 30W
Baotou China **59** B4 40 38N 109 59E
BARBADOS 79 P2
Barbuda *i.* Antigua & Barbuda **84** C9 17 41N 61 48W
Barcelona Spain **50** G4 41 25N 2 10E
Bareilly India **58** C3 28 20N 79 24E
Barents Sea Arctic Ocean **86** 75 00N 40 00E
Barfleur France **41** F2 49 40N 1 16W
Bari Italy **51** F4 41 07N 16 52E
Barito *r.* Indonesia **60** C2 2 00S 115 00E
Barking England **39** E2 51 33N 0 06E
Barletta Italy **51** F4 41 20N 16 17E
Barmouth Wales **36** C2 52 43N 4 03W
Barnard Castle England **34** C3 54 33N 1 55W
Barnau Russia **56** J3 53 21N 83 45E
Barnet England **38** D2 51 39N 0 12W
Barnoldswick England **34** C2 53 56N 2 16W
Barnsley England **35** D2 53 34N 1 28W
Barnstaple England **40** C4 51 05N 4 04W
Barquisimeto Venezuela **84** C9 10 03N 69 18W
Barra *i.* Scotland **30** B1/2 57 00N 7 25W
Barranquilla Colombia **84** B9 11 10N 74 50W
Barreiras Brazil **84** E6 12 09S 44 58W
Barrow-in-Furness England **34** B3 54 07N 3 14W
Barry Wales **36** D1 51 24N 3 18W
Barton-upon-Humber England **35** E2 53 41N 0 27W
Basel Switzerland **49** D3 47 33N 7 36E
Basildon England **39** E2 51 34N 0 25W
Basingstoke England **38** C2 51 16N 1 05W
Basra Iraq **61** E4 30 30N 47 50E
Bassein Myanmar **58** E2 16 46N 94 45E
Bass Strait Australia **72** E2 39 51S 145 53E
Bastia France **51** B5 42 14N 9 26E
Bata Equatorial Guinea **66** C3 1 51N 9 49E
Batang China **59** A3 30 02N 99 01E
Batangas The Philippines **60** D4 13 46N 121 01E
Bath England **38** B2 51 23N 2 22W
Bath and North East Somerset *u.a.* England **38** B2 51 25N 2 30W
Bathgate Scotland **33** F3 55 55N 3 39W
Baton Rouge USA **79** K4 30 30N 91 10W
Batumi Georgia **56** E2 41 37N 41 36E
Baykal, Lake Russia **57** L3 54 00N 109 00E
Bayeux France **48** C4 49 16N 0 42W
Bayonne France **48** C1 43 30N 1 28W
Bayreuth Germany **49** F3 49 27N 11 35E
Beachy Head *c.* England **39** E1 50 44N 0 16E
Bearsden Scotland **33** E3 55 56N 4 20W
Beaufort Sea Arctic Ocean **78** E7 72 00N 140 00W
Beauly *r.* Scotland **31** E2 57 30N 4 30W
Beauvais France **48** E4 49 26N 2 05E
Beccles England **39** F3 52 28N 1 34E
Bechar Algeria **66** B6 31 35N 2 17W
Bedford England **38** D3 52 08N 0 29W
Bedfordshire *co.* England **38** D3 52 08N 0 29W
Bedworth England **37** F2 52 29N 1 28W
Beersheba Israel **43** N2 31 15N 34 47E
Beida Libya **66** E6 32 00N 21 30E
Beijing China **59** D3 39 55N 116 26E
Beinn Dearg *mt.* Scotland **31** E2 57 47N 4 56W
Beira Mozambique **67** D3 19 49S 34 52E
Beirut Lebanon **61** D4 33 52N 35 30E
Beja Portugal **50** B3 38 01N 7 52W
Bejaïa Algeria **42** H3 36 49N 5 03E
BELARUS 56 C3
Belém Brazil **84** E7 1 27S 48 29W
Belfast Northern Ireland **32** D2 54 35N 5 55W
Belfast *district* Northern Ireland **32** C2/D2 54 30N 5 58W
Belfast Lough *est.* Northern Ireland **32** D2 54 40N 5 45W
Belfort France **48** G3 47 38N 6 52E
Belgaum India **58** C2 15 54N 74 36E
BELGIUM 49
Belgrade Serbia and Montenegro **42** L4 44 50N 20 30E
Belitung *i.* Indonesia **60** B2 2 30S 107 30E
BELIZE 79 L2
Belize Belize **79** L2 17 29N 88 10W
Belle Isle *i.* France **48** B3 47 20N 3 10W
Bellingshausen Sea Southern Ocean **86** 71 00S 85 00W
Belmopan Belize **79** L2 17 13N 88 48W
Belo Horizonte Brazil **84** E6 19 54S 43 54W
Ben Alder *mt.* Scotland **31** E1 56 49N 4 28W

Benavente Spain **50** C5 42 00N 5 40W
Benbecula *i.* Scotland **30** B2 57 25N 7 20W
Ben Cruachan *mt.* Scotland **30** D1 56 26N 5 09W
Bengal, Bay of Indian Ocean **58** D2 17 00N 88 00E
Benghazi Libya **66** E6 32 07N 20 04E
Benguela Angola **67** B3 12 34S 13 24E
Ben Hope *mt.* Scotland **31** E3 58 24N 4 37W
BENIN 66 C4
Ben Klibreck *mt.* Scotland **31** E3 58 14N 4 22W
Ben Lawers *mt.* Scotland **31** E1 56 33N 4 15W
Ben Lomond *mt.* Scotland **33** E4 56 12N 4 38W
Ben More *mt.* Argyll and Bute Scotland **30** C1 56 25N 6 02W
Ben More *mt.* Stirling Scotland **31** E1 56 25N 6 02W
Ben More Assynt *mt.* Scotland **31** E3 58 07N 4 52W
Ben Nevis *mt.* Scotland **31** D1 56 48N 5 00W
Benue *r.* Nigeria/Cameroon **66** C3/D3 9 00N 10 00E
Ben Wyvis *mt.* Scotland **31** E2 57 40N 4 35W
Berbera Somalia **66** H4 10 28N 45 02E
Berezniki Russia **43** T7 59 26N 56 49E
Bérgamo Italy **51** B6 45 42N 9 40E
Bergen Norway **42** H8 60 23N 5 20E
Bergerac France **48** D2 44 50N 0 29E
Bering Sea Pacific Ocean **57** S3 58 00N 170 00W
Bering Strait Russia/USA **78** C7 69 00N 169 00W
Berlin Germany **49** G5 52 32N 13 25E
Bermuda *i.* Atlantic Ocean **79** N4 32 50N 64 20W
Bern Switzerland **49** D2 46 57N 7 26E
Berneray *i.* Scotland **30** B2 57 45N 7 10W
Bernina *mt.* Europe **42** E2 46 23N 9 54E
Berwick-upon-Tweed England **33** G3 55 46N 2 00W
Besançon France **48** F3 47 14N 6 02E
Bethesda Wales **36** C3 53 11N 4 03W
Béthune France **48** E5 50 32N 2 38E
Beverley England **35** E2 53 51N 0 26W
Bewdley England **37** E2 52 22N 2 19W
Bexley England **39** E2 51 27N 0 09E
BHUTAN 58 D3/E3
Białystok Poland **42** L6 53 09N 23 10E
Biarritz France **48** C1 43 29N 1 33W
Bicester England **38** C2 51 54N 1 09W
Bideford England **40** C4 51 01N 4 13W
Bideford Bay England **40** C4 51 05N 4 25W
Bielefeld Germany **49** E5 52 02N 8 32E
Bigbury Bay England **40** D3 50 17N 4 00W
Biggar Scotland **33** F3 55 38N 3 32W
Biggleswade England **38** D3 52 06N 0 17W
Bikaner India **58** C3 28 01N 73 22E
Bilbao Spain **50** D5 43 15N 2 56W
Bintan *i.* Indonesia **60** B3 0 50N 104 30E
Birdum Australia **72** D4 15 39S 133 13E
Birkenhead England **34** B2 53 24N 3 02W
Birmingham England **37** F2 52 30N 1 50W
Birmingham USA **79** L4 33 30N 86 55W
Biscay, Bay of Atlantic Ocean **48** B2 45 30N 2 50W
Bishkek Kyrgyzstan **56** H2 42 53N 74 46E
Bishop Auckland England **34** D3 54 40N 1 40W
Bishop's Stortford England **39** E2 51 53N 0 09E
Biskra Algeria **42** H2 34 50N 5 41E
Bissau Guinea-Bissau **66** A4 11 52N 15 39W
Biwa, Lake Japan **59** M2 35 20N 135 20E
Bizerte Tunisia **51** B2 37 18N 9 52E
Blackburn England **34** C2 53 45N 2 29W
Blackburn with Darwen *u.a.* England **34** C2 53 43N 2 25W
Black Forest *mts.* Germany **49** E3 47 00N 8 00E
Black Mountains Wales **36** D1 51 55N 3 10W
Blackpool England **34** B2 53 50N 3 03W
Blackpool *u.a.* England **34** B2 53 51N 3 10W
Black Sea Europe **43** P4 43 00N 35 00E
Black Volta *r.* Africa **66** B3/4 10 00N 3 00W
Blackwater *r.* Northern Ireland **32** C2 54 30N 6 45W
Blackwater Reservoir Scotland **30** C1 56 41N 4 46W
Blaenau Ffestiniog Wales **36** D2 52 59N 3 56W
Blaenau Gwent *u.a.* Wales **36** D1 51 45N 3 10W
Blagoveshchensk Russia **57** N3 50 19N 127 30E
Blairgowrie Scotland **31** F1 56 36N 3 21W
Blandford Forum England **41** E3 50 52N 2 11W
Blantyre Malawi **67** D3 15 46S 35 00E
Blenheim New Zealand **73** C2 41 31S 173 57E
Blida Algeria **42** H3 36 30N 2 50E
Blois France **48** D3 47 36N 1 20E
Bloemfontein Republic of South Africa **67** C2 29 07S 26 14E
Blue Nile *r.* Ethiopia/Sudan **61** D2 12 00N 33 00E
Blyth England **33** H3 55 07N 1 30W
Blyth *r.* England **33** H3 55 10N 1 45W
Boa Vista Brazil **84** C8 2 23S 55 30W
Bobo Dioulasso Burkina **66** B4 11 11N 4 18W
Bochum Germany **49** D4 51 28N 7 11E
Bodele Depression Chad **66** E4 17 00N 17 50E
Bodmin England **40** C3 50 29N 4 43W
Bodmin Moor England **40** C3 50 35N 4 40W
Bodø Norway **42** J9 67 18N 14 26E
Bognor Regis England **38** D1 50 47N 0 41W
Bogor Indonesia **60** B2 6 34S 106 48E
Bogotá Colombia **84** B8 4 38N 74 05W
Boise USA **79** H5 43 38N 116 12W
BOLIVIA 84 C6
Bologna Italy **51** C6 44 30N 11 20E
Bolton England **34** C2 53 35N 2 26W
Bolzano Italy **51** C7 46 30N 11 22E
Bonaire *i.* Lesser Antilles **79** N2 12 15N 68 27W
Bonar Bridge *tn.* Scotland **31** E2 57 53N 4 21W
Bo'ness Scotland **33** F4 56 01N 3 37W
Bonifacio Corsica **51** B4 41 23N 9 10E
Bonn Germany **49** D4 50 44N 7 06E
Bootle England **34** B2 53 28N 3 00W
Bordeaux France **48** C2 44 50N 0 34W
Borneo *i.* Indonesia/Malaysia **60** C3 1 00N 113 00E
Bornholm *i.* Denmark **42** K6 55 02N 15 00E
Boscastle England **40** C3 50 41N 4 42W
BOSNIA-HERZEGOVINA 42 K4
Boston England **35** E2 52 29N 0 01W
Boston USA **79** M5 42 20N 71 05W
Bothnia, Gulf of Finland/Sweden **42** L8 61 00N 19 10E
BOTSWANA 67 C2

Bouaké Côte d'Ivoire **66** B3 7 42N 5 00W
Bougainville *i.* Papua New Guinea **72** F5 6 15S 155 00E
Boulogne-sur-Mer France **48** D5 50 43N 1 37E
Bourges France **48** E3 47 05N 2 23E
Bourke Australia **72** E2 30 05S 145 58E
Bournemouth England **41** F3 50 43N 1 54W
Bournemouth *u.a.* England **41** F3 50 46N 1 52W
Bou Saâda Algeria **42** G3 35 10N 4 09E
Bovey Tracey England **40** D3 50 36N 3 40W
Boyoma Falls Congo Dem.Rep. **67** C5 0 18N 25 30E
Bracknell England **38** D2 51 26N 0 46W
Bracknell Forest *u.a.* England **38** D2 51 22N 0 43W
Bradford England **34** C2 53 48N 1 45W
Braemar Scotland **31** F2 57 01N 3 23W
Brahmaputra *r.* India/Bangladesh **58** E3 27 00N 94 00E
Brăila Romania **42** M5 45 17N 27 58E
Braintree England **39** E2 51 53N 0 32E
Brampton England **34** C3 54 57 2 43W
Brandenburg Germany **49** G5 52 25N 12 34E
Branderburgh Scotland **31** F2 57 43N 3 18W
Brasília Brazil **84** E6 15 45S 47 57W
Braşov Romania **42** M5 45 39N 25 35E
Bratislava Slovakia **42** K5 48 10N 17 10E
Bratsk Russia **57** L3 56 20N 101 50E
Braunton England **40** C4 51 07N 4 10W
Bray Republic of Ireland **36** A3 53 12N 6 06W
BRAZIL 84 C7/E7
Brazilian Plateau Brazil **84** E6 17 00S 44 00W
Brazzaville Congo **66** D2 4 14S 15 14E
Brechin Scotland **31** G1 56 44N 2 40W
Brecon Wales **36** D1 51 57N 3 24W
Brecon Beacons *mts.* Wales **36** D1 51 53N 3 30W
Breda Netherlands **49** C4 51 35N 4 46E
Bremen Germany **49** E5 53 05N 8 48E
Bremerhaven Germany **49** E5 53 33N 8 35E
Brenner Pass Austria/Italy **49** F2 47 02N 11 32E
Brent England **38** D2 51 34N 0 17W
Brentwood England **39** E2 51 38N 0 18E
Bréscia Italy **51** C6 45 33N 10 13E
Bressay *i.* Scotland **29** D3 60 08N 1 05W
Brest Belarus **42** L6 52 08N 23 40E
Brest France **48** A4 48 23N 4 30W
Bridgend Wales **36** D1 51 31N 3 35W
Bridgend *u.a.* Wales **36** D1 51 32N 3 35W
Bridgnorth England **37** E2 52 33N 2 25W
Bridgwater England **41** E4 51 08N 3 00W
Bridgwater Bay England **41** D4 51 15N 3 20W
Bridlington England **35** D3 54 05N 0 12W
Bridport England **41** E3 50 44N 2 46W
Brigg England **35** E2 53 34N 0 30W
Brighouse England **34** D2 53 42N 1 47W
Brighton England **38** D1 50 50N 0 10W
Brighton & Hove *u.a.* England **38** D1 50 52N 0 13W
Brindisi Italy **51** F4 40 37N 17 57E
Brisbane Australia **72** F3 27 28S 153 03E
Bristol England **38** B2 51 27N 2 35W
Bristol *u.a.* England **38** B2 51 30N 2 30W
Bristol Channel United Kingdom **36** C1/D1 51 20N 3 50W
British Columbia *province* Canada **78** G6 55 00N 128 00W
Brittany *geog. reg.* France **48** B4 48 00N 3 00W
Brive France **48** D2 45 09N 1 32E
Brixham England **40** D3 50 23N 3 30W
Brno Czech Republic **42** K5 49 13N 16 40E
Broad Bay Scotland **30** C3 58 15N 6 10W
Broadford England **37** F2 52 02N 1 50W
Broad Law *mt.* Scotland **33** F3 55 30N 3 22W
Broadway England **37** F2 52 02N 1 50W
Brodick Scotland **32** D3 55 35N 5 09W
Broken Hill *tn.* Australia **72** E2 31 57S 141 28E
Bromley England **39** E2 51 31N 0 01W
Bromsgrove England **37** E2 52 20N 2 03W
Bromyard England **37** E2 52 11N 2 30W
Brooks Range *mts.* U.S.A. **78** D7/E7 67 55N 155 00W
Broome Australia **72** C4 17 55S 122 13E
Brora Scotland **31** F3 58 01N 3 51W
Brough England **34** C3 54 32N 2 19W
Brough Head Scotland **29** B2 59 09N 3 19W
Brown Clee Hill England **37** E2 52 27N 2 35W
Brown Willy *sum.* England **40** C3 50 35N 4 36W
Brugge Belgium **49** B4 51 13N 3 14E
BRUNEI 60 C3
Brunswick Germany **49** F5 52 15N 10 30E
Brussels Belgium **49** C4 50 50N 4 21E
Bryansk Russia **56** D3 53 15N 34 09E
Bryher *i.* England **40** A2 49 57N 6 21W
Bucaramanga Colombia **84** B8 7 08N 73 10W
Bucharest Romania **42** M4 44 25N 26 07E
Buckfastleigh England **40** D3 50 29N 3 46W
Buckhaven Scotland **33** F4 56 11N 3 03W
Buckie Scotland **31** G2 57 40N 2 58W
Buckingham England **38** D2 52 00N 1 00W
Buckinghamshire *co.* England **38** D2 51 50N 0 50W
Budapest Hungary **42** K5 47 30N 19 03E
Bude England **40** C3 50 50N 4 33W
Bude Bay England **40** C3 50 50N 4 40W
Buenaventura Colombia **84** B8 3 54N 77 02W
Buenos Aires Argentina **85** D4 34 40S 58 30W
Buffalo USA **79** M5 42 52N 78 55W
Builth Wells Wales **36** D2 52 09N 3 24W
Bujumbura Burundi **67** C4 3 22S 29 19E
Bukavu Congo Dem. Rep. **67** C4 2 30S 28 50E
Bukhara Uzbekistan **56** G1 39 47N 64 26E
Bulawayo Zimbabwe **67** C2 20 10S 28 43E
BULGARIA 42 M4
Bunbury Australia **72** B2 33 20S 115 39E
Buncrana Republic of Ireland **32** B3 55 08N 7 27W
Bundaberg Australia **72** F3 24 53S 152 21E
Bungay England **39** F3 52 28N 1 26E
Buraida Saudi Arabia **61** E3 26 20N 43 59E
Bure *r.* England **39** F3 52 47N 1 20E
Burgas Bulgaria **42** M4 42 30N 27 29E
Burghead *tn.* Scotland **31** F2 57 42N 3 30W
Burgos Spain **50** D5 42 21N 3 41W
Burgundy *geog. reg.* France **48** F3 47 00N 5 00E
BURKINA 66 B4

BURMA *see* MYANMAR
Burnie Australia **72** E1 41 03S 145 55E
Burnley England **34** C2 53 48N 2 14W
Burry Port Wales **36** C1 51 42N 4 15W
Bursa Turkey **42** M4 40 12N 29 04E
Burton upon Trent England **37** F2 52 48N 1 36W
Buru *i.* Indonesia **60** D2 3 30S 126 30E
BURUNDI **67** C4
Bury England **34** C2 53 36N 2 17W
Bury St. Edmunds England **39** E3 52 15N 0 43E
Bush *r.* Northern Ireland **32** C3 55 10N 6 30W
Bute *i.* Scotland **32** D3 55 50N 5 05W
Bute, Sound of Scotland **32** D3 55 45N 5 10W
Buton *i.* Indonesia **60** D2 5 00S 122 45E
Butt of Lewis *c.* Scotland **30** C3 58 30N 6 20W
Butuan The Philippines **60** D3 8 56N 125 31E
Buxton England **37** F3 53 15N 1 55W
Bydgoszcz Poland **42** K6 53 16N 18 00E

C
Cabanatuan The Philippines **60** D4 15 30N 120 58E
Cabinda *province* Angola **66** D2 5 00S 12 00E
Cabora Bassa, Lake Mozambique **67** D3 15 40S 31 40E
Cabrera *i.* Balearic Islands **50** G3 39 00N 2 59E
Cader Idris *mt.* Wales **36** D2 52 42N 3 54W
Cádiz Spain **50** B2 36 32N 6 18W
Caen France **48** C4 49 11N 0 22W
Caernarfon Wales **36** C3 53 08N 4 16W
Caernarfon Bay Wales **36** C3 53 05N 4 30W
Caerphilly Wales **36** D1 51 35N 3 14W
Caerphilly *u.a.* Wales **36** D1 51 37N 3 15W
Cagayan de Oro The Philippines **60** D3 8 29N 124 40E
Cagliari Italy **51** B3 39 13N 9 08E
Cairn Gorm *mt.* Scotland **31** F2 57 07N 3 40W
Cairngorms *mts.* Scotland **31** F2 57 10N 3 30W
Cairns Australia **72** E4 16 54S 145 45E
Cairo Egypt **61** D4 30 03N 31 15E
Calais France **48** D5 50 57N 1 52E
Cala Ratjada Balearic Islands **50** G3 39 43N 3 27E
Calatayud Spain **50** E4 41 21N 1 39W
Calbayog The Philippines **60** D4 12 04N 124 38E
Calcutta India **58** D3 22 35N 88 21E
Calgary Canada **78** H6 51 05N 114 05W
Cali Colombia **84** B8 3 24N 76 30W
Calicut India **58** C1 11 15N 75 45E
California *state* USA **79** H4 35 00N 119 00W
California, Gulf of Mexico **79** H3 27 00N 111 00W
Callander Scotland **33** E4 56 15N 4 13W
Callao Peru **84** B6 12 05S 77 08W
Calne England **38** B2 51 27N 2 00W
Cam *r.* England **39** E3 52 15N 0 15W
Camagüey Cuba **79** M3 21 25N 77 55W
Camberley England **38** D2 51 21N 0 45W
CAMBODIA **60** B4
Camborne England **40** B3 50 12N 5 19W
Cambrai France **48** E5 50 10N 3 14E
Cambrian Mountains Wales **36** D2 52 15N 3 45W
Cambridge England **39** E3 52 12N 0 07E
Cambridgeshire *co.* England **38/39** D3/E3 52 30N 0 00
Camel *r.* England **40** C3 50 30N 4 45W
CAMEROON **66** D3
Cameroun, Mount Cameroon **66** C3 4 13N 9 10E
Campbeltown Scotland **32** D3 55 26N 5 36W
Campina Grande Brazil **84** F7 7 15S 35 50W
Campinas Brazil **84** E5 22 54S 47 06W
Campo Grande Brazil **84** D5 20 24S 54 35W
Campos Brazil **84** E5 21 46S 41 21W
Campsie Fells *hills* Scotland **33** E4 56 00N 4 15W
CANADA **78**
Canary Islands Spain **66** A5 28 30N 15 10W
Canaveral, Cape USA **79** L3 28 28N 80 28W
Canberra Australia **72** E2 35 17S 149 09E
Canisp *mt.* Scotland **31** D3 58 07N 5 03W
Cannes France **48** G1 43 33N 7 00E
Cannock England **37** E2 52 42N 2 01W
Cantabrian Mountains Spain **50** B5/C5 43 00N 5 30W
Canterbury England **39** F2 51 17N 1 05E
Canterbury Bight *b.* New Zealand **73** C2 44 00S 172 00E
Canterbury Plains New Zealand **73** C2 43 45S 171 56E
Can Tho Vietnam **60** B4 10 03N 105 46E
Cap de la Hague *c.* France **41** F2 49 44N 1 56W
Cape Gris-Nez *c.* France **39** F1 50 52N 1 35E
CAPE VERDE **4**
Caracas Venezuela **84** C9 10 35N 66 56W
Carcassonne France **48** E1 43 13N 2 21E
Cardiff Wales **36** D1 51 30N 3 13W
Cardiff *u.a.* Wales **36** D1 51 32N 3 14W
Cardigan Wales **36** C2 52 06N 4 40W
Cardigan Bay Wales **36** C2 52 30N 4 30W
Carentan France **41** F2 49 18N 1 14W
Caribbean Sea Central America **79** M2 15 00N 75 00W
Carlingford Lough *est.* Northern Ireland/ Republic of Ireland **32** C2 54 05N 6 10W
Carlisle England **34** C3 54 54N 2 55W
Carmarthen Wales **36** C1 51 51N 4 20W
Carmarthen Bay Wales **36** C1 51 40N 4 30W
Carmarthenshire *u.a.* Wales **36** C1/D1 51 55N 4 00W
Carmel Head Wales **36** C3 53 24N 4 34W
Carnarvon Australia **72** B3 24 53S 113 40E
Carn Eige *mt.* Scotland **31** D2 57 22N 5 07W
Carnforth England **34** C3 54 08N 2 46W
Carnoustie Scotland **31** G1 56 30N 2 44W
Carpathians *mts.* Europe **42** L5/M5 49 00N 22 00E
Carpentaria, Gulf of Australia **72** D4 14 00S 139 11E
Carrickfergus Northern Ireland **32** D2 54 43N 5 49W
Carrickfergus *district* Northern Ireland **32** D2 54 40N 5 50W
Cartagena Colombia **84** B9 10 24N 75 33W
Cartagena Spain **50** E2 37 36N 0 59W
Carteret France **41** F2 49 22N 1 48W
Casablanca Morocco **66** B6 33 39N 7 35W
Caspian Sea Asia **56** F2 41 00N 50 00E
Cassel France **39** G1 51 40N 2 28E

Cassino Italy **51** D4 41 29N 13 50E
Castlebay Scotland **30** B1 56 57N 7 28W
Castleblaney Republic of Ireland **32** C2 54 07N 6 44W
Castle Douglas Scotland **33** F2 54 57N 3 56W
Castleford England **35** D2 43 44N 1 21W
Castlereagh *district* Northern Ireland **32** D2 54 35N 5 50W
Castletown Isle of Man British Isles **33** E2 54 04N 4 38W
Castrovillari Italy **51** F3 39 48N 16 12E
Catánia Italy **51** E2 37 31N 15 06E
Catanzaro Italy **51** F3 38 54N 16 36E
Cat Island The Bahamas **79** M3 24 30N 75 30W
Cauca *r.* Colombia **84** B8 7 40N 75 00W
Caucasus *mts.* Asia **56** E2 43 00N 43 00E
Cavan Republic of Ireland **32** B1 53 58N 7 21W
Caxias do Sul Brazil **85** D5 29 14S 51 10W
Cayenne French Guiana **84** D8 4 55N 52 18W
Cayman Islands Caribbean Sea **79** L2 19 20N 81 15W
Cebollera *mt.* Spain **50** D4 42 00N 2 40W
Cebu The Philippines **60** D4 10 17N 123 56E
Celebes Sea Indonesia **60** D3 3 00N 122 00E
Cemaes Head Wales **36** C2 53 10N 4 50W
CENTRAL AFRICAN REPUBLIC **67** B5/C5
Central Siberian Plateau Russia **57** L4 65 00N 110 00E
Ceredigion *u.a.* Wales **36** C2/D2 52 20N 4 00W
Ceuta *territory* Spain **50** C1 35 53N 5 19W
CHAD **66** D4
Chad, Lake West Africa **66** D4 13 50N 14 00E
Chagos Archipelago *is.* Indian Ocean **5** 6 00S 72 00E
Châlons-sur-Marne France **48** F4 48 58N 4 22E
Chalon-sur-Saône France **48** F3 46 47N 4 51E
Chambéry France **48** F2 45 34N 5 55E
Changchun China **59** D4 43 50N 125 20E
Chang Jiang *(Yangtze) r.* China **59** C3 30 00N 116 00E
Changsha China **59** C2 28 10N 113 00E
Channel Islands British Isles **41** E2 49 30N 2 30W
Channel Tunnel United Kingdom/France **39** F1/2 5 00N 1 30E
Chard England **41** E3 50 53N 2 58W
Chardzhev Turkmenistan **56** G1 39 09N 63 34E
Chari *r.* Chad/Sudan **66** D4 11 00N 16 00E
Charleroi Belgium **49** C4 50 25N 4 27E
Charlestown of Aberlour Scotland **31** F2 57 28N 3 14W
Charleville Australia **72** E3 26 24S 146 14E
Charleville France **48** F4 49 46N 4 43E
Charlotte USA **79** L4 35 03N 80 50W
Charters Towers Australia **72** E3 20 04S 146 16E
Chartres France **48** D4 48 27N 1 30E
Châteauroux France **48** D3 46 49N 1 41E
Chatham England **39** E2 51 23N 0 32E
Cheadle England **34** C2 53 24N 2 13W
Cheb Czech Republic **49** G4 50 08N 12 28E
Cheboksary Russia **56** E3 56 08N 47 12E
Chelmsford England **39** E2 51 44N 0 28E
Cheltenham England **38** B2 51 54N 2 04W
Chelyabinsk Russia **56** G3 55 12N 61 25E
Chemnitz Germany **49** G4 50 50N 12 55E
Chengdu China **59** B3 30 37N 104 06E
Chennai India **58** D2 13 05N 80 18E
Chepstow Wales **37** E1 51 39N 2 41W
Cher *r.* France **48** D3 47 15N 1 30E
Cherbourg France **48** C4 49 38N 1 37W
Chernivtsi Ukraine **42** M5 48 19N 25 52E
Cherwell *r.* England **38** C2 51 55N 1 20W
Cheshire *co.* England **34** C2 53 30N 2 30W
Cheshunt England **38** D2 51 43N 0 02W
Chester England **34** C2 53 12N 2 54W
Chesterfield England **37** F3 53 15N 1 25W
Chester-le-Street England **34** D3 54 52N 1 34W
Cheviot Hills England/Scotland **33** G3 55 25 N2 20W
Cheviot, The *sum.* England **33** G3 55 29N 2 20W
Cheyenne USA **79** J5 41 08N 104 50W
Chiang Mai Thailand **60** A4 18 48N 98 59E
Chiba Japan **59** N2 35 38N 140 07E
Chicago USA **79** L5 41 50N 87 45W
Chichester England **38** D1 50 50N 0 48W
Chiclayo Peru **84** B7 6 47S 79 47W
Chicoutimi Canada **79** M5 48 26N 71 06W
Chieti Italy **51** E4 42 21N 14 10E
Chihuahua Mexico **79** J3 28 40N 106 06W
CHILE **84/85** B6/C2
Chillán Chile **85** B4 36 37S 72 10W
Chiloé Island Chile **85** B3 42 30S 74 00W
Chiltern Hills England **38** C2/D2 51 40N 1 00W
Chimbote Peru **84** B7 9 04S 78 34W
CHINA **59**
Chippenham England **38** B2 51 28N 2 07W
Chipping Norton England **38** C2 51 56N 1 32W
Chipping Sodbury England **38** B2 51 33N 2 24W
Chişinău Moldova **42** M5 47 00N 28 50E
Chita Russia **57** M3 52 03N 113 35E
Chittagong Bangladesh **58** E3 22 20N 91 48E
Cholet France **48** C3 47 04N 0 53W
Chongjin North Korea **59** D4 41 50N 129 55E
Chongqing China **59** B2 29 30N 106 35E
Chorley England **34** C2 53 40N 2 38W
Christchurch England **41** F3 50 44N 1 45W
Christchurch New Zealand **73** C2 43 32S 172 38E
Christmas Island Indian Ocean **60** B1 10 28S 105 35E
Churchill Canada **78** K6 58 45N 94 00W
Churchill Falls *tn.* Canada **78** N6 53 35N 64 00W
Cincinnati USA **79** L4 39 10N 83 30W
Cirencester England **38** C2 51 44N 1 59W
Citlaltépetl *mt.* Mexico **79** K2 19 00N 97 18W
City of Edinburgh *u.a.* Scotland **33** F3 55 55N 3 15W
City of Kingston upon Hull *u.a.* England **35** E2 53 45N 0 25W
Ciudad Bolivar Venezuela **84** C8 8 06N 63 36W
Ciudadela Balearic Islands **50** G3 40 00N 3 50E
Ciudad Guayana Venezuela **84** C8 8 22N 62 37W
Ciudad Juárez Mexico **79** J4 31 42N 106 29W
Ciudad Obregón Mexico **79** J3 27 28N 109 59W
Ciudad Rodrigo Spain **50** B4 40 36N 6 33W
Clachan Scotland **32** D3 55 45N 5 34W
Clackmannanshire *u.a.* England **33** F4 56 10N 3 40W
Clacton on Sea England **39** F2 51 48N 1 09E
Claonaig Scotland **32** D3 55 46N 5 22W
Cleethorpes England **35** E2 53 34N 0 02W

Clermont-Ferrand France **48** E2 45 47N 3 05E
Clevedon England **38** B2 51 27N 2 51W
Cleveland Hills England **35** D3 54 25N 1 15W
Clisham *mt.* Scotland **30** C2 57 58N 6 50W
Clitheroe England **34** C2 53 53N 2 23W
Clones Republic of Ireland **32** B2 54 11N 7 15W
Cluj-Napoca Romania **42** L5 46 47N 23 37E
Clutha *r.* New Zealand **73** B1 46 00S 169 30E
Clwyd *r.* Wales **36** D3 53 15N 3 25W
Clyde *r.* Scotland **33** E3 55 45N 3 55W
Clydebank Scotland **33** E3 55 54N 4 24W
Coalisland Northern Ireland **32** C2 54 32N 6 42W
Coalville England **37** F2 52 44N 1 20W
Coast Mountains Canada **78** G6 58 10N 132 40W
Coatbridge Scotland **33** E3 55 52N 4 01W
Coburg Germany **49** F4 50 15N 10 58E
Cochabamba Bolivia **84** C6 17 26S 66 10W
Cochin India **58** C1 9 56N 76 15E
Cockermouth England **34** B3 54 40N 3 21W
Cognac France **48** C2 45 42N 0 19W
Coimbatore India **58** C1 11 00N 76 57E
Coimbra Portugal **50** A4 40 12N 8 25W
Colchester England **39** E2 51 54N 0 54E
Coldstream *tn.* Scotland **33** G3 55 39N 2 15W
Coleraine Northern Ireland **32** C3 55 08N 6 40W
Coleraine *district* Northern Ireland **32** C3 55 00N 6 40W
Coll *i.* Scotland **30** C1 56 40N 6 35W
Colmar France **48** G4 48 05N 7 21E
Colne England **34** C2 53 52N 2 09W
Colne *r.* England **39** E2 51 53N 0 45E
Cologne Germany **49** D4 50 56N 6 57E
COLOMBIA **84** B8
Colombo Sri Lanka **58** C1 6 55N 79 52E
Colonsay *i.* Scotland **32** C4 56 05N 6 15W
Colorado *r.* Argentina **85** C4 37 30S 69 00W
Colorado *r.* USA/Mexico **79** J4 38 00N 109 00W
Colorado *state* USA **79** J4 39 00N 106 00W
Columbia USA **79** L4 34 00N 81 00W
Columbia *r.* Canada/USA **78** H6 50 30N 119 00W
Columbus USA **79** L4 39 59N 83 03W
Colwyn Bay *tn.* Wales **36** D3 53 18N 3 43W
Communism Peak Tajikistan **56** H1 38 59N 72 01E
Como Italy **51** B6 45 48N 9 05E
Comodoro Rivadavia Argentina **85** C3 45 50S 67 30W
Como, Lake Italy **51** B6/7 46 00N 9 00E
COMOROS **67** E3
Conakry Guinea **66** A3 9 30N 13 43W
Concepción Chile **85** B4 36 50S 73 03W
Conejara *i.* Balearic Islands **50** G3 39 11N 2 58E
CONGO **66** D2
Congo *r.* Africa **67** B4 3 00S 16 00E
CONGO DEMOCRATIC REPUBLIC **67** C4
Coniston Water *l.* England **34** B3 54 20N 3 05W
Connecticut *state* USA **79** M5 41 00N 73 00W
Consett England **34** D3 54 51N 1 49W
Constance, Lake Europe **49** E2 47 40N 9 30E
Constanţa Romania **42** M4 44 12N 28 40E
Constantine Algeria **66** C6 36 22N 6 40E
Conwy Wales **36** D3 53 17N 3 50W
Conwy *r.* Wales **36** D3 53 20N 3 55W
Conwy *u.a.* Wales **36** D3 53 10N 3 55W
Cook Islands Pacific Ocean **4** 19 30S 159 50W
Cook, Mount New Zealand **73** C2 43 36S 170 09E
Cookstown Northern Ireland **32** C2 54 39N 6 45W
Cookstown *district* Northern Ireland **32** C2 54 35N 6 55W
Cook Strait New Zealand **73** C2 41 24S 174 36E
Cooktown Australia **72** E4 15 28S 145 15E
Cooper Creek Australia **72** E3 26 10S 142 20E
Copenhagen Denmark **42** J7 55 43N 12 34E
Coquet *r.* England **33** H3 55 20N 1 50W
Coral Sea Pacific Ocean **72** F4 15 00S 154 00E
Corby England **38** D3 52 49N 0 32W
Córdoba Argentina **85** C4 31 25S 64 11W
Córdoba Spain **50** C2 37 53N 4 46W
Corfu *i.* Greece **42** K3 39 00N 19 00E
Cornwall *co.* England **40** B3/C3 50 25N 4 50W
Corpus Christi USA **79** K3 27 47N 97 26W
Corrientes Argentina **85** D5 27 30S 58 48W
Corsewall Point Scotland **32** D3 55 00N 5 10W
Corsica *i.* France **51** B5 42 00N 9 00E
Cosenza Italy **51** F3 39 17N 16 16E
Costa Brava *geog. reg.* Spain **50** G4/5 41 40N 3 50E
Costa del Sol *geog. reg.* Spain **50** C2/D2 36 40N 4 40W
COSTA RICA **79** L1
CÔTE D'IVOIRE **66** B3
Cotonou Benin **66** C3 6 24N 2 31E
Cotopaxi *vol.* Ecuador **84** B7 0 40S 78 28W
Cotswold Hills England **38** B2/C2 51 40N 2 10W
Cottbus Germany **49** H4 51 43N 14 21E
Coupar Angus Scotland **31** F1 56 33N 3 17W
Coutainville France **41** F2 49 03N 1 34W
Coutances France **41** F2 49 03N 1 29W
Coventry England **37** F2 52 25N 1 30W
Cowes England **38** C1 50 45N 1 18W
Craigavon Northern Ireland **32** C2 54 28N 6 25W
Craigavon *district* Northern Ireland **32** C2 54 30N 6 30W
Craighouse Scotland **32** D3 55 51N 5 57W
Craignure Scotland **30** D1 56 28N 5 42W
Crail Scotland **33** G4 56 16N 2 38W
Craiova Romania **42** L4 44 18N 23 47E
Cramlington England **33** H3 55 05N 1 35W
Crawley England **38** D2 51 07N 0 12W
Crediton England **40** D3 50 47N 3 39W
Cree *r.* Scotland **33** E3 55 00N 4 30W
Creeslough Republic of Ireland **32** B3 55 07N 7 55W
Cremona Italy **51** C6 45 08N 10 01E
Crete *i.* Greece **42** M3 35 00N 25 00E
Crewe England **34** C2 53 05N 2 27W
Crewkerne England **41** E3 50 53N 2 48W
Crianlarich Scotland **31** E1 56 23N 4 37W
Crieff Scotland **31** F1 56 23N 3 52W
Crimea *pen.* Ukraine **43** N5 46 00N 34 00E
CROATIA **42** K5
Cromarty Scotland **31** E2 57 40N 4 02W
Cromarty Firth *est.* Scotland **31** E2 57 40N 4 20W
Cromer England **39** F3 52 56N 1 18E

Cross Fell *sum.* England **34** C3 54 43N 2 29W
Crossmaglen Northern Ireland **32** C2 54 05N 6 37W
Crotone Italy **51** F3 39 05N 17 08E
Croydon England **38** D2 51 23N 0 06W
Crumlin Northern Ireland **32** C2 54 37N 6 14W
Cruzeiro do Sul Brazil **84** B7 7 40S 72 39W
Cuanza *r.* Angola **67** B4 9 40S 15 00E
CUBA **79** M3
Cubango *r.* Southern Africa **67** B3 17 00S 18 00E
Cúcuta Colombia **84** B8 7 55N 73 31W
Cuenca Ecuador **84** B7 2 54S 79 00W
Cuiabá Brazil **84** D6 15 32S 56 05W
Cuillin Hills Scotland **30** C2 57 15N 6 15W
Culiacán Mexico **79** J3 24 50N 107 23W
Cullen Scotland **31** G2 57 41N 2 49W
Cullompton England **40** D3 50 52N 3 24W
Cumaná Venezuela **84** C9 10 29N 64 12W
Cumbernauld Scotland **33** F3 55 57N 4 00W
Cumbria *co.* England **34** B3/C3 54 30N 2 50W
Cumnock Scotland **33** E3 55 27N 4 16W
Cunene *r.* Angola/Namibia **67** B3 17 00S 15 00E
Cuneo Italy **51** A6 44 24N 7 33E
Cunnamulla Australia **72** E3 28 03S 145 43E
Cupar Scotland **33** F4 56 19N 3 01W
Curaçao *i.* Lesser Antilles **79** N2 12 20N 68 20W
Curitiba Brazil **85** E5 25 25S 49 25W
Cuttack India **58** D3 20 26N 85 56E
Cuzco Peru **84** B6 13 32S 1 57W
Cwmbran Wales **36** D1 51 39N 3 00W
Cyclades *is.* Greece **42** L3/L4 36 00N 25 00E
CYPRUS **43** N2
CZECH REPUBLIC **42** K5
Częstochowa Poland **42** K6 50 49N 19 07E

D
Daer Reservoir Scotland **33** F3 55 25N 3 30W
Dakar Senegal **66** A4 14 38N 17 27W
Dalbeattie Scotland **33** F2 54 56N 3 49W
Dalian China **59** D3 38 53N 121 37E
Dallas USA **79** K4 32 47N 96 48W
Dalmally Scotland **31** E1 56 24N 4 58W
Dalton-in-Furness England **34** B3 54 09N 3 11W
Daly *r.* Australia **72** D4 13 30S 130 30E
Damascus Syria **61** D4 33 30N 36 19E
Dammam Saudi Arabia **61** E3 26 25N 50 06E
Da Nang Vietnam **60** B4 16 04N 108 14E
Danube *r.* Europe **42** L4 44 00N 25 00E
Dar es Salaam Tanzania **67** D4 6 51S 39 18E
Darfur *mts.* Sudan **61** C2 12 40N 24 20E
Dargaville New Zealand **73** C3 35 56S 173 52E
Darling *r.* Australia **72** E3 31 00S 144 00E
Darlington England **34** D3 54 31N 1 34W
Darlington *u.a.* England **34** D3 54 35N 1 34W
Darmstadt Germany **49** E3 49 52N 8 39E
Darnah Libya **42** L2 32 46N 22 39E
Dart *r.* England **40** D3 50 30N 3 50W
Dartford England **39** E2 51 27N 0 13E
Dartmoor *geog. reg.* England **40** D3 50 35N 3 50W
Dartmouth England **40** D3 50 21N 3 35W
Darvel Scotland **33** E3 55 37N 4 18W
Darwin Australia **72** D4 12 24S 130 52E
Daugava *r.* Belarus **42** M7 55 00N 29 00E
Daugavpils Latvia **42** M7 55 52N 26 31E
Dauphine *geog. reg.* France **48** F2 45 00N 5 00E
Davao The Philippines **60** D3 7 05N 125 38E
Daventry England **38** C3 52 16N 1 09W
Dawlish England **40** D3 50 35N 3 28W
Dawson Canada **78** F7 64 04N 139 24W
Deal England **39** F2 51 14N 1 24E
Debrecen Hungary **42** L5 47 30N 21 37E
Deccan *plat.* India **58** C2 18 00N 78 00E
Dee *r.* Aberdeenshire/Aberdeen City Scotland **31** G2 57 05N 2 10W
Dee *r.* Dumfries and Galloway Scotland **33** E2/F2 54 55N 4 00W
Dee *r.* England/Wales **36** D3 53 20N 3 10W
Deeps, The *b.* Scotland **29** D3 60 10N 1 25W
Delaware *state* USA **79** M4 39 00N 75 00W
Delhi India **58** C3 28 40N 77 14E
Demavand, Mount Iran **61** F4 35 56N 52 08E
Denbigh Wales **36** D3 53 11N 3 25W
Denbighshire *u.a.* Wales **36** D3 53 10N 3 10W
DENMARK **42** H7
Denver USA **79** J4 39 45N 105 00W
De Panne Belgium **39** G2 51 06N 2 35E
Derby Australia **72** C4 17 18S 123 37E
Derby England **37** F2 52 55N 1 30W
Derby City *u.a.* England **37** F2 52 53N 1 30W
Derbyshire *co.* England **37** F2 52 55N 1 30W
Derg *r.* Northern Ireland **32** B2 54 40N 7 45E
Derwent *r.* Cumbria England **34** B3 54 40N 3 30W
Derwent *r.* Derbyshire England **37** F3 53 20N 1 40W
Derwent *r.* Northumberland/Durham/Tyne and Wear England **34** D3 54 50N 2 05W
Derwent *r.* North Yorkshire/York/East Riding of Yorkshire England **35** D2 54 00N 0 55W
Derwent Water *l.* England **34** B3 54 35N 3 09W
Des Moines USA **79** K5 41 35N 93 35W
Dessau Germany **49** G4 51 51N 12 15E
Detroit USA **79** L5 42 23N 83 05W
Deveron *r.* Scotland **31** G2 57 35N 2 40W
Devizes England **38** C2 51 22N 1 59W
Devon *co.* England **40** C3/D3 50 45N 3 50W
Devon Island Canada **78** L8 75 47N 88 00W
Dewsbury England **35** D2 53 42N 1 37W
Dezful Iran **61** E4 32 23N 48 28E
Dhaka Bangladesh **58** E3 23 42N 90 22E
Dibrugarh India **58** E3 27 29N 94 56E
Didcot England **38** C2 51 37N 1 15W
Dieppe France **48** D4 49 55N 1 05E
Dijon France **48** F3 47 20N 5 02E
Dili East Timor **60** D2 8 33S 125 34E
Dingwall Scotland **31** E2 57 35N 4 29W
Dire Dawa Ethiopia **61** E1 9 35N 41 50E
Diss England **39** F3 52 23N 1 06E
Diyarbakir Turkey **43** Q3 37 55N 40 14E
Djelfa Algeria **42** G2 34 43N 3 14E
DJIBOUTI **61** E2
Djibouti Djibouti **61** E2 11 35N 43 11E

Dnieper r. Ukraine/Belarus 56 D3 51 00N 30 00E
Dniester r. Europe 42 M5 48 00N 27 00E
Dnipropetrovsk Ukraine 56 D2 48 29N 35 00E
Dodoma Tanzania 67 D4 6 10S 35 40E
Doha Qatar 61 F3 25 15N 51 36E
Dolgellau Wales 36 D2 52 44N 3 53W
Dolomites mts. Italy 49 F2 46 00N 12 00E
DOMINICA 79 N2
DOMINICAN REPUBLIC 79 M2
Don r. Russia 56 E3 50 00N 40 30E
Don r. Scotland 31 G2 57 15N 2 10W
Donaghadee Northern Ireland 32 D2 54 39N 5 33W
Doncaster England 35 D2 53 32N 1 07W
Donegal Republic of Ireland 32 A2 54 39N 8 07W
Donegal co. Republic of Ireland 32 A2/B2 54 55N 8 00W
Donetsk Ukraine 56 D2 48 00N 37 50E
Dongting Hu l. China 59 C2 29 00N 113 30E
Doon r. Scotland 33 E3 55 20N 4 30W
Dorchester England 41 E3 50 43N 2 26W
Dordogne r. France 48 D2 45 00N 1 30E
Dordrecht Netherlands 49 C4 51 48N 4 40E
Dorking England 38 D2 51 14N 0 20W
Dornoch Scotland 31 E2 57 52N 4 02W
Dornoch Firth est. Scotland 31 E2 57 55N 3 55W
Dorset co. England 41 E3 50 50N 2 20W
Dortmund Germany 49 D4 51 32N 7 27E
Douai France 48 E5 50 22N 3 05E
Douala Cameroon 66 C3 4 04N 9 43E
Douglas Isle of Man British Isles 33 E2 54 09N 4 29W
Douro r. Spain/Portugal 50 B4 41 30N 6 30W
Dove r. England 37 F3 53 10N 1 50W
Dover England 39 F2 51 08N 1 19E
Dover, Strait of English Channel 39 F1/2 51 00N 1 20W
Down district Northern Ireland 32 D2 54 25N 5 55W
Downham Market England 39 E3 52 36N 0 23E
Downpatrick Northern Ireland 32 D2 54 20N 5 43W
Drakensberg mts. Republic of South Africa 67 C2 30 00S 28 00E
Drava r. Europe 49 G2 46 45N 13 30E
Dresden Germany 49 G4 51 03N 13 45E
Droitwich England 37 E2 52 16N 2 09W
Dromore Northern Ireland 32 C2 54 25N 6 09W
Dronning Maud Land geog. reg. Antarctica 86 73 00S 10 00E
Drummore Scotland 32 E2 54 42N 4 54W
Drumnadrochit Scotland 31 E2 57 20N 4 30W
Dubai United Arab Emirates 61 F3 25 14N 55 17E
Dubbo Australia 72 E2 32 15S 148 38E
Dublin Republic of Ireland 36 A3 53 20N 6 15W
Dudley England 37 E2 52 30N 2 05W
Dufftown Scotland 31 F2 57 26N 3 08W
Duisburg Germany 49 D4 51 26N 6 45E
Duluth USA 79 K5 46 45N 92 10W
Dumbarton Scotland 33 E3 55 57N 4 35W
Dumfries Scotland 33 F3 55 04N 3 37W
Dumfries and Galloway u.a. Scotland 33 E3/F3 55 10N 4 00W
Dunbar Scotland 33 G4 56 00N 2 31W
Dunblane Scotland 33 F4 56 12N 3 59W
Duncansby Head c. Scotland 29 B1 58 39N 3 02W
Dundalk Republic of Ireland 32 C2 54 01N 6 25W
Dundee Scotland 31 G1 56 28N 3 00W
Dundee City u.a. Scotland 31 F1/G1 56 30N 2 55W
Dunedin New Zealand 73 C1 45 53S 170 30E
Dunfermline Scotland 33 F4 56 04N 3 29W
Dungannon Northern Ireland 32 C2 54 31N 6 46W
Dungannon district Northern Ireland 32 B2/C2 54 30N 7 00W
Dungeness c. England 39 E1 50 55N 0 58E
Dungiven Northern Ireland 32 C2 54 56N 6 55W
Dunkery Beacon sum. England 40 D4 51 11N 3 35W
Dún Laoghaire Republic of Ireland 36 A3 53 17N 6 08W
Dunnett Head Scotland 29 B1 58 40N 3 25W
Dunoon Scotland 32 E3 55 57N 4 56W
Duns Scotland 33 G3 55 47N 2 20W
Dunstable England 38 D2 51 53N 0 32W
Dunvegan Scotland 30 C2 57 26N 6 35W
Durance r. France 48 F1 43 50N 5 15E
Durango Mexico 79 J3 24 01N 104 40W
Durban Republic of South Africa 67 D2 29 53S 31 00E
Durham England 34 D3 54 47N 1 34W
Durham co. England 34 C3/D3 54 40N 2 00W
Dursley England 37 E1 51 42N 2 21W
Dushanbe Tajikistan 56 E2 54 40N 2 00W
Düsseldorf Germany 49 D4 51 13N 6 47E
Dyce Scotland 31 G2 57 12N 2 11W
Dyfi r. Wales 36 D2 52 38N 3 50W

E

Ealing England 38 D2 51 31N 0 18W
Earn r. Scotland 31 F1 56 15N 3 40W
East Ayrshire u.a. Scotland 33 E3 55 35N 4 15W
Eastbourne England 39 E1 50 46N 0 17E
East Cape New Zealand 73 D3 37 41S 178 33E
East Dereham England 39 E3 52 41N 0 56E
East Dunbartonshire u.a. Scotland 33 E3 55 55N 4 15W
Eastern Rift Valley East Africa 67 D4/5 4 00N 36 00E
East Friesian Islands Netherlands 49 D5 53 00N 7 00E
East Kilbride Scotland 33 E3 55 46N 4 10W
Eastleigh England 38 C1 50 58N 1 22W
East London Republic of South Africa 67 C1 33 00S 27 54E
East Lothian u.a. Scotland 33 G3 55 56N 2 42W
East Renfrewshire u.a. Scotland 33 E3 55 45N 4 25E
East Riding of Yorkshire u.a. England 35 E2 53 54N 0 40W
East Sussex co. England 39 E1 50 55N 0 10E
EAST TIMOR 60 D2
Ebbw Vale Wales 36 D1 51 47N 3 12W
Ebro r. Spain 50 E4 42 00N 1 15W
Ech Cheliff Algeria 42 G3 36 05N 1 15E
ECUADOR 84 B7

Eday i. Scotland 29 C2 59 11N 2 47W
Eddrachillis Bay Scotland 30 D3 58 25N 5 15W
Eden r. Cumbria England 34 C3 54 45N 2 40W
Eden r. Surrey/Kent England 39 E2 51 11N 0 05E
Edinburgh Scotland 33 F3 55 57N 3 13W
Edmonton Canada 78 H6 53 34N 113 25W
Edward, Lake Congo Dem. Rep./Uganda 67 C4 0 30S 29 00E
EGYPT 61 C3
Eigg i. Scotland 30 C1 56 55N 6 10W
Eindhoven Netherlands 49 C4 51 26N 5 30E
Elba i. Italy 51 C5 42 00N 10 00E
El Bayadh Algeria 42 G2 33 40N 1 00E
Elbe r. Europe 49 F5 53 15N 11 00E
Elbrus, Mount Russia 43 Q4 43 21N 42 29E
Elche Spain 50 E3 38 16N 0 41W
Eleuthera i. The Bahamas 79 M3 25 05N 76 30W
El Faiyum Egypt 61 D3 29 19N 30 50E
El Fasher Sudan 61 C2 13 37N 25 22E
Elgin Scotland 31 F2 57 39N 3 20W
El Giza Egypt 61 D4 30 01N 31 12E
Elgol Scotland 30 C2 57 09N 6 06W
El Kharga Egypt 61 D3 25 27N 30 32E
Ellen r. England 34 B3 54 45N 3 25W
Ellesmere Island Canada 78 L8 77 30N 82 30W
Ellesmere Port England 34 C2 53 17N 2 54W
Ellon Scotland 31 G2 57 22N 2 05W
El Minya Egypt 61 D3 28 06N 30 45E
El Paso USA 79 J4 31 45N 106 30W
EL SALVADOR 79 L2
Elvas Portugal 50 B3 38 53N 7 10W
Ely England 39 E3 52 24N 0 16E
Emden Germany 49 D5 53 23N 7 13E
Emi Koussi mt. Chad 66 D4 19 52N 18 31E
Ems r. Germany 49 D5 53 00N 7 00E
Enard Bay Scotland 30 D3 58 10N 5 25W
Enfield England 38 D2 51 39N 0 05W
Enggano i. Indonesia 60 B2 5 20S 102 20E
England country United Kingdom 28 53 00N 2 00W
English Channel United Kingdom/France 28 50 00N 2 00W
Enniskillen Northern Ireland 32 B2 54 21N 7 38W
Enschede Netherlands 49 D5 52 13N 6 55E
Entebbe Uganda 67 D5 0 04N 32 27E
Épinal France 48 G4 48 10N 6 28E
Epsom England 38 D2 51 20N 0 16W
EQUATORIAL GUINEA 66 B3
Erebus, Mount Antarctica 86 77 40S 167 20E
Erfurt Germany 49 F4 50 58N 11 02E
Erie, Lake Canada/USA 79 L5 42 15N 81 00W
Erlangen Germany 49 F3 49 36N 11 02E
ERITREA 61 D2
Erlangen Germany 49 F3 49 36N 11 02E
Erne r. Northern Ireland/Republic of Ireland 32 B2 54 10N 7 30W
Errigal Mountain Republic of Ireland 32 A3 55 02N 8 07W
Erzurum Turkey 43 Q3 39 57N 41 17E
Esfahan Iran 61 F4 32 41N 51 41E
Esha Ness pt. Scotland 29 D3 60 29N 1 37W
Esk r. England 35 E3 54 30N 0 45W
Esk r. Scotland/England 33 F3 55 15N 3 05W
Eskisehir Turkey 43 N3 39 46N 30 30E
Esperance Australia 72 C3 33 51S 121 54E
Esquel Argentina 85 B3 42 55S 71 20W
Essen Germany 49 D4 51 27N 6 57E
Essex co. England 39 E2 51 46N 0 30E
ESTONIA 42 M7
ETHIOPIA 61 E1
Ethiopian Highlands Africa 61 D1 8 00N 37 00E
Etna, Mount Italy 51 E2 37 45N 15 00E
Etosha Pan salt l. Namibia 67 B3 18 30S 16 30E
Eyre, Lake Australia 72 D3 28 43S 137 11E
Euphrates r. Iraq/Syria/Turkey 61 D4/E4 35 00N 40 00E
Europa i. Mozambique Channel 67 E2 22 20S 40 20E
Everest, Mount China/Nepal 58 E3 27 59N 86 56E
Evesham England 37 F2 52 06N 1 56W
Evreux France 48 D4 49 03N 1 11E
Evvoia i. Greece 42 L3 38 00N 24 00E
Exe r. England 40 D4 51 10N 3 35W
Exeter England 40 D4 50 43N 3 31W
Exmoor geog. reg. England 40 D4 51 08N 3 40W
Exmouth England 40 D3 50 37N 3 25W
Eyemouth Scotland 33 G3 55 25N 2 06W
Eye Peninsula Scotland 30 C3 58 10N 6 10W

F

Faroe Islands Atlantic Ocean 42 E8 62 00N 7 00W
Fairbanks USA 78 E7 64 50N 147 50W
Fair Head c. Northern Ireland 32 C3 55 15N 6 10W
Fair Isle i. Shetland Islands Scotland 29 D2 59 32N 1 38W
Faisalabad Pakistan 58 C4 31 25N 73 09E
Fakenham England 39 E3 52 50N 0 51E
Fal r. England 40 C3 50 15N 4 55W
Falkirk Scotland 33 F3 55 59N 3 48W
Falkirk u.a. Scotland 33 F3/4 56 05N 3 53W
Falkland Islands South Atlantic Ocean 85 D2 52 30S 60 00W
Falmouth England 40 B3 50 08N 5 04W
Falster i. Denmark 49 F6/G6 54 00N 12 00E
Fareham England 38 C1 50 51N 1 10W
Farewell, Cape Greenland 78 Q6 60 00N 44 00W
Farewell, Cape New Zealand 73 C2 40 30S 172 41E
Faringdon England 38 C2 51 40N 1 35W
Farnborough England 38 D2 51 17N 0 46W
Farnham England 38 D2 51 13N 0 49W
Faro Portugal 50 B2 37 01N 7 56W
Fawley England 38 C1 50 49N 1 20W
FEDERATED STATES OF MICRONESIA 5
Fehmarn i. Germany 49 F6 54 00N 11 00E
Feilding New Zealand 73 C2 40 14S 175 34E
Feira de Santana Brazil 84 F6 12 17S 38 53W
Felixstowe England 39 F2 51 58N 1 20E
Fens, The geog. reg. England 35 E1/F1 52 45N 0 05E
Fergana Uzbekistan 56 H2 40 23N 71 19E

Fermanagh district Northern Ireland 32 B2 54 25N 7 45W
Ferrara Italy 51 C6 44 50N 11 38E
Fès Morocco 66 B6 34 05N 5 00W
Fethaland, Point of Scotland 29 D3 60 35N 1 18W
Fetlar i. Scotland 29 E3 60 37N 0 52W
Fife u.a. Scotland 33 F4/G4 56 10N 3 00W
FIJI 5
Filchner Ice Shelf Antarctica 86 80 00S 37 00W
Finke r. Australia 72 D3 25 00S 135 00E
FINLAND 42 M8
Finland, Gulf of Finland/Russia 42 L7 59 40N 23 30E
Finn r. Northern Ireland/Republic of Ireland 32 B2 54 50N 7 50W
Fionnphort Scotland 30 C1 56 19N 6 23W
Firth of Clyde est. Scotland 32 E3 55 40N 5 00W
Firth of Forth est. Scotland 33 F4/G4 56 05N 3 00W
Firth of Lorn est. Scotland 30 D1 56 15N 6 00W
Firth of Tay est. Scotland 31 F1 56 25N 3 00W
Fishguard Wales 36 C1 51 59N 4 59W
Fitzroy r. Australia 72 C4 17 00S 126 00E
Flamborough Head c. England 35 E3 54 06N 0 04W
Fleetwood England 34 B2 53 56N 3 01W
Flinders r. Australia 72 E3/4 20 00S 142 00E
Flinders Range Australia 72 D2 31 20S 138 45E
Flint Wales 36 D3 53 15N 3 07W
Flintshire u.a. Wales 36 D3 53 25N 3 10W
Florence Italy 51 C5 43 47N 11 15E
Flores i. Indonesia 60 D2 8 40S 121 00E
Flores Sea Indonesia 60 D2 7 00S 119 00E
Florianópolis Brazil 85 E5 27 35S 48 31W
Florida state USA 79 L3 28 00N 82 00W
Florida, Straits of sd. Cuba/USA 79 L3 24 00N 81 00W
Fly r. Papua New Guinea 72 E5 8 00S 142 00E
Fochabers Scotland 31 F2 57 37N 3 05W
Fóggia Italy 51 E4 41 28N 15 33E
Folkestone England 39 F2 51 05N 1 11E
Fontainebleau France 48 E4 48 24N 2 42E
Forel, Mount Greenland 86 67 00N 37 00W
Forest of Bowland hills England 34 C2 54 00N 2 35W
Forfar Scotland 31 G1 56 38N 2 54W
Forlì Italy 51 D6 44 13N 12 02E
Formby England 34 B2 53 34N 3 05W
Formentera i. Balearic Islands 50 F3 38 41N 1 30E
Fornells Balearic Islands 50 H3 40 04N 4 07E
Forres Scotland 31 F2 57 37N 3 38W
Fortaleza Brazil 84 F7 3 45S 38 35W
Fort Augustus Scotland 31 E2 57 09N 4 41W
Forth r. Scotland 33 E4 56 07N 4 10W
Fort McMurray Canada 78 H6 56 45N 111 27W
Fort Peck Reservoir USA 79 J5 48 01N 106 28W
Fort Simpson Canada 78 G7 61 46N 121 15W
Fort William Scotland 31 D1 56 49N 5 07W
Fort Worth USA 79 K4 32 45N 97 20W
Foula i. Scotland 29 C3 60 08N 2 05W
Foveaux Strait New Zealand 73 B1 46 42S 167 59E
Fowey England 40 C3 50 20N 4 38W
Fowey r. England 40 C3 50 25N 4 30W
Foyle r. Northern Ireland/Republic of Ireland 32 B2 54 58N 7 35W
FRANCE 48
Frankfurt Germany 49 E4 50 06N 8 41E
Franz Josef Land is. Russia 57 G6 80 00N 50 00E
Fraser r. Canada 78 G6 52 00N 122 00W
Fraserburgh Scotland 31 G2 57 42N 2 00W
Freetown Sierra Leone 66 A3 8 30N 13 17W
Freiburg Germany 49 D3 48 00N 7 52E
Fréjus France 48 G1 43 26N 6 44E
French Guiana territory France 84 D8 5 00N 53 00W
French Polynesia is. Pacific Ocean 4 21 00S 150 00W
Fresno USA 79 H4 36 41N 119 47W
Frome England 41 E4 51 14N 2 20W
Frome r. England 41 E3 50 40N 2 05W
Fuji, Mount Japan 59 M2 35 23N 138 42E
Fukui Japan 59 M2 36 04N 136 12E
Fukuoka Japan 59 L1 33 39N 130 21E
Fukushima Japan 59 N2 37 44N 140 28E
Fukuyama Japan 59 L1 34 29N 133 21E
Furnace Scotland 32 D4 56 09N 5 12W
Fushun China 59 D3 41 50N 123 54E
Fuxin China 59 D3 42 08N 121 39E
Fuzhou China 59 C2 26 09N 119 17E
Fyn i. Denmark 49 F6 55 30N 10 00E
FYROM see MACEDONIA, FORMER YUGOSLAV REPUBLIC OF

G

Gabès Tunisia 42 J2 33 52N 10 06E
GABON 66 D2
Gaborone Botswana 67 C2 24 45S 25 55E
Gafsa Tunisia 42 H2 34 28N 8 43E
Gainsborough England 35 E2 53 24N 0 48W
Gairloch tn. Scotland 30 D2 57 42N 5 40W
Galapagos Islands Pacific Ocean 4 12 00S 87 00W
Galashiels Scotland 33 G3 55 37N 2 49W
Galați Romania 42 M5 45 27N 28 02E
Gallipoli Italy 51 G4 40 03N 17 59E
GAMBIA, THE 66 A4
Gäncä Azerbaijan 56 E2 40 39N 46 20E
Gander Canada 79 P5 49 00N 54 15W
Ganges r. India/Bangladesh 58 D3 24 00N 88 00E
Gap France 48 G2 44 33N 6 05E
Garda, Lake Italy 51 C6 45 40N 10 00E
Garelochhead Scotland 33 E4 56 05N 4 50W
Garonne r. France 48 D2 44 45N 0 15E
Gatehouse of Fleet Scotland 33 E2 54 53N 4 11W
Gateshead England 34 D3 54 58N 1 35W
Gaziantep Turkey 43 P3 37 04N 37 21E
Gdańsk Poland 42 K6 54 22N 18 41E
Gdynia Poland 42 K6 54 31N 18 30E
Geelong Australia 72 E2 38 08S 144 20E
Gelsenkirchen Germany 49 D4 51 30N 7 05E
Geneva Switzerland 49 D2 46 13N 6 09E
Geneva, Lake France/Switzerland 49 D2 46 20N 6 20E
Genoa Italy 51 B6 44 24N 8 56E
Gent Belgium 49 B4 51 02N 3 42E
Georgetown Guyana 84 D8 6 46N 58 10W
George Town Malaysia 60 B3 5 25N 100 20E
GEORGIA 56 E2

Georgia state USA 79 L4 33 00N 83 00W
Gera Germany 49 G4 50 51N 12 11E
Geraldton Australia 72 B3 28 46S 114 36E
GERMANY 49
GHANA 66 B3
Gibraltar territory UK 50 C2 36 09N 5 21W
Gibraltar, Strait of Spain/Morocco 50 C1 35 58N 5 30W
Gibson Desert Australia 72 C3 24 00S 122 00E
Giessen Germany 49 E4 50 35N 8 42E
Gifu Japan 59 M2 35 27N 136 46E
Gigha is. Scotland 32 D3 55 40N 5 45W
Gijón Spain 50 C5 43 32N 5 40W
Gillingham England 39 E2 51 24N 0 33E
Gironde r. France 48 C2 45 30N 1 00W
Girvan Scotland 32 D3 55 15N 4 51W
Gisborne New Zealand 73 D3 38 40S 178 01E
Glasgow Scotland 33 E3 55 53N 4 15W
Glasgow City u.a. Scotland 33 E3 55 50N 4 20W
Glastonbury England 41 E4 51 09N 2 43W
Glenluce Scotland 33 E2 54 53N 4 49W
Glenrothes Scotland 33 F4 56 12N 3 10W
Gloucester England 38 B2 51 53N 2 14W
Gloucestershire co. England 38 B2 51 50N 2 20W
Goat Fell mt. Scotland 32 D3 55 39N 5 11W
Gobi Desert Mongolia 59 B3 44 30N 100 00E
Godavari r. India 58 C2/D2 19 00N 80 00E
Godthåb see Nuuk
Goiânia Brazil 84 E6 16 43S 49 18W
Gold Coast tn. Australia 72 F3 28 04S 153 25E
Gongga Shan mt. China 59 B2 29 34N 101 53E
Good Hope, Cape of Republic of South Africa 67 B1 34 30S 19 00E
Goole England 35 E2 53 42N 0 52W
Gore New Zealand 73 B1 46 06S 168 56E
Goroka Papua New Guinea 72 E5 6 02S 145 22E
Göteborg Sweden 42 J7 57 45N 12 00E
Gotland i. Sweden 42 K7 57 30N 18 40E
Göttingen Germany 49 E4 51 32N 9 57E
Governador Valadares Brazil 84 E6 18 51S 41 57W
Gower p. Wales 36 C1 51 35N 4 10W
Grafton Australia 72 F3 29 40S 152 58E
Grampian Mountains Scotland 31 E1/F1 56 45N 4 00W
Granada Spain 50 D2 37 10N 3 35W
Grand Bahama i. The Bahamas 79 M3 27 00N 78 00W
Grand Canyon USA 79 H4 36 04N 112 07W
Grand Rapids tn. USA 79 L5 42 57N 86 40W
Grangemouth Scotland 33 F4 56 01N 3 44W
Grantham England 35 E1 52 55N 0 39W
Grantown-on-Spey Scotland 31 F2 57 20N 3 58W
Gravesend England 39 E2 51 27N 0 24E
Grays England 39 E2 51 29N 0 20E
Graz Austria 42 K5 47 05N 15 22E
Great Abaco i. The Bahamas 79 M3 26 40N 77 00W
Great Australian Bight b. Australia 72 C2 32 31S 130 00E
Great Barrier Island New Zealand 73 D3 36 13S 175 24E
Great Barrier Reef Australia 72 E4/F3 15 00S 146 00E
Great Bear Lake Canada 78 H7 66 00N 120 00W
Great Dividing Range mts. Australia 72 E2/F3 35 00N 148 00E
Great Driffield England 35 E3 54 01N 0 26W
Greater Antilles is. West Indies 79 M2/N2 19 00N 78 00W
Greater London co. England 38 D2 51 30N 0 10W
Greater Manchester co. England 34 C2 53 30N 2 15W
Great Inagua i. The Bahamas 79 M3 21 40N 73 00W
Great Karoo mts. Republic of South Africa 67 C1 32 30S 22 30E
Great Malvern England 37 E2 52 07N 2 19W
Great Ouse r. England 39 E3 52 40N 0 20E
Great St. Bernard Pass France/Italy 48 G2 45 50N 7 10E
Great Salt Lake USA 79 H5 41 10N 112 40W
Great Sandy Desert Australia 72 C3 21 00S 121 00
Great Slave Lake Canada 78 H7 62 00N 114 00W
Great Stour r. England 39 F2 51 18N 1 10E
Great Torrington England 40 C3 51 57N 4 09W
Great Victoria Desert Australia 72 C3/D3 28 00S 129 00E
Great Wall China 59 B3 39 00N 109 00E
Great Whernside sum. England 34 D3 54 10N 1 59W
Great Yarmouth England 39 F3 52 37N 1 44E
GREECE 42 L3
GREENLAND 78 Q8
Greenock Scotland 33 E3 55 57N 4 45W
Greenwich England 38 D2 51 29N 0 00
GRENADA 79 N2
Grenoble France 48 F2 45 11N 5 43E
Greta r. England 34 C3 54 10N 2 30W
Greymouth New Zealand 73 C2 42 27S 171 12E
Greystones Republic of Ireland 36 A3 53 09N 6 04W
Grimsby England 35 E2 53 35N 0 05W
Groningen Netherlands 49 D5 53 13N 6 35E
Grosseto Italy 51 C5 42 46N 11 07E
Gross Glockner mt. Austria 49 G2 47 05N 12 44E
Groznyy Russia 43 Q3 43 21N 45 42E
Guadalajara Mexico 79 J3 20 40N 103 20W
Guadalquivir r. Spain 50 C2 37 45N 5 30W
Guadalupe i. Mexico 79 H3 29 00N 118 24W
Guadeloupe i. Lesser Antilles 79 N2 16 30N 61 30W
Guadiana r. Spain/Portugal 50 C3 39 00N 5 30W
GUAM 5
Guangzhou China 59 C2 23 08N 113 20E
Guantánamo Cuba 79 M3 20 09N 75 14W
Guarda Portugal 50 B4 40 32N 7 17W
GUATEMALA 79 K2
Guatemala Guatemala 79 K2 14 38N 90 22W
Guayaquil Ecuador 84 B7 2 13S 79 54W
Guernsey i. Channel Islands British Isles 41 E2 46 27N 2 35W
GUINEA 66 A4
GUINEA-BISSAU 66 A4
Guinea, Gulf of Atlantic Ocean 66 C3 2 00N 2 30E
Guisborough England 35 D3 54 32N 1 04W
Guiyang China 59 B2 26 35N 106 40E

ulf, The Middle East 61 F3 27 20N 51 00E
uwahati India 58 E3 26 10N 91 45E
UYANA 84 D8
wadar Pakistan 58 B3 25 07N 62 19E
walior India 58 C3 26 12N 78 09E
wynedd u.a. Wales 36 D2 52 45N 3 55W

H
aarlem Netherlands 49 C5 52 23N 4 39E
achinohe Japan 59 N3 40 30N 141 30E
aifa Israel 61 D4 32 49N 34 59E
ail Saudi Arabia 61 E3 27 31N 41 45E
ainan i. China 59 B1 18 50N 109 50E
ai Phong Vietnam 60 B5 20 50N 106 41E
AITI 79 M2
akodate Japan 59 N3 41 46N 140 44E
alesowen England 37 E2 52 26N 2 05W
alifax Canada 79 N5 44 38N 63 35W
alifax England 34 D2 53 44N 1 52W
alkirk Scotland 31 F3 58 00N 3 47W
alle Germany 49 F4 51 28N 11 58E
almahera i. Indonesia 60 D3 0 30S 127 00E
alton England 34 C2 53 20N 2 40W
altwhistle England 34 C3 54 58N 2 27W
amadan Iran 61 E4 34 46N 48 35E
amah Syria 43 P3 35 10N 36 45E
amamatsu Japan 59 M1 34 42N 137 42E
amburg Germany 49 F5 53 33N 10 00E
amersley Range Australia 72 B3 22 04S 117 37E
ami China 58 E5 42 37N 93 32E
amilton Canada 79 M5 43 15N 79 50W
amilton New Zealand 73 D3 37 47S 175 17E
amilton Scotland 33 E3 55 47N 4 03W
amm Germany 49 D4 51 40N 7 49E
ampshire co. England 38 C2 51 10N 1 15W
angzhou China 59 D3 30 18N 120 07E
annover Germany 49 E5 52 23N 9 44E
anoi Vietnam 60 B5 21 01N 105 52E
arare Zimbabwe 67 D3 17 50S 31 03E
arbin China 59 D4 45 45N 126 41E
argeysa Somalia 67 E5 9 31N 44 02E
arlech Wales 36 C2 52 52N 4 07W
arlow England 39 E2 51 47N 0 08E
aroldswick Scotland 29 E3 60 47N 0 50W
arris i. Scotland 30 C2 57 50N 6 55W
arris, Sound of Scotland 30 B2 57 45N 7 10W
arrogate England 34 D2 54 00N 1 33W
arrow England 38 D2 51 34N 0 20W
artland Point England 40 C4 51 02N 4 31W
artlepool England 35 D3 54 41N 1 13W
artlepool u.a. England 35 D3 54 41N 1 13W
arwich England 39 F2 51 57N 1 17E
arz mts. Europe 49 F4 52 00N 10 00E
aslemere England 38 D2 51 06N 0 43W
astings England 39 E1 50 51N 0 36E
astings New Zealand 73 D3 39 39S 176 51E
atherleigh England 40 C3 50 49N 4 04W
avering England 39 E2 51 34N 0 14E
awaiian Islands Pacific Ocean 4 20 00N 156 00W
awera New Zealand 73 C3 39 35S 174 17E
awke Bay New Zealand 73 D3 39 23S 177 12E
awick Scotland 33 G3 55 25N 2 47W
aywards Heath England 38 D2 51 00N 0 06W
ay River tn. Canada 78 H7 60 51N 115 42W
efei China 59 C3 31 55N 117 18E
egang China 59 E4 47 36N 130 30E
eidelberg Germany 49 E3 49 25N 8 42E
eilbronn Germany 49 E3 49 08N 9 14E
ellin Spain 50 E3 38 31N 1 43W
elmsdale Scotland 31 F3 58 07N 3 40W
elmsdale r. Scotland 31 F3 58 10N 3 50W
elsinki Finland 42 L8 60 08N 25 00E
elston England 40 B3 50 05N 5 16W
elvellyn mt. England 34 B3 54 32N 3 02W
emel Hempstead England 38 D2 51 46N 0 28W
emsworth England 35 D2 53 38N 1 21W
engelo Netherlands 49 D5 52 16N 6 46E
enley-on-Thames England 38 D2 51 32N 0 56W
erat Afghanistan 58 B4 34 20N 62 12E
ereford England 37 E2 52 04N 2 43W
erefordshire u.a. England 37 E2 52 12N 2 40W
erma Ness c. Scotland 29 E3 60 50N 0 54W
ermosillo Mexico 79 H3 29 15N 110 59W
ertfordshire co. England 38 D2 51 50N 0 05W
exham England 35 C3 54 58N 2 07W
eysham England 34 C3 54 02N 2 54W
ghland u.a. Scotland 30/31 D2/E2 57 00N 5 00W
igh Veld mts. Republic of South Africa 67 C2 28 00S 28 00E
igh Wycombe England 38 D2 51 38N 0 46W
illingdon England 38 D2 51 32N 0 27W
Iversum Netherlands 49 C5 52 14N 5 10E
malaya mts. Asia 58 D3 28 00N 85 00E
meji Japan 59 L1 34 50N 134 40E
nckley England 37 E2 52 33N 1 21W
ndu Kush mts. Afghanistan 58 B4 35 00N 70 00E
iroshima Japan 59 L1 34 23N 132 27E
itchin England 38 D2 51 57N 0 17W
obart Australia 72 E1 42 53S 147 19E
o Chi Minh Vietnam 60 B4 10 46N 106 43E
odeida Yemen Republic 61 E2 14 50N 42 58E
ófn Iceland 42 C8 64 16N 15 10W
oggar mts. Algeria 66 C5 23 50N 6 00E
ohhot China 59 C4 40 49N 117 37E
olderness p. England 35 E2 53 45N 0 05W
olguín Cuba 79 M3 20 54N 76 15W
ollywood USA 79 H4 34 05N 118 21W

Holsworthy England 40 C3 50 49N 4 21W
Holyhead Wales 36 C3 53 19N 4 38W
Holy Island England 33 H3 55 41N 1 48W
Holy Island Wales 36 C3 53 16N 4 39W
Homs Syria 61 D4 34 42N 36 40E
Homyel' Belarus 56 D3 52 25N 31 00E
HONDURAS 79 L2
Hong Kong China 59 C2 23 00N 114 00E
Honiara Solomon Islands 72 F5 9 28S 159 57E
Honiton England 41 D3 50 48N 3 13W
Honshu i. Japan 59 M2 37 15N 138 00E
Horn, Cape Chile 85 C2 56 00S 67 15W
Horncastle England 35 E2 53 13N 0 07W
Hornsea England 35 E2 53 55N 0 10W
Horsham England 38 D2 51 04N 0 21W
Hospitalet Spain 50 G4 41 21N 2 06E
Hounslow England 38 D2 51 28N 0 21W
Houston USA 79 K3 29 45N 95 25W
Hove England 38 D1 50 49N 0 11W
Howe, Cape Australia 72 E2 37 29S 149 59E
Howth Republic of Ireland 36 A3 53 23N 6 04W
Hoy i. Scotland 29 B1 58 48N 3 20W
Huainan China 59 C3 32 41N 117 06E
Huambo Angola 67 B3 12 44S 15 47E
Huancayo Peru 84 B6 12 05S 75 12W
Huang He r. China 59 C3 36 00N 116 00E
Hubli India 58 C2 15 20N 75 14E
Huddersfield England 34 D2 53 39N 1 47W
Hudson r. USA 79 M5 43 20N 73 50W
Hudson Bay Canada 78 L6/ 60 00N 89 00W
Hue Vietnam 60 B4 16 28N 107 35E
Huelva Spain 50 B2 37 15N 6 56W
Hufuf Saudi Arabia 61 E3 25 20N 49 34E
Hugh Town England 40 A2 49 55N 6 19W
Hull r. England 35 E2 53 50N 0 25W
Humber r. England 35 E2 53 40N 0 10W
HUNGARY 42 K5
Hungnam North Korea 59 D3 39 49N 127 40E
Hunstanton England 39 E3 52 57N 0 30E
Huntingdon England 38 D3 52 20N 0 12W
Huntly Scotland 31 G2 57 27N 2 47W
Huron, Lake Canada/USA 79 L5 45 00N 83 00W
Hyderabad India 58 C2 17 22N 78 26E
Hyderabad Pakistan 58 B3 25 22N 68 22E

I
Iaşi Romania 42 M5 47 09N 27 38E
Ibadan Nigeria 66 C3 7 23N 3 56E
Ibagué Colombia 84 B8 4 25N 75 20W
Ibiza Balearic Islands 50 F3 38 54N 1 26E
Ibiza i. Balearic Islands 50 F3 39 00N 1 20E
ICELAND 42 C9
Idaho state USA 79 H5 44 00N 115 00W
Ieper (Ypres) Belgium 39 G1 50 51N 2 53E
IJsselmeer l. Netherlands 49 C5 52 50N 5 15E
Ilchester England 41 E3 51 01N 2 41W
Ilebo Congo Dem. Rep. 67 C4 4 20S 20 35E
Ilfracombe England 40 C4 51 13N 4 08W
Ilhéus Brazil 84 F6 14 50S 39 06W
Ilkeston England 37 F2 52 59N 1 18W
Ilkley England 34 D2 53 55N 1 50W
Illinois state USA 79 L5 40 00N 89 00W
Ilminster England 41 E3 50 56N 2 55W
Iloilo The Philippines 60 D4 10 41N 122 33E
Immingham England 35 E2 53 36N 0 11W
Imphal India 58 E3 24 47N 93 55E
Inca Balearic Islands 50 G3 39 43N 2 54E
Inchon South Korea 59 D3 37 30N 126 38E
INDIA 58 C3
Indiana state USA 79 L5 40 00N 86 00W
Indianapolis USA 79 L4 39 45N 86 10W
Indian Ocean 7
INDONESIA 60 A3/D2
Indore India 58 C3 22 42N 75 54E
Indus r. Asia 58 B3 27 00N 68 00E
Ingleborough sum. England 34 C3 54 10N 2 23W
Ingolstadt Germany 49 F3 48 46N 11 27E
Inishowen Peninsula Republic of Ireland 32 B3 55 15N 7 15W
Inland Sea sd. Japan 59 L1 34 00N 132 30E
Inn r. Europe 49 G3 48 15N 12 30E
Inner Hebrides is. Scotland 30 C1/2 56 45N 6 45W
Innerleithen Scotland 33 F3 55 38N 3 05W
Inner Sound Scotland 30 D2 57 25N 5 55W
Innsbruck Austria 49 F2 47 17N 11 25E
Inuvik Canada 78 F7 68 16N 133 40W
Inveraray Scotland 32 D4 56 13N 5 05W
Inverbervie Scotland 31 G2 56 51N 2 17W
Invercargill New Zealand 73 B1 46 25S 168 22E
Inverclyde u.a. Scotland 33 E3 55 50N 4 45W
Invergarry Scotland 31 E2 57 02N 4 47W
Invergordon Scotland 31 E2 57 42N 4 10W
Inverkeithing Scotland 33 F4 56 02N 3 25W
Invermoriston Scotland 31 E2 57 13N 4 38W
Inverness Scotland 31 E2 57 27N 4 15W
Inverurie Scotland 31 G2 57 17N 2 23W
Iona i. Scotland 30 C1 56 19N 6 25W
Ionian Island Greece 42 L3 39 40N 20 51E
Ionian Sea Mediterranean Sea 42 K3 38 00N 27 00E
Iowa state USA 79 K5 42 00N 94 00W
Ipoh Malaysia 60 B3 4 36N 101 05E
Ipswich England 39 F3 52 04N 1 10E
Iquique Chile 84 B5 20 15S 70 08W
Iquitos Peru 84 B7 3 51S 73 13W
Iraklion Greece 42 M3 35 20N 25 08E
IRAN 61 F4
IRAQ 61 F4
Irbid Jordan 43 P2 32 33N 35 51E
Irian Jaya admin. Indonesia 72 D5 3 00S 133 00E
Irish Sea British Isles 28 53 30N 5 30W
Irkutsk Russia 57 L3 52 18N 104 15E
Irrawaddy r. Myanmar 60 A4 20 00N 97 30E
Irthing r. England 34 C3 55 00N 2 40W
Irtysh r. Russia 56 H3 57 30N 72 30E
Irvine Scotland 33 E3 55 37N 4 40W
Ísafjördour Iceland 42 B9 66 05N 23 08W
Ishikari r. Japan 59 N3 43 30N 142 00E
Isigny-sur-Mer France 41 F2 49 18N 1 06W

Isla r. Scotland 31 F1 56 40N 3 15W
Islamabad Pakistan 58 C4 33 42N 73 10E
Island Magee p. Northern Ireland 32 D2 53 45N 5 45W
Islay i. Scotland 32 C3 55 48N 6 12W
Isle of Anglesey u.a. Wales 36 C3 53 18N 4 25W
Isle of Man British Isles 33 E2 54 15N 4 30W
Isle of Wight u.a. England 38 C1 50 40N 1 20W
ISRAEL 61 D4
Istanbul Turkey 42 M4 41 02N 28 57E
Istria p. Croatia 49 G1 45 00N 14 00E
Itabuna Brazil 84 F6 14 48S 39 18W
ITALY 51
Itchen r. England 38 C2 51 05N 1 15W
Ivanovo Russia 56 E3 57 00N 41 00E
Iwaki Japan 59 N2 37 03N 140 58E
Izhevsk Russia 43 S7 56 49N 53 11E
Izmir Turkey 42 M3 38 25N 27 10E
Izu Islands Japan 59 M1 34 20N 139 20E

J
Jabalpur India 58 C3 23 10N 79 59E
Jackson USA 79 K4 32 20N 90 11W
Jacksonville USA 79 L4 30 20N 81 40W
Jaffna Sri Lanka 58 D1 9 40N 80 01E
Jaipur India 58 C3 26 53N 75 50E
Jakarta Indonesia 60 B2 6 08S 106 45E
JAMAICA 79 M2
Jambi Indonesia 60 B2 1 34S 103 37E
James Bay Canada 78 L6 53 45N 81 00W
Jammu & Kashmir state Southern Asia 58 C4 29 40N 76 30E
Jamshedpur India 58 D3 22 47N 86 12E
JAPAN 59
Japan, Sea of Pacific Ocean 59 M3 39 00N 137 00E
Jauf Saudi Arabia 61 D3 29 49N 39 52E
Java i. Indonesia 60 B2/C2 7 00S 110 00E
Javalambre mt. Spain 50 E4 40 05N 1 02W
Java Sea Indonesia 60 C2 5 00S 112 00E
Jaya Peak Indonesia 72 D5 4 05S 137 09E
Jedburgh Scotland 33 G3 55 29N 2 34W
Jedda Saudi Arabia 61 D3 21 30N 39 10E
Jena Germany 49 F4 50 56N 11 35E
Jerez de la Frontera Spain 50 B2 36 41N 6 08W
Jersey i. Channel Islands British Isles 41 E2 49 13N 2 07W
Jerusalem Israel/Jordan 61 D4 31 47N 35 13E
Jiamusi China 59 E4 46 50N 130 29E
Jiayuguan China 59 A4 39 47N 98 14E
Jilin China 59 D4 43 53N 126 35E
Jinan China 59 C3 36 41N 117 00E
Jinsha Jiang (Yangtze) r. China 59 B2 27 30N 103 00E
Jixi China 59 E4 45 17N 131 00E
Jizan Saudi Arabia 61 E2 16 56N 42 33E
João Pessoa Brazil 84 F7 7 06S 34 53W
Johannesburg Republic of South Africa 67 C2 26 10S 28 02E
John o'Groats Scotland 31 F3 58 38N 3 05W
Johnstone Scotland 33 E3 55 50N 4 31W
Johor Bahru Malaysia 60 B3 1 27N 103 45E
Joinville Brazil 85 E5 26 20S 48 55W
Jönköping Sweden 42 J7 57 45N 14 10E
JORDAN 61 D4
Jos Plateau Nigeria 66 C3/4 9 30N 8 55E
Juan Fernández Islands Chile 85 B4 33 30S 80 00W
Juba Sudan 61 D1 4 50N 31 35E
Juba r. Somalia/Ethiopia 67 E5 5 00N 41 00E
Juiz de Fora Brazil 85 E4 21 47S 43 23W
Jungfrau mt. Switzerland 49 D2 46 33N 7 58E
Jura i. Scotland 32 D3/D4 55 55N 6 00W
Jura mts. France/Switzerland 48 F3 46 30N 6 00E
Jura, Sound of Scotland 32 D3/4 56 00N 5 45W
Jutland p. Denmark 49 E6 55 00N 9 00E

K
Kabul Afghanistan 58 B4 34 30N 70 00E
Kabwe Zambia 67 C3 14 29S 28 25E
Kaduna Nigeria 66 C4 10 28N 7 25E
Kaesong South Korea 59 D3 37 59N 126 30E
Kagoshima Japan 59 L1 31 37N 130 32E
Kainji Reservoir Nigeria 66 C4 10 25N 4 56E
Kaipara Harbour New Zealand 73 C3 36 12S 174 06E
Kaiserslautern Germany 49 D3 49 27N 7 47E
Kalahari Desert Southern Africa 67 C2 23 30S 23 00E
Kalemie Congo Dem. Rep. 67 C4 5 57S 29 10E
Kalgoorlie Australia 72 C2 30 49S 121 29E
Kaliningrad Russia 56 C3 54 40N 20 30E
Kamchatka Peninsula Russia 57 R3 57 30N 160 00E
Kampala Uganda 67 D5 0 19N 32 35E
Kananga Congo Dem. Rep. 67 C4 5 53S 22 26E
Kanazawa Japan 59 M2 36 35N 136 38E
Kandahar Afghanistan 58 B4 31 35N 65 45E
Kandalaksha Russia 42 N9 67 09N 32 31E
Kandla India 58 C3 23 03N 70 11E
Kandy Sri Lanka 58 D1 7 17N 80 40E
Kankan Guinea 66 B4 10 22N 9 11W
Kanpur India 58 D3 26 27N 80 14E
Kansas state USA 79 K4 38 00N 98 00W
Kansas City USA 79 K4 39 02N 94 33W
Kaohsiung Taiwan 59 D2 22 36N 120 17E
Kapuas r. Indonesia 60 C3 0 30N 112 00E
Karachi Pakistan 58 B3 24 52N 67 03E
Karaganda Kazakhstan 56 H2 49 53N 73 07E
Karbala Iraq 61 E4 32 37N 44 03E
Kariba, Lake Zambia/Zimbabwe 67 C3 17 00S 28 00E
Karlovac Croatia 51 E6 45 30N 15 34E
Karlsruhe Germany 49 E3 49 00N 8 24E
Karun r. Iran 61 E4 32 00N 48 00E
Kasai r. Angola/Congo Dem. Rep. 67 B4 4 00S 19 00E
Kashi China 58 C4 39 29N 76 02E
Kassala Sudan 61 D2 15 24N 36 30E
Kassel Germany 49 E4 51 18N 9 30E
Kasserine Tunisia 51 B1 35 13N 8 43E
Katherine Australia 72 D4 14 27S 132 15E

Kathmandu Nepal 58 D3 27 42N 85 19E
Katowice Poland 42 K6 50 15N 18 59E
Kaunas Lithuania 42 L6 54 52N 23 55E
Kayes Mali 66 A4 14 26N 11 28W
Kayseri Turkey 43 P3 38 42N 35 28E
KAZAKHSTAN 56 G2
Kazan' Russia 56 E3 55 45N 49 10E
Keady Northern Ireland 32 C2 54 15N 6 42W
Keighley England 34 D2 53 52N 1 54W
Keith Scotland 31 G2 57 32N 2 57W
Kelso Scotland 33 G3 55 36N 2 25W
Kemerovo Russia 56 J3 55 25N 86 05E
Kendal England 34 C3 54 20N 2 45W
Kenilworth England 37 F2 52 21N 1 34W
Kenitra Morocco 66 B6 34 20N 6 34W
Kennet r. England 38 C2 51 30N 1 45W
Kent co. England 39 E2 51 15N 0 09E
KENTUCKY state USA 79 L4 37 00N 85 00W
KENYA 67 D5
Kenya, Mount Kenya 67 D4 0 10S 37 19E
Kerema Papua New Guinea 72 E5 7 59S 145 46E
Kerguelen is. Indian Ocean 5 49 15N 69 10E
Kerman Iran 61 F4 30 18N 57 05E
Kermanshah Iran 61 E4 34 19N 47 04E
Kerrera i. Scotland 32 D1 56 24N 5 33W
Keswick England 34 B3 54 37N 3 08W
Kettering England 38 D3 52 24N 0 44W
Keynsham England 38 B2 51 26N 2 30W
Khabarovsk Russia 57 P2 48 32N 135 08E
Khaniá Greece 42 L3 35 31N 24 01E
Khanka, Lake Asia 57 P2 45 00N 132 30E
Kharkiv Ukraine 56 D2 50 00N 36 15E
Khartoum Sudan 61 D2 15 33N 32 35E
Kherson Ukraine 56 D2 46 39N 32 38E
Khulna Bangladesh 58 D3 22 49N 89 34E
Khyber Pass Afghanistan/Pakistan 58 C4 34 06N 71 05E
Kidderminster England 37 E2 52 23N 2 14W
Kidsgrove England 34 D3 53 05N 2 14W
Kidwelly Wales 36 C1 51 45N 4 18W
Kiel Germany 49 F6 54 20N 10 08E
Kielder Water res. England 33 G3 55 10N 2 30W
Kiev Ukraine 56 D3 50 25N 30 30E
Kigali Rwanda 67 D4 1 56S 30 04E
Kigoma Tanzania 67 C4 4 52S 29 36E
Kikwit Congo Dem. Rep. 67 B4 5 02S 18 51E
Kilbrannan Sound Scotland 32 D3 55 30N 5 30W
Kilimanjaro, Mount Tanzania 67 D4 3 04S 37 22E
Kilkeel Northern Ireland 32 C2 54 04N 6 00W
Kilmacrenan Republic of Ireland 32 B3 55 02N 7 47W
Kilmaluag Scotland 30 C2 57 41N 6 17W
Kilmarnock Scotland 33 E3 55 36N 4 30W
Kilmory Scotland 32 D3 55 55N 5 41W
Kimberley Republic of South Africa 67 C2 28 45S 24 46E
Kinabalu, Mount Malaysia 60 C3 6 03N 116 32E
Kinbrace Scotland 31 F3 58 15N 3 56W
Kingsbridge England 40 D3 50 17N 3 46W
King's Lynn England 39 E3 52 45N 0 24E
Kingston Jamaica 79 M2 17 58N 76 48W
Kingston upon Hull England 35 E2 53 45N 0 20W
Kingston upon Thames England 38 D2 51 25N 0 18W
Kingswood England 38 B2 51 28N 2 30W
Kington England 36 D2 52 12N 3 01W
Kingussie Scotland 31 E2 57 05N 4 03W
Kinloch Scotland 30 C2 57 01N 6 17W
Kinross Scotland 31 F1 56 13N 3 27W
Kinshasa Congo Dem. Rep. 67 B4 4 18S 15 18E
Kintyre p. Scotland 32 D3 55 30N 5 35W
KIRIBATI 4/5
Kirkbean Scotland 33 F2 54 55N 3 36W
Kirkby England 34 C2 53 29N 2 54W
Kirkby Stephen England 34 C3 54 28N 2 20W
Kirkcaldy Scotland 33 F4 56 07N 3 10W
Kirkcudbright Scotland 33 E2 54 50N 4 03W
Kirkintilloch Scotland 33 E3 55 57N 4 10W
Kirk Michael Isle of Man British Isles 33 E2 54 17N 4 35W
Kirkpatrick, Mount Antarctica 86 84 25S 165 30E
Kirkuk Iraq 61 E4 35 28N 44 26E
Kirkwall Scotland 29 C1 58 59N 2 58W
Kirov Russia 56 E3 58 00N 49 38E
Kirriemuir Scotland 31 F1 56 41N 3 01W
Kisangani Congo Dem. Rep. 67 C5 0 33N 25 14E
Kisumu Kenya 67 D4 0 08S 34 47E
Kitakami r. Japan 59 N2 39 00N 141 20E
Kita Kyushu Japan 59 L1 33 52N 130 49E
Kitwe Zambia 67 C3 12 48S 28 14E
Kitzbühel Austria 51 D7 47 27N 12 23E
Kivu, Lake Congo Dem. Rep./Rwanda 67 C4 2 00S 29 00E
Klagenfurt Austria 49 H2 46 38N 14 20E
Klaipėda Lithuania 42 L7 55 43N 21 07E
Knaresborough England 35 D3 54 00N 1 27W
Knighton England 36 D2 52 21N 3 03W
Kobe Japan 59 M1 34 40N 135 12E
Koblenz Germany 49 D4 50 21N 7 36E
Kochi Japan 59 L1 33 33N 133 32E
Kodiak Island USA 78 D6 57 20N 153 40W
Kokand Uzbekistan 56 H2 40 33N 70 55E
Kola Peninsula Russia 42 P9 67 00N 39 00E
Kolhapur India 58 C2 16 40N 74 20E
Kolkata India 58 D3 22 30N 88 20E
Kolyma r. Russia 57 R4 68 00N 152 00E
Komsomolsk-on-Amur Russia 57 P3 50 32N 136 59E
Konya Turkey 43 N3 37 51N 32 30E
Koriyama Japan 59 N2 37 23N 140 22E
Kosciusko, Mount Australia 72 E2 36 27S 148 17E
Kota Bharu Malaysia 60 B3 6 08N 102 14E
Kota Kinabalu Malaysia 60 C3 5 59N 116 04E
Kotlas Russia 43 R8 61 15N 46 35E
Kragujevac Serbia and Montenegro 42 L4 44 01N 20 55E
Kra, Isthmus of Myanmar/Thailand 60 A4 10 20N 99 00E
Kraków Poland 42 K6 50 03N 19 55E
Kranj Slovenia 51 E7 46 15N 14 20E
Krasnodar Russia 56 D2 45 02N 39 00E
Krasnovodsk Turkmenistan 56 F2 40 01N 53 00E

Krasnoyarsk Russia **57** K3 56 05N 92 46E
Kratie Cambodia **60** B4 12 30N 106 03E
Krefeld Germany **49** D4 51 20N 6 32E
Krishna r. India **58** C2 16 00N 79 00E
Kryvyy Rih Ukraine **56** D2 47 55N 33 24E
Kuala Lumpur Malaysia **60** B3 3 09N 101 42E
Kuala Terengganu Malaysia **60** B3 5 20N 103 09E
Kuantan Malaysia **60** B3 3 48N 103 19E
Kuching Malaysia **60** C3 1 35N 110 21E
Kuh-e-Hazaran mt. Iran **61** F3 29 35N 57 20E
Kumamoto Japan **59** L1 32 50N 130 42E
Kumasi Ghana **66** B3 6 45N 1 35W
Kunlun Shan mts. China **58** D4 36 30N 85 00E
Kunming China **59** B2 25 04N 102 41E
Kupang Indonesia **60** D1 10 13S 123 38E
Kurgan Russia **56** G3 55 30N 65 20E
Kuril Islands Russia **57** R2 50 00N 155 00E
Kursk Russia **56** D3 51 45N 36 14E
Kushiro Japan **59** N4 42 58N 144 24E
Kutaisi Georgia **43** Q4 42 15N 42 44E
KUWAIT 61 E3
Kuwait Kuwait **61** E3 29 20N 48 00E
Kwangju South Korea **59** D3 35 07N 126 52E
Kyle of Lochalsh Scotland **30** D2 57 17N 5 43W
Kyoga, Lake Uganda **67** D5 2 00N 34 00E
Kyoto Japan **59** M2 35 02N 135 45E
KYRGYZSTAN 56 H2
Kyushu i. Japan **59** L1 32 20N 131 00E

L

Laâyoune Western Sahara **66** A5 27 10N 13 11W
Ladoga, Lake Russia **56** D4 61 00N 30 00E
Lae Papua New Guinea **72** E5 6 45S 147 00E
Lagos Nigeria **66** C3 6 27N 3 28E
La Grande Rivière r. Canada **78** L6 53 34N 74 36W
Lahore Pakistan **58** C4 31 35N 74 18E
Lairg Scotland **31** E3 58 01N 4 25W
Lake District geog. reg. England **34** B3/C3 54 30N 3 00W
Lakshadweep (Laccadive Islands) India **58** C2 9 30N 73 00E
Lambert Glacier Antarctica **86** 73 00S 70 00E
Lambourn r. England **38** C2 51 30N 1 30W
Lammermuir Hills Scotland **33** G3 55 50N 2 45W
Lampedusa i. Italy **51** D1 35 00N 12 00E
Lampeter Wales **36** C2 52 07N 4 05W
Lanark Scotland **33** F3 55 41N 3 48W
Lancang Jiang (Mekong) r. China/Myanmar/ Laos/Cambodia **59** A3 32 00N 98 00E
Lancashire co. England **34** C2 53 50N 2 30W
Lancaster England **34** C3 54 03N 2 48W
Land's End c. England **40** B3 50 03N 5 44W
Langholm Scotland **33** G3 55 09N 3 00W
Languedoc geog. reg. France **48** E1/F2 44 00N 4 00E
Lanzhou China **59** B3 36 01N 103 45E
LAOS 60 B4
La Paz Bolivia **84** C6 16 30S 68 10W
La Plata Argentina **85** D4 34 52S 57 55W
La Puebla Balearic Islands **50** G3 39 46N 3 01E
Largs Scotland **32** E3 55 48N 4 52W
Lárisa Greece **42** L3 39 38N 22 25E
Larne Northern Ireland **32** D2 54 51N 5 49W
Larne district Northern Ireland **32** D2 54 50N 5 50W
Larsen Ice Shelf Antarctica **86** F7 00S 62 00W
La Rochelle France **48** C3 46 10N 1 10W
Las Palmas Canary Islands **66** A5 28 08N 15 27W
La Spezia Italy **51** B6 44 07N 9 48E
Las Vegas USA **79** H4 36 10N 115 10W
Latakia Syria **61** D4 35 31N 35 47E
Latina Italy **51** D4 41 28N 12 53E
LATVIA 42 M7
Launceston Australia **72** E1 41 27S 147 09E
Launceston England **40** C3 50 38N 4 21W
Laurencekirk Scotland **31** G1 56 50N 2 29W
Lausanne Switzerland **49** D2 46 32N 6 39E
Laval France **48** C4 48 04N 0 45W
Leader Water r. Scotland **33** G3 55 45N 2 50W
LEBANON 61 D4
Ledbury England **37** E2 52 02N 2 25W
Leeds England **34** D2 53 50N 1 35W
Leeuwin, Cape Australia **72** B2 34 21S 115 08E
le Havre France **48** D4 49 30N 0 06E
Leicester England **37** F2 52 38N 1 05W
Leicester City u.a. England **37** F2 52 36N 1 08W
Leicestershire co. England **37** F2/G2 52 38N 1 00W
Leiden Netherlands **49** C5 52 10N 4 30E
Leighton Buzzard England **38** D2 51 55N 0 41W
Leipzig Germany **49** G4 51 20N 12 25E
Leith Hill England **38** D2 51 11N 0 23W
Leitrim co. Republic of Ireland **32** A2 54 05N 8 00W
le Mans France **48** D4 48 00N 0 12E
Lena r. Russia **57** N4 64 30N 127 00E
Lens France **48** E5 50 26N 2 50E
Leominster England **37** E2 52 14N 2 45W
León Mexico **79** J3 21 10N 101 42W
León Spain **50** C5 42 35N 5 34W
le Puy France **48** E2 45 03N 3 53E
Lerwick Scotland **29** D3 60 09N 1 09W
LESOTHO 67 C2
Lessay France **41** F2 49 13N 1 32W
Lesser Antilles is. West Indies **79** N2 18 00N 65 00W
Letchworth England **38** D2 51 58N 0 14W
le Touquet-Paris-Plage France **39** F1 50 13N 1 36E
Letterkenny Republic of Ireland **32** B2 54 57N 7 44W
Leverkusen Germany **49** D4 51 02N 6 59E
Levin New Zealand **73** D2 40 37S 175 17E
Lewes England **38** E1 50 52N 0 01E
Lewis i. Scotland **30** C3 58 15N 6 30W
Leyburn England **34** D3 54 19N 1 49W
Leyland England **34** C2 53 42N 2 42W
Leyte i. The Philippines **60** D4 11 00N 125 00E
Lhasa China **58** E3 29 08N 91 43E
Lianyungang China **59** D3 34 37N 119 10E
Liao He r. China **59** D4 42 30N 122 00E
Liard r. Canada **78** G7 61 00N 122 00W
LIBERIA 66 B3
Libreville Gabon **66** C3 0 30N 9 25E

LIBYA 66 D5
Libyan Desert North Africa **61** C3 25 00N 25 00E
Lichfield England **37** F2 52 42N 1 48W
Liddel Water r. England/Scotland **33** G3 55 15N 2 50W
LIECHTENSTEIN 49 E2
Liège Belgium **49** C4 50 38N 5 35E
Liepāja Latvia **42** L7 56 30N 21 00E
Likasi Congo Dem. Rep. **67** C3 10 58S 26 47E
Lille France **48** E5 50 39N 3 05E
Lillers France **39** G1 50 34N 2 29E
Lilongwe Malawi **67** D3 13 58S 33 49E
Lima Peru **84** B6 12 06S 8 40W
Limassol Cyprus **43** N2 34 04N 33 03E
Limavady Northern Ireland **32** C3 55 03N 6 57W
Limavady district Northern Ireland **32** B2/C2 54 50N 7 00W
Limoges France **48** D2 45 50N 1 15E
Limpopo r. Southern Africa **67** C2 22 30S 28 00E
Lincoln England **35** E2 53 14N 0 33W
Lincolnshire co. England **35** E2 53 10N 0 20W
Lincoln Wolds hills England **35** E2 53 25N 0 05W
Lingga i. Indonesia **60** B2 0 10S 104 40E
Linköping Sweden **42** K7 58 25N 15 35E
Linlithgow Scotland **33** F3 55 59N 3 37W
Linz Austria **42** J5 48 19N 14 18E
Lipetsk Russia **56** D3 52 37N 39 36E
Lisbon Portugal **50** A3 38 44N 9 08W
Lisburn Northern Ireland **32** C2 54 31N 6 03W
Lisburn district Northern Ireland **32** C2 54 30N 6 10W
Lisieux France **48** D4 49 09N 0 14E
Liskeard England **40** C3 50 28N 4 28W
Lismore i. Scotland **30** D1 56 30N 5 30W
LITHUANIA 42 L7
Littlehampton England **38** D1 50 48N 0 33W
Little Minch sd. Scotland **30** C2 57 45N 6 30W
Little Ouse r. England **39** E3 52 30N 0 30E
Little Rock USA **79** K4 34 42N 92 17W
Liuzhou China **59** B2 24 17N 109 15E
Liverpool England **34** C2 53 25N 2 55W
Livingston Scotland **33** F3 55 53N 3 32W
Livorno Italy **51** C5 43 33N 10 18E
Lizard England **40** B2 49 57N 5 13W
Lizard Point England **40** B2 49 56N 5 13W
Ljubljana Slovenia **51** E7 46 04N 14 30E
Llandeilo Wales **36** D1 51 53N 3 59W
Llandovery Wales **36** D1 51 59N 3 48W
Llandrindod Wells Wales **36** D2 52 15N 3 23W
Llandudno Wales **36** D3 53 19N 3 49W
Llanelli Wales **36** C1 51 42N 4 10W
Llangollen Wales **36** D2 52 58N 3 10W
Llanidloes Wales **36** D2 52 27N 3 32W
Lleida Spain **50** F4 41 37N 0 38E
Lleyn Peninsula Wales **36** C2 52 53N 4 30W
Lobito Angola **67** B3 12 20S 13 34E
Lochaline tn. Scotland **30** D1 56 32N 5 47W
Loch Arkaig l. Scotland **30** D1 56 59N 5 10W
Loch Awe l. Scotland **30/31** D1 56 15N 5 17W
Lochdon tn. Scotland **30** D1 56 25N 5 38W
Loch Doon l. Scotland **33** E3 55 26N 4 38W
Loch Earn l. Scotland **31** E1 56 25N 4 10W
Loch Eishort est. Scotland **30** D2 57 08N 6 00W
Loch Eriboll b. Scotland **31** E3 58 31N 4 41W
Loch Ericht l. Scotland **31** E1 56 48N 4 25W
Loch Etive l. Scotland **30/31** D1 56 30N 5 10W
Loch Fyne b. Scotland **32** D4 56 10N 5 05W
Lochgilphead tn. Scotland **32** D4 56 03N 5 26W
Loch Katrine l. Scotland **33** E4 56 16N 4 30W
Loch Ken l. Scotland **33** E3 55 02N 4 07W
Loch Leven l. Scotland **31** F1 56 15N 3 23W
Loch Linnhe b. Scotland **30** D1 56 35N 5 25W
Loch Lochy l. Scotland **31** E1 56 58N 4 55W
Loch Lomond l. Scotland **33** E4 56 10N 4 35W
Loch Long l. Scotland **32/33** E4 56 10N 4 50W
Lochmaben tn. Scotland **33** F3 55 08N 3 27W
Lochmaddy tn. Scotland **30** B2 57 36N 7 08W
Loch Nan Clar l. Scotland **31** E3 58 30N 4 00W
Loch Maree l. Scotland **30** D2 57 40N 5 30W
Loch Mullardoch l. Scotland **31** E2 57 27N 4 58W
Lochnagar mt. Scotland **31** F1 56 57N 3 16W
Loch Ness l. Scotland **31** E2 57 02N 4 30W
Lochranza tn. Scotland **32** D3 55 42N 5 18W
Loch Shiel l. Scotland **30** D1 56 45N 5 35W
Loch Shin l. Scotland **31** E3 58 05N 4 30W
Loch Snizort b. Scotland **30** C2 57 30N 6 30W
Loch Tay l. Scotland **31** E1 56 31N 4 10W
Loch Torridon b. Scotland **30** D2 57 35N 5 46W
Lockerbie Scotland **33** F3 55 07N 3 22W
Łódź Poland **42** L6 51 49N 19 28E
Logan, Mount Canada **78** E7 60 34N 140 25W
Logroño Spain **50** D5 42 28N 2 26W
Loire r. France **48** D3 47 30N 1 30W
Lolland i. Denmark **49** F6 54 45N 12 20E
Lombok i. Indonesia **60** C2 8 30S 116 30E
Lomé Togo **66** C3 6 10N 1 21E
London England **38** D2 51 30N 0 10W
Londonderry Northern Ireland **32** B2 54 59N 7 19W
Londonderry district Northern Ireland **32** B2 54 55N 7 20W
Londrina Brazil **84** D5 23 18S 51 13W
Long Eaton England **37** F2 52 54N 1 15W
Long Island The Bahamas **79** M3 23 20N 75 00W
Long Mynd sum. England **37** E2 52 32N 2 52W
Longreach Australia **72** E3 23 26S 144 15E
Longs Peak USA **79** J5 40 20N 105 50W
Looe England **40** C3 51 21N 4 27W
Lorient France **48** B3 47 45N 3 21W
Los Angeles USA **79** H4 34 00N 118 15W
Lossiemouth Scotland **31** F2 57 43N 3 18W
Lostwithiel England **40** C3 50 25N 4 40W
Lot r. France **48** E2 44 30N 2 15E
Louangphrabang Laos **60** B4 19 53N 102 10E
Lough Allen l. Republic of Ireland **32** A2 54 15N 8 00W
Lough Beg l. Northern Ireland **32** C2 54 48N 6 16W
Loughborough England **37** F2 52 47N 1 11W
Lough Derg l. Republic of Ireland **32** B2 52 55N 8 15W

Lough Foyle est. Northern Ireland/Republic of Ireland **32** B3 55 10N 7 10W
Lough Macnean Lower l. Northern Ireland **32** B2 54 17N 7 50W
Lough Macnean Upper l. Northern Ireland/ Republic of Ireland **32** B2 54 18N 7 55W
Lough Melvin l. Northern Ireland/Republic of Ireland **32** A2 54 25N 8 05W
Lough Neagh l. Northern Ireland **32** C2 54 35N 6 30W
Lough Oughter l. Republic of Ireland **32** B2 54 00N 7 30W
Lough Swilly b. Republic of Ireland **32** B3 55 20N 7 35W
Louisiana state USA **79** K4 32 00N 92 00W
Louisville USA **79** L4 38 13N 85 48W
Lourdes France **48** C1 43 06N 0 02W
Louth England **35** E2 53 22N 0 01W
Louth co. Republic of Ireland **32** C1/2 53 55N 6 25W
Lower California p. Mexico **79** H3 27 30N 113 00W
Lower Lough Erne l. Northern Ireland **32** B2 54 25N 7 45W
Lowestoft England **39** F3 52 29N 1 45E
Lowther Hills Scotland **33** F3 55 25N 3 45W
Lualaba r. Congo Dem. Rep. **67** C4 4 00S 26 30E
Luanda Angola **67** B4 8 50S 13 15E
Lubango Angola **67** B3 14 55S 13 30E
Lübeck Germany **49** F5 53 52N 10 40E
Lublin Poland **42** L6 51 18N 22 31E
Lubumbashi Congo Dem. Rep. **67** C3 11 41S 27 29E
Luce Bay Scotland **32/33** E2 54 47N 4 50W
Lucerne Switzerland **49** E2 47 03N 8 17E
Lucknow India **58** D3 26 50N 80 54E
Lüderitz Namibia **67** B2 26 38S 15 10E
Ludhiana India **58** C4 30 56N 75 52E
Ludlow England **37** E2 52 22N 2 43W
Ludwigshafen Germany **49** E3 49 29N 8 27E
Lugano Switzerland **49** E2 46 01N 8 57E
Luhans'k Ukraine **56** D2 48 35N 39 20E
Luleå Sweden **42** L9 65 35N 22 10E
Lundy i. England **40** C4 51 11N 4 40W
Lune r. England **34** C3 54 10N 2 40W
Luoyang China **59** C3 34 47N 112 26E
Lurgan Northern Ireland **32** C2 54 28N 6 20W
Lusaka Zambia **67** C3 15 26S 28 20E
Luton England **38** D2 51 53N 0 25W
Luton u.a. England **38** D2 51 53N 0 30W
LUXEMBOURG 49 C3/D3
Luxembourg Luxembourg **49** D3 49 37N 6 08E
Luxor Egypt **61** D3 25 41N 32 24E
Luzon i. The Philippines **60** D4 15 00N 122 00E
L'viv Ukraine **56** C2 49 50N 24 00E
Lybster Scotland **31** F3 58 18N 3 13W
Lyme Bay England **41** E3 50 40N 2 55W
Lyme Regis England **41** E3 50 44N 2 57W
Lymington England **38** C1 50 46N 1 33W
Lynn Lake tn. Canada **78** J6 56 51N 101 01W
Lynton England **40** D4 51 15N 3 50W
Lyons France **48** F2 45 46N 4 50E
Lys r. France **39** G1 50 40N 2 10E
Lytham St. Anne's England **34** B2 53 45N 3 01W

M

Maas r. Netherlands **49** C4 51 50N 5 45E
Maastricht Netherlands **49** C4 50 51N 5 42E
Mablethorpe England **35** F2 53 21N 0 15E
Macao China **59** C2 22 10N 113 40E
Macapá Brazil **84** D8 0 04N 51 04W
Macclesfield England **34** C2 53 16N 2 07W
Macdonnell Ranges Australia **72** D3 23 42S 128 42E
Macduff Scotland **31** G2 57 40N 2 29W
MACEDONIA, FORMER YUGOSLAV REPUBLIC OF (FYROM) 42 L4
Maceió Brazil **84** F7 9 40S 35 44W
Machynlleth Wales **36** D2 52 35N 3 51W
Mackay, Lake Australia **72** C3 22 25S 128 42E
Mackenzie r. Canada **78** G7 66 00N 123 00W
Mackenzie Mountains Canada **78** G7 66 00N 132 00W
McKinley, Mount USA **78** E7 62 02N 151 01W
Mâcon France **48** F3 46 18N 4 50E
MADAGASCAR 67 E2/3
Madang Papua New Guinea **72** E5 5 14S 145 45E
Madeira r. Brazil **84** C7 6 00S 61 30W
Madeira Islands Atlantic Ocean **5** 32 45N 17 00W
Madrid Spain **50** D4 40 25N 3 43W
Madura i. Indonesia **60** C2 7 00S 113 00E
Madurai India **58** C1 9 55N 78 07E
Maebashi Japan **59** M2 36 24N 139 04E
Magadan Russia **57** R3 59 38N 150 50E
Magdalena r. Colombia **84** B8 3 00N 75 40W
Magdeburg Germany **49** F5 52 08N 11 37E
Maggiore, Lake Italy **51** B6/7 46 00N 8 00E
Maghera Northern Ireland **32** C2 54 51N 6 40W
Magherafelt Northern Ireland **32** C2 54 45N 6 36W
Magherafelt district Northern Ireland **32** C2 54 45N 6 50W
Magnitogorsk Russia **56** F3 53 28N 59 06E
Mahajanga Madagascar **67** E3 15 40S 46 20E
Mahakam r. Indonesia **60** C3 0 30N 116 00E
Mahilyow Belarus **56** D3 53 54N 30 20E
Mahón Balearic Islands **50** H3 39 54N 4 15E
Maidenhead England **38** D2 51 32N 0 44W
Maidstone England **39** E2 51 17N 0 32E
Maiduguri Nigeria **66** D3 11 53N 13 16E
Main r. Germany **49** F4 50 00N 10 00E
Main r. Northern Ireland **32** C2 54 50N 6 25W
Mai-Ndombe, Lake Congo Dem. Rep. **67** B4 2 00S 18 20E
Maine state USA **79** N5 45 00N 70 00W
Mainland i. Orkney Islands Scotland **29** B1/B2 59 00N 3 15W
Mainland i. Shetland Islands Scotland **29** D3 60 15N 1 20W
Mainz Germany **49** D3 50 00N 8 16E
Makassar Strait Indonesia **60** C2 0 00N 119 00E
Makeyevka Ukraine **56** D2 48 01N 38 00E
Makhachkala Russia **56** E2 42 59N 47 30E
Malabo Equatorial Guinea **66** C3 3 45N 8 48E
Malacca, Strait of Indonesia **60** B3 4 00N 100 00E

Málaga Spain **50** C2 36 43N 4 25W
Malahide Republic of Ireland **36** A3 53 27N 6 09W
Malakal Sudan **61** D1 9 31N 31 40E
Malang Indonesia **60** C2 7 59S 112 45E
Malanje Angola **67** B4 9 32S 16 20E
Malatya Turkey **43** P3 38 22N 38 18E
MALAWI 67 D3
Malawi, Lake see Nyasa, Lake
Malaya admin. Malaysia **60** B3 5 00N 102 00E
MALAYSIA 60 B3/C3
MALDIVES 58 C1
MALI 66 C4
Malin Head c. Republic of Ireland **32** B3 55 30N 7 20W
Mallaig Scotland **30** D2 57 00N 5 50W
Mallorca i. Balearic Islands **50** G3 39 50N 2 30E
Malmesbury England **38** B2 51 36N 2 06W
Malmö Sweden **42** J7 55 35N 13 00E
MALTA 51 E1
Malton England **35** E3 54 08N 0 48W
Manacor Balearic Islands **50** G3 39 35N 3 12E
Manado Indonesia **60** D3 1 32N 124 55E
Managua Nicaragua **79** L2 12 06N 86 18W
Manaus Brazil **84** D7 3 06S 60 00W
Manawatu r. New Zealand **73** D2 40 30S 176 00E
Manchester England **34** C2 53 30N 2 15W
Mandalay Myanmar **58** B3 21 57N 96 04E
Manfredonia Italy **51** E4 41 37N 15 55E
Mangalore India **58** C2 12 54N 74 51E
Mangotsfield England **38** B2 51 29N 2 31W
Manila The Philippines **60** D4 14 37N 120 58E
Manitoba province Canada **78** K6 55 00N 98 00W
Manizales Colombia **84** B8 5 03N 75 32W
Mannheim Germany **49** E3 49 30N 8 28E
Mansfield England **37** F3 53 09N 1 11W
Manzanares Spain **50** D3 39 00N 3 23W
Maputo Mozambique **67** D2 25 58S 32 35E
Maracaibo Venezuela **84** B9 10 44N 71 37W
Maracaibo, Lake Venezuela **84** B9 9 50N 71 30W
Marañón r. Peru **84** B7 7 00S 77 40W
Marbella Spain **50** C2 36 31N 4 53W
Marble Bar Australia **72** B3 21 10S 119 43E
Mar del Plata Argentina **85** D4 38 00S 57 32W
Marden England **39** E2 51 11N 0 30E
Margarita i. Venezuela **79** N2 11 30N 64 00W
Margate England **39** F2 51 24N 1 24E
Maribor Slovenia **51** E7 46 34N 15 38E
Marie Byrd Land geog. reg. Antarctica **86** 77 00S 130 00W
Mariscal Estigarribia Paraguay **84** C5 22 03S 60 35W
Mariupol Ukraine **56** D2 47 05N 37 34E
Market Drayton England **37** E2 52 54N 2 29W
Market Harborough England **37** G2 52 29N 0 55W
Market Rasen England **35** E2 53 24N 0 21W
Markham, Mount Antarctica **86** 82 45S 160 25E
Marlborough England **38** C2 51 26N 1 43W
Marlow England **38** D2 51 35N 0 48W
Marne r. France **48** E4 49 00N 4 00E
Marrakesh Morocco **66** B6 31 49N 8 00W
Marsala Italy **51** D2 37 48N 12 27E
Marseille France **48** F1 43 18N 5 22E
MARSHALL ISLANDS 5
Martinique i. Lesser Antilles **79** N2 14 30N 61 00W
Maryborough Australia **72** F3 25 33S 152 42E
Maryland state USA **79** M4 39 00N 77 00W
Maryport England **34** B3 54 43N 3 30W
Maseru Lesotho **67** C2 29 19S 27 29E
Mashhad Iran **61** F4 36 16N 59 34E
Massachusetts state USA **79** M5 42 00N 72 00W
Massawa Eritrea **61** D2 15 42N 39 25E
Massif Central mts. France **48** E2 45 00N 3 30E
Masterton New Zealand **73** D2 40 57S 175 39E
Matadi Congo Dem. Rep. **67** B4 5 50S 13 32E
Matamoros Mexico **79** K3 25 33N 103 51W
Matlock England **37** F3 53 08N 1 32W
Mato Grosso geog. reg. Brazil **84** D6 14 00S 56 00W
Matsue Japan **59** L2 35 29N 133 04E
Matsuyama Japan **59** L1 33 50N 132 47E
Matterhorn mt. Switzerland **49** D1 45 59N 7 39E
MAURITANIA 66 A5
MAURITIUS 5
Maybole Scotland **33** E3 55 21N 4 41W
Mazatlán Mexico **79** J3 23 11N 106 25W
Mbandaka Congo Dem. Rep. **67** B5 0 03N 18 28E
Mbuji-Mayi Congo Dem. Rep. **67** C4 6 10S 23 39E
Mecca Saudi Arabia **61** D3 21 26N 39 49E
Medan Indonesia **60** A3 3 35N 98 39E
Medellín Colombia **84** B8 6 15N 75 36W
Medina Saudi Arabia **61** D3 24 30N 39 35E
Mediterranean Sea Africa/Europe **42/43** 35 00N 15 00E
Medway r. England **39** E2 51 24N 0 30E
Medway u.a. England **39** E2 51 28N 0 35E
Meekatharra Australia **72** B3 26 35S 118 30E
Meerut India **58** C3 29 00N 77 42E
Mega Ethiopia **61** D1 4 02N 38 19E
Meharry, Mount Australia **72** B3 22 58S 118 35E
Meig r. Scotland **31** E2 57 40N 4 50W
Meknes Morocco **66** B6 33 53N 5 37W
Mekong (Lancang Jiang) r. Cambodia/Laos/ Myanmar/China **59** B1 15 00N 105 00E
Melbourne Australia **72** E2 37 45S 144 58E
Melrose Scotland **33** G3 55 36N 2 44W
Melton Mowbray England **37** G2 52 46N 0 53W
Melville Island Canada **78** H5 75 30N 112 00W
Memphis USA **79** K4 35 10N 90 00W
Menam r. Thailand **60** B4 15 00N 100 00E
Mendip Hills England **41** E4 51 18N 2 45W
Mendoza Argentina **85** C4 32 48S 68 52W
Menorca i. Balearic Islands **50** H3 39 45N 4 15E
Mentawai Islands Indonesia **60** A2 2 00N 99 00E
Menzies, Mount Antarctica **86** 73 30S 62 00E
Meon r. England **38** C1 50 55N 1 10W
Mere England **38** B2 51 06N 2 16W
Mérida Mexico **79** L3 20 59N 89 39W
Mersey r. England **34** C2 53 20N 2 55W
Merseyside co. England **34** C2 53 30N 3 20W
Mersin Turkey **43** N3 36 47N 34 37E
Merthyr Tydfil Wales **36** D1 51 46N 3 23W
Merthyr Tydfil u.a. Wales **36** D1 51 48N 3 20W
Merton England **38** D2 51 25N 0 12W

essina Italy 51 E3 38 13N 15 33E
etz France 48 G4 49 07N 6 11E
euse r. Belgium/France 49 C4 50 30N 5 00E
exicali Mexico 79 H4 32 36N 115 30W
EXICO 79 H4/K2
exico City Mexico 79 K2 19 25N 99 10W
exico, Gulf of Mexico 79 L3 25 00N 90 00W
iami USA 79 L3 25 45N 80 15W
ichigan state USA 79 L5 45 00N 85 00W
ichigan, Lake Canada/USA 79 L5 44 00N 87 00W
ickle Fell sum. England 34 C3 54 38N 2 18W
iddlesbrough England 35 D3 54 35N 1 14W
iddlesbrough u.a. England 35 D3 54 33N 1 04W
idlothian u.a. Scotland 33 F3 55 50N 3 05W
ilan Italy 51 B6 45 28N 9 12E
ildenhall England 39 E3 52 21N 0 30E
ildura Australia 72 E2 34 12S 142 09E
ilford Haven Wales 36 B1 51 44N 5 02W
ilford Sound New Zealand 73 B2 44 41S 167 56E
ilton Keynes England 38 D3 52 02N 0 42W
ilton Keynes u.a. England 38 D3 52 10N 0 40W
ilton Ness c. Scotland 31 G1 56 40N 2 20W
ilwaukee USA 79 L5 43 03N 87 56W
inch, The sd. Scotland 30 C3/D3 58 00N 6 00W
indanao i. The Philippines 60 D3 8 00N 125 00E
indoro i. The Philippines 60 D4 13 00N 121 00E
inehead England 40 D4 51 13N 3 29W
ingulay i. Scotland 30 B1 56 49N 7 38W
inneapolis USA 79 K5 45 00N 93 15W
innesota state USA 79 K5 47 00N 95 00W
insk Belarus 56 C3 53 51N 27 30E
iskolc Hungary 42 L5 48 07N 20 47E
isool i. Indonesia 60 E2 1 50S 129 55E
isratah Libya 66 D6 32 23N 15 06E
ississippi r. USA 79 K4 33 00N 90 30W
ississippi state USA 79 K4 32 00N 90 00W
issouri r. USA 79 J5 48 00N 109 00W
issouri state USA 79 K4 38 00N 93 00W
iyazaki Japan 59 L1 31 56N 131 27E
obile USA 79 L4 30 40N 88 05W
oçambique Mozambique 67 E3 15 03S 40 45E
ódena Italy 51 C6 44 39N 10 55E
offat Scotland 33 F3 55 20N 3 27W
ogadishu Somalia 67 E5 2 02N 45 21E
old Wales 36 D3 53 10N 3 08W
oldau r. Czech Republic 49 H3 49 30N 14 15E
OLDOVA 42 M5
oluccas is. Indonesia 60 D3/E2 4 00S 127 00E
olucca Sea Indonesia 60 D2 0 30S 125 30E
ombasa Kenya 67 D4 4 04S 39 40E
ONACO 48 G1
onadhliath Mountains Scotland 31 E2 57 10N 4 00W
onaghan Republic of Ireland 32 C2 54 15N 6 58W
onaghan co. Republic of Ireland 32 B2/C2 54 10N 7 00W
onforte Spain 50 B5 42 32N 7 30W
ONGOLIA 57 L2
onmouth Wales 37 E1 51 50N 2 43W
onmouthshire u.a. Wales 37 E1 51 47N 2 55W
onopoli Italy 51 F4 40 57N 17 18E
onrovia Liberia 66 A3 6 20N 10 46W
ontana state USA 79 H5 47 00N 111 00W
ontauban France 48 D2 44 01N 1 20E
ontbéliard France 48 G3 47 31N 6 48E
ont Blanc mt. France/Italy 48 G2 45 50N 6 52E
onterrey Mexico 79 J3 25 40N 100 20W
ontes Claros tn. Brazil 84 E6 16 45N 43 52W
ontevideo Uruguay 85 D4 34 55S 56 10W
ontgomery Wales 36 D2 52 34N 3 10W
ontluçon France 48 E3 46 20N 2 36E
ontpellier France 48 E1 43 36N 3 53E
ontréal Canada 79 M5 45 32N 73 36W
ontreux Switzerland 49 D2 46 27N 6 55E
ontrose Scotland 31 G1 56 43N 2 29W
onza Italy 51 B6 45 35N 9 16E
oosonee Canada 79 L6 51 18N 80 39W
oray u.a. Scotland 31 F2 57 20N 3 10W
oray Firth est. Scotland 31 F2 57 45N 3 45W
orecambe England 34 C3 54 04N 2 53W
orecambe Bay England 34 B3/C3 54 00N 3 00W
orelia Mexico 79 J2 19 40N 101 11W
oreton-in-Marsh England 38 C2 51 59N 1 42W
orioka Japan 59 N2 39 43N 141 08E
orlaix France 48 B4 48 35N 3 50W
OROCCO 66 B6
oroni Comoros 67 E3 11 40S 43 16E
orotai i. Indonesia 60 D3 2 30N 128 30E
orven mt. Scotland 31 F3 58 14N 3 42W
oscow Russia 56 D3 55 45N 37 42E
osel r. Germany/France 49 D3 50 00N 7 00E
óstoles Spain 50 D4 40 19N 3 53W
osul Iraq 61 E4 36 21N 43 08E
otherwell Scotland 33 E3 55 48N 3 59W
oulmein Myanmar 58 E2 16 30N 97 39E
ount Hagen tn. Papua New Guinea 72 E5 5 54S 114 13E
ount Isa tn. Australia 72 D3 20 44S 139 29E
ount Magnet tn. Australia 72 B3 28 02S 117 50E
ounts Bay England 40 B3 50 05N 5 30W
oyale Kenya 66 D5 3 31N 39 04E
oyle district Northern Ireland 32 C3 55 10N 6 10W
OZAMBIQUE 67 D3
ozambique Channel Mozambique/Madagascar 67 E3 18 00S 34 00E
uck i. Scotland 30 C1 56 50N 6 15W
uckle Roe i. Scotland 29 D3 60 22N 1 26W
udanjiang China 59 D4 44 36N 129 42E
ukalla Yemen Republic 61 E2 14 34N 49 09E
ulhacén mt. Spain 50 D2 37 04N 3 19W
ulhouse France 48 G3 47 45N 7 21E
ull i. Scotland 30 C1/D1 56 25N 6 00W
ull Head c. Scotland 29 C2 59 20N 2 58W
ullion England 40 B3 50 01N 5 14W
ull of Galloway c. Scotland 32 E2 54 38N 4 50W
ull of Kintyre c. Scotland 32 D3 55 17N 5 55W
ull of Oa c. Scotland 32 C3 55 35N 6 20W
ultan Pakistan 58 C4 30 10N 71 36E

Mumbai India 58 C2 18 56N 72 51E
München Gladbach Germany 49 D4 51 12N 6 25E
Munich Germany 49 F3 48 08N 11 35E
Münster Germany 49 D4 51 58N 7 37E
Mur r. Europe 49 H2 47 00N 14 00E
Murchison r. Australia 72 B3 26 00S 117 00E
Murcia Spain 50 E2 37 59N 1 08W
Murmansk Russia 56 D4 68 59N 33 08E
Muroran Japan 59 N3 42 21N 140 59E
Murray r. Australia 72 E2 35 40S 144 00E
Murrumbidgee r. Australia 72 E2 35 00S 145 00E
Muscat Oman 61 F3 23 37N 58 38E
Musi r. Indonesia 60 B2 3 00S 104 00E
Musselburgh Scotland 33 F3 55 57N 3 04W
Mwanza Tanzania 67 D4 2 31S 32 56E
Mweru, Lake Congo Dem. Rep./Zambia 67 C4 8 30S 28 30E
MYANMAR (BURMA) 58 E3
Mykolayiv Ukraine 56 D2 46 57N 32 00E
Mynydd Eppynt hills Wales 36 D2 52 02N 3 35W
Mynydd Preseli hills Wales 36 C1 51 58N 4 45W
Mysore India 58 C2 12 18N 76 37E

N

Naberezhnyye Chelny Russia 56 F3 55 42N 52 19E
Nabeul Tunisia 42 J3 36 30N 10 44E
Nador Morocco 50 D1 35 10N 3 00W
Nagano Japan 59 M2 36 39N 138 10E
Nagasaki Japan 59 K1 32 45N 129 52E
Nagoya Japan 59 M2 35 08N 136 53E
Nagpur India 58 C3 21 10N 79 12E
Nairn Scotland 31 F2 57 35N 3 53W
Nairn r. Scotland 31 E2 57 28N 4 10W
Nairobi Kenya 67 D4 1 17S 36 50E
Najran Saudi Arabia 61 E2 17 37N 44 40E
Namangan Uzbekistan 56 H2 40 59N 71 41E
Namib Desert Namibia 67 B2 22 00S 14 00E
NAMIBIA 67 B2
Nampo North Korea 59 D3 38 51N 125 10E
Nampula Mozambique 67 D3 15 09S 39 14E
Namur Belgium 49 C4 50 28N 4 52E
Nanchang China 59 C2 28 33N 115 58E
Nancy France 48 G4 48 42N 6 12E
Nanjing China 59 C2 32 03N 118 47E
Nanning China 59 B2 22 50N 108 19E
Nan Shan mts. China 59 A3 38 00N 99 00E
Nantes France 48 C3 47 14N 1 35W
Napier New Zealand 73 D3 39 30S 176 54E
Naples Italy 51 E4 40 50N 14 15E
Napo r. Ecuador/Peru 84 B7 1 30S 74 30W
Narbonne France 48 E1 43 11N 3 00E
Narmada r. India 58 C3 22 00N 78 00E
Narvik Norway 42 K9 68 26N 17 25E
Nassau The Bahamas 79 M3 25 05N 77 20W
Nasser, Lake Egypt 61 D3 22 35N 31 40E
Natal Brazil 84 F5 5 46S 35 15W
Natuna Islands Indonesia 60 B3 3 40N 108 00E
NAURU 5
Ndjamena Chad 66 D4 12 10N 14 59E
Ndola Zambia 67 C3 13 00S 28 39E
Neath Wales 36 D1 51 40N 3 48W
Neath Port Talbot u.a. Wales 36 D1 51 40N 3 45W
Nebraska state USA 79 J5 42 00N 102 00W
Negro r. Argentina 85 C4 39 39S 67 30W
Negro r. Bolivia/Brazil 84 C7 1 00S 62 20W
Negros i. The Philippines 60 D3 10 00N 123 00E
Neiva Colombia 84 B8 2 58N 75 15W
Nelson England 34 C2 53 51N 2 13W
Nelson New Zealand 73 C2 41 30S 172 30E
Nelson r. Canada 79 K6 57 00N 94 00W
Nemuro Japan 59 P3 43 22N 145 36E
Nene r. England 39 E3 52 45N 0 10E
Nen Jiang r. China 59 D4 45 00N 124 00E
NEPAL 58 D3
NETHERLANDS 49 C5/D5
Nevada state USA 79 H4 39 00N 118 00W
Nevers France 48 E3 47 00N 3 09E
Nevis i. St. Kitts and Nevis 79 N2 17 00N 62 30W
Newark USA 79 M5 40 43N 74 11W
Newark-on-Trent England 37 G3 53 05N 0 49W
New Britain i. Papua New Guinea 72 F5 4 45S 150 30E
New Brunswick province Canada 79 N5 47 30N 66 00W
Newburgh Scotland 33 F4 57 18N 2 00W
Newbury England 38 C2 51 25N 1 20W
New Caledonia i. Pacific Ocean 5 22 00S 165 00E
Newcastle Australia 72 F2 32 57S 151 43E
Newcastle Northern Ireland 32 D2 54 12N 5 54W
Newcastle Emlyn Wales 36 C2 52 02N 4 28W
Newcastle-under-Lyme England 37 E3 53 00N 2 14W
Newcastle upon Tyne England 34 D3 54 59N 1 35W
New Cumnock Scotland 33 E3 55 24N 4 12W
Newfoundland i. Canada 79 P5 53 51N 56 56W
Newfoundland and Labrador province Canada 78 P6 56 00N 60 00W
New Galloway Scotland 33 E3 55 05N 4 10W
New Hampshire state USA 79 M5 43 00N 72 00W
New Ireland i. Papua New Guinea 72 F5 3 15S 152 30E
New Jersey state USA 79 M4 40 00N 75 00W
Newman Australia 72 B3 23 22S 119 43E
Newmarket England 39 E3 52 15N 0 25E
New Mexico state USA 79 J4 35 00N 107 00W
New Orleans USA 79 K3 30 00N 90 03W
New Plymouth New Zealand 73 C3 39 04S 174 04E
Newport Isle of Wight England 38 C1 50 42N 1 18W
Newport Telford and Wrekin England 37 E2 52 47N 2 22W
Newport Wales 36 D1 51 35N 3 00W
Newport r. u.a. Wales 36 D1/E1 51 33N 3 00W
Newquay England 40 B3 50 25N 5 05W
New Quay Wales 36 C2 52 13N 4 22W
Newry Northern Ireland 32 C2 54 11N 6 20W
Newry and Mourne district Northern Ireland 32 C2 54 10N 6 20W
New Siberian Islands Russia 57 Q5 75 00N 145 00E
New South Wales state Australia 72 E2 32 00S 145 00E
Newton Abbot England 40 D3 50 32N 3 36W

Newton Aycliffe England 34 D3 54 37N 1 34W
Newtonmore Scotland 31 E2 57 04N 4 08W
Newton Stewart Scotland 33 E2 54 57N 4 29W
Newtown Wales 36 D2 52 32N 3 19W
Newtownabbey Northern Ireland 32 D2 54 40N 5 54W
Newtownabbey district Northern Ireland 32 D2 54 45N 5 55W
Newtownards Northern Ireland 32 D2 54 36N 5 41W
Newtownhamilton Northern Ireland 32 C2 54 12N 6 35W
Newtownstewart Northern Ireland 32 B2 54 43N 7 24W
New York USA 79 M5 40 40N 73 50W
New York state USA 79 M5 43 00N 76 00W
NEW ZEALAND 73
Ngaoundéré Cameroon 66 D3 7 20N 13 35E
Nguru Nigeria 66 D4 12 53N 10 30E
Nha-Trang Vietnam 58 C2 12 15N 109 10E
Niamey Niger 66 C4 13 32N 2 05E
Nias i. Indonesia 60 A3 1 00N 97 30E
NICARAGUA 79 L2
Nicaragua, Lake Nicaragua 79 L2 11 50N 86 00W
Nice France 48 G1 43 42N 7 16E
Nicobar Islands India 58 E1 8 30N 94 00E
Nicosia Cyprus 43 N3 35 11N 33 23E
Nidd r. England 34 D3 54 00N 1 40W
Nieuwpoort Belgium 39 G2 51 08N 2 45E
NIGER 66 C4
Niger r. Africa 66 B4 11 00N 5 00W
NIGERIA 66 C3
Niigata Japan 59 M2 37 58N 139 02E
Nijmegen Netherlands 49 C4 51 50N 5 52E
Nile r. Sudan/Egypt 61 D3 28 00N 31 00E
Nimba, Mount Guinea/Liberia 66 B3 7 39N 8 30W
Nîmes France 48 F1 43 50N 4 21E
Niort France 48 C3 46 19N 0 27W
Niš Serbia and Montenegro 42 L4 43 20N 21 54E
Niteroi Brazil 84 E5 22 54S 43 06W
Nith r. Scotland 33 F3 55 15N 3 50W
Nizhniy Novgorod Russia 56 E3 56 20N 44 00E
Nizhniy Tagil Russia 56 F3 58 00N 59 58E
Norfolk USA 79 M4 36 54N 76 18W
Norfolk co. England 39 E3/F3 52 40N 1 00E
Norfolk Broads geog. reg. England 39 F3 52 45N 1 30E
Norilsk Russia 57 J4 69 21N 88 02E
Normandy geog. reg. France 48 C4/D4 49 00N 0 00
Norrköping Sweden 42 K7 58 35N 16 10E
Northallerton England 35 D3 54 20N 1 26W
Northampton England 38 D3 52 14N 0 54W
Northamptonshire co. England 38 C3/D3 52 20N 1 00W
North Ayrshire u.a. Scotland 32/33 D3/E3 55 30N 5 05W
North Berwick Scotland 33 G4 56 04N 2 44W
North Cape New Zealand 73 C4 34 25S 173 03E
North Carolina state USA 79 M4 36 00N 80 00W
North Channel British Isles 32 D3 55 20N 5 50W
North Dakota state USA 79 J5 47 00N 102 00W
North Down district Northern Ireland 32 D2 54 35N 5 50W
North Downs hills England 38/39 D2/E2 51 15N 0 30E
North Dvina r. Russia 56 E4 63 00N 43 00E
North East Lincolnshire u.a. England 35 E2 53 30N 0 10W
Northern Ireland province United Kingdom 32 B2 54 40N 7 00W
NORTHERN MARIANAS 5
Northern Territory Australia 72 D4 19 00S 132 00E
North Esk r. Scotland 31 G1 56 50N 2 50W
North Foreland c. England 39 F2 51 23N 1 27E
North Friesian Islands Germany 49 E6 54 00N 8 00E
North Island New Zealand 73 D3 39 00N 176 00E
NORTH KOREA 59 D4
North Lanarkshire u.a. Scotland 33 F3 55 50N 3 55W
North Lincolnshire u.a. England 35 E2 53 40N 0 40W
North Pole Arctic Ocean 86 90 00N
North Ronaldsay i. Scotland 29 C2 59 23N 2 26W
North Sea Atlantic Ocean 42 G7 57 00N 4 00E
North Shields England 35 D4 55 01N 1 26W
North Uist i. Scotland 30 B2 57 04N 7 16W
Northumberland co. England 34 C3/D3/H3 55 10N 2 00W
Northwest Highlands Scotland 30/31 D2/E3 58 00N 5 00W
North West Somerset u.a. England 38 B2 51 25N 2 50W
Northwest Territories territory Canada 78 H7 64 00N 110 30W
Northwich England 34 C2 53 16N 2 32W
North York Moors England 35 E3 54 25N 0 45W
North Yorkshire co. England 34/35 D3/E3 54 00N 1 20W
Norton England 35 E3 54 08N 0 48W
NORWAY 42 H7/M9
Norwich England 39 F3 52 38N 1 18E
Nottingham England 37 F2 52 58N 1 10W
Nottingham City u.a. England 37 F2 52 58N 1 10W
Nottinghamshire co. England 37 F3/G3 53 20N 1 00W
Nouadhibou Mauritania 66 A5 20 54N 17 01W
Nouakchott Mauritania 66 A4 18 09N 15 58W
Novara Italy 51 B6 45 27N 8 37E
Nova Scotia province Canada 79 N5 45 30N 63 00W
Novaya Zemlya is. Russia 56 F5 74 00N 56 00E
Novgorod Russia 42 N7 58 30N 31 20E
Novokuznetsk Russia 57 J3 53 45N 87 12E
Novosibirsk Russia 56 J3 55 04N 83 05E
Nuevo Laredo Mexico 79 K3 27 39N 99 30W
Nu Jiang (Salween) r. China/Myanmar 58 E4 31 30N 94 00E
Nullarbor Plain Australia 72 C2 30 30S 129 00E
Nunavut territory Canada 78 K7 67 30N 95 30W
Nuneaton England 38 C3 52 32N 1 28W
Nunivak i. USA 78 C6 60 00N 166 00W
Nuremberg Germany 49 F3 49 27N 11 05E
Nuuk (Godthåb) Greenland 78 P7 64 10N 51 40W
Nyala Sudan 61 C2 12 01N 24 50E
Nyasa, Lake (Lake Malawi) Malawi/Mozambique 67 D3 12 00S 35 00E

O

Oahe, Lake USA 79 J5 45 00N 100 00W
Oamaru New Zealand 73 C1 45 06S 170 58E
Ob r. Russia 56 G4 64 00N 65 00E
Oban Scotland 30 D1 56 25N 5 29W
Oberammergau Germany 49 F2 47 35N 11 07E
Obihiro Japan 59 N3 42 56N 143 10E
Obi i. Indonesia 60 D3 1 30S 127 30E
Ochil Hills Scotland 31 F1 56 15N 3 30W
Odense Denmark 42 J7 55 24N 10 25E
Oder r. Europe 49 H5 53 00N 14 00E
Odessa Ukraine 56 D2 46 30N 30 46E
Ogbomoso Nigeria 66 C3 8 05N 4 11E
Ohio r. USA 79 L4 39 00N 86 00W
Ohio state USA 79 L5 40 00N 83 00W
Oiapoque Brazil 84 D8 3 54N 51 46W
Oise r. France 48 E4 49 30N 3 00E
Oita Japan 59 L1 33 15N 131 36E
Okavango Swamp Botswana 67 C3 19 00S 23 00E
Okayama Japan 59 L1 34 40N 133 54E
Okehampton England 40 C3 50 44N 4 00W
Okhotsk, Sea of Russia 57 Q3 56 00N 145 00E
Oki Islands Japan 59 L2 36 05N 133 00E
Oklahoma state USA 79 K4 36 00N 98 00W
Oklahoma City USA 79 K4 35 28N 97 33W
Öland i. Sweden 42 K6 56 45N 51 50E
Olbia Italy 51 B4 40 56N 9 30E
Oldenburg Germany 49 E5 53 08N 8 13E
Oldham England 34 C2 53 33N 2 07W
Oldmeldrum Scotland 31 G2 57 20N 2 20W
Olongapo The Philippines 60 D4 14 49N 120 17E
Olympus, Mt. Greece 42 L4 40 05N 22 21E
Omagh Northern Ireland 32 B2 54 36N 7 18W
Omagh district Northern Ireland 32 B2 54 30N 7 30W
Omaha USA 79 K5 41 15N 96 00W
OMAN 61 F3
Oman, Gulf of Iran/Oman 61 F3 24 30N 58 30E
Omdurman Sudan 61 D2 15 37N 32 29E
Omsk Russia 56 H3 55 00N 73 22E
Onega, Lake r. Russia 56 D4 62 00N 40 00E
Onitsha Nigeria 66 C3 6 10N 6 47E
Ontario province Canada 79 L6 55 00N 85 00W
Ontario, Lake Canada/USA 79 M5 43 45N 78 00W
Oostende Belgium 49 B4 51 13N 2 55E
Oporto Portugal 50 A4 41 09N 8 37W
Oran Algeria 66 B6 35 45N 0 38W
Orange France 48 F2 44 08N 4 48E
Orange r. Southern Africa 67 B2 29 00S 19 00E
Ord r. Australia 72 C4 15 00S 129 00E
Örebro Sweden 42 K7 59 17N 15 13E
Oregon state USA 79 H5 44 00N 120 00W
Orel Russia 56 D3 52 58N 36 04E
Orenburg Russia 56 F3 51 50N 55 00E
Orford Ness c. England 39 F3 52 05N 1 34E
Orinoco r. Venezuela/Colombia 84 C8 6 40N 64 30W
Oristano Italy 51 B3 39 54N 8 36E
Orkney Islands u.a. Scotland 29 B1/C2 59 00N 3 00W
Orléans France 48 D3 47 54N 1 54E
Orne r. France 41 G1/2 49 00N 1 30W
Oronsay i. Scotland 32 C4 56 00N 6 15W
Orsk Russia 56 F3 51 13N 58 35E
Ortles mt. Italy 49 F2 46 31N 10 33E
Oruro Bolivia 84 C6 17 59S 67 08W
Osaka Japan 59 M1 34 40N 135 30E
Osh Kyrgyzstan 56 H2 40 37N 72 49E
Oslo Norway 42 J7 59 56N 10 45E
Osnabrück Germany 49 E5 52 17N 8 03E
Osorno Chile 85 B3 40 35S 73 14W
Ostrava Czech Republic 42 K5 49 50N 18 15E
Osumi Islands Japan 59 L1 30 30N 130 30E
Oswestry England 37 D2 52 52N 3 03W
Otranto Italy 51 G4 40 08N 18 30E
Ottawa Canada 79 M5 46 00N 77 00W
Ouagadougou Burkina 66 B4 12 20N 1 40W
Oubangui r. Central Africa 67 C4 4 00N 21 00E
Oujda Morocco 66 B6 34 41N 1 45W
Oulu Finland 42 M9 65 02N 25 27E
Oundle England 38 D3 52 29N 0 29W
Ouse r. England 35 D2 53 40N 1 05W
Outer Hebrides is. Scotland 30 B1/C3 58 00N 7 00W
Out Skerries is. Scotland 29 E3 60 25N 0 46W
Oviedo Spain 50 C5 43 21N 7 18W
Oxford England 38 C2 51 46N 1 15W
Oxfordshire co. England 38 C2 51 50N 1 25W

P

Pabbay i. Scotland 30 B2 57 47N 7 14W
Pacific Ocean 79 J2
Padang Indonesia 60 B2 1 00S 100 21E
Paderborn Germany 49 E4 51 43N 8 44E
Padstow England 40 C3 50 33N 4 56W
Padua Italy 51 C6 45 24N 11 53E
Paisley Scotland 33 E3 55 50N 4 26W
Pakanbaru Indonesia 60 B3 0 33N 101 30E
PAKISTAN 58 B3
Palau Islands Pacific Ocean 60 E3 7 30N 134 30E
Palawan i. The Philippines 60 C3 10 00N 119 00E
Palembang Indonesia 60 B2 2 59S 104 45E
Palermo Italy 51 D3 38 08N 13 23E
Palma Balearic Islands 50 G3 39 35N 2 39E
Palmerston North New Zealand 73 D2 40 22S 175 37E
Pamirs mts. Asia 58 C4 38 00N 74 00E
Pamplona Spain 50 E5 42 49N 1 39W
PANAMA 79 L1
Panamá Panama 79 M1 8 57N 19 30W
Panama Canal Panama 79 L1 9 00N 80 00W
Panay i. The Philippines 60 D4 11 00N 122 00E
Pantelleria i. Italy 51 C2 36 47N 12 00E
Papa Stour i. Scotland 29 D3 60 20N 1 42W
Papa Westray i. Scotland 29 C2 59 22N 2 54W
PAPUA NEW GUINEA 72 E5
PARAGUAY 84 D5
Paraguay r. South America 84 D5 21 20S 58 20W
Paramaribo Suriname 84 D8 5 52N 55 14W

Paraná Argentina **85** C4 31 45S 60 30W
Paraná r. South America **85** D5 30 00S 59 50W
Paris France **48** E4 48 52N 2 20E
Parma Italy **51** C6 44 48N 10 19E
Parnaíba Brazil **84** E7 2 58S 41 46W
Parrett r. England **41** E4 51 05N 2 55W
Parry Islands Canada **78** J8 75 15N 109 00W
Pasto Colombia **84** B8 1 12N 77 17W
Patagonia geog. reg. Argentina **85** C3 48 00S 70 00W
Patna India **58** D3 25 37N 85 12E
Patra Greece **42** L3 38 14N 21 44E
Pau France **48** C1 43 18N 0 22W
Peace r. Canada **78** H4 57 30N 117 00W
Pechora Russia **43** T9 65 14N 57 18E
Pechora r. Russia **43** S9 66 00N 53 00E
Peebles Scotland **33** F3 55 39N 3 12W
Peel Isle of Man British Isles **33** E2 54 14N 4 42W
Peel Fell sum. Scotland/England **33** F3 55 17N 2 35W
Pegasus Bay New Zealand **73** C2 43 22S 172 55E
Pegu Myanmar **58** E2 17 18N 96 31E
Peipus, Lake Estonia/Russia **42** M7 58 00N 27 45E
Peloponnese geog. reg. Greece **42** L3 37 00N 22 00E
Pelotas Brazil **85** D4 31 45S 52 20W
Pematangsiantar Indonesia **60** A3 2 59N 99 01E
Pembroke Wales **36** C1 51 41N 4 55W
Pembrokeshire u.a. Wales **36** B1/C1 51 50N 5 00W
Peñalara mt. Spain **50** G4 40 51N 3 57W
Penicuik Scotland **33** F3 55 50N 3 14W
Pennines hills England **34** C3 54 30N 2 10W
Pennsylvania state USA **79** M5 41 00N 78 00W
Penrith England **34** C3 54 40N 2 44W
Penryn England **40** B3 50 09N 5 06W
Pentland Firth sd. Scotland **29** B1 58 45N 3 10W
Pentland Hills Scotland **33** F3 55 45N 3 30W
Pen-y-ghent sum. England **34** C3 54 10N 2 14W
Penza Russia **56** E3 53 11N 45 00E
Penzance England **40** B3 50 07N 5 33W
Perm Russia **56** F3 58 01N 56 10E
Perpignan France **48** E1 42 42N 2 54E
Perth Australia **72** B2 31 57S 115 52E
Perth Scotland **31** F1 56 42N 3 28W
Perth and Kinross u.a. Scotland **31** E1/F1 56 45N 3 50W
PERU **84** B6
Perugia Italy **51** D5 43 07N 12 23E
Pescara Italy **51** E5 42 27N 14 13E
Peshawar Pakistan **58** C4 34 01N 71 33E
Peterborough England **38** D3 52 35N 0 15W
Peterborough u.a. England **38** D3 52 40N 0 15W
Peterhead Scotland **31** H2 57 30N 1 46W
Peterlee England **35** D3 54 46N 1 19W
Petersfield England **38** D1 51 00N 0 56W
Petropavlovsk Kazakhstan **56** G3 54 53N 69 13E
Petropavlovsk-Kamchatskiy Russia **57** R3 53 03N 158 43E
Petrozavodsk Russia **42** N8 61 46N 34 19E
Pforzheim Germany **49** E3 48 53N 8 41E
Philadelphia USA **79** M4 40 00N 75 10W
PHILIPPINES **60** D3/4
Phnom Penh Cambodia **60** B4 11 35N 104 55E
Phoenix USA **79** H4 33 30N 112 03W
Piacenza Italy **51** B6 45 03N 9 41E
Pickering England **35** D3 54 14N 0 46W
Pickering, Vale of England **35** E3 54 10N 0 45W
Pietermaritzburg Republic of South Africa **67** D2 29 36S 30 24E
Pilcomayo r. South America **84** C5 24 00S 61 00W
Piraeus Greece **42** L3 37 57N 23 42E
Pisa Italy **51** C5 43 43N 10 24E
Pitcairn Islands Pacific Ocean **4** 25 04S 130 06W
Pitlochry Scotland **31** F1 56 43N 3 45W
Piura Peru **84** A7 5 15S 80 38W
Plenty, Bay of New Zealand **73** D3 37 48S 177 12E
Ploieşti Romania **42** M4 44 57N 26 01E
Plovdiv Bulgaria **42** L4 42 08N 24 45E
Plymouth England **40** C3 50 23N 4 10W
Plymouth u.a. England **40** C3 50 24N 4 10W
Plynlimon mt. Wales **36** D2 52 28N 3 47W
Po r. Italy **51** C6/D6 45 00N 12 00E
Pobeda Peak Kyrgyzstan **56** J2 42 25N 80 15E
Pointe Noire tn. Congo **66** C2 4 46S 11 53E
Poitiers France **48** D3 46 35N 0 20E
POLAND **42** K6
Ponta Grossa Brazil **85** D5 25 07S 50 09W
Pontardulais Wales **36** C1 51 43N 4 02W
Pontefract England **35** D2 53 42N 1 18W
Pontianak Indonesia **60** B2 0 05S 109 16E
Pontypool Wales **36** D1 51 43N 3 02W
Pontypridd Wales **36** D1 51 37N 3 22W
Poole England **41** F3 50 43N 1 59W
Poole u.a. England **41** F3 50 43N 1 58W
Poolewe Scotland **30** D2 57 45N 5 37W
Poopo, Lake Bolivia **84** C6 18 30S 67 20W
Popocatepetl vol. Mexico **79** K2 19 02N 98 38W
Porbandar India **58** B3 21 04N 69 40E
Portadown Northern Ireland **32** C2 54 26N 6 27W
Port Askaig Scotland **32** C3 55 51N 6 07W
Port Augusta Australia **72** D2 32 30S 137 48E
Port-au-Prince Haiti **79** M2 18 33N 72 20W
Port Elizabeth Republic of South Africa **67** C1 33 58S 25 36E
Port Ellen Scotland **32** C3 55 39N 6 12W
Port Gentil Gabon **66** C2 0 40S 8 50E
Port Glasgow Scotland **33** E3 55 56N 4 41W
Port Harcourt Nigeria **66** C3 4 43N 7 05E
Port Hedland Australia **72** B3 20 18S 118 35E
Porthmadog Wales **36** C2 52 55N 4 08W
Portknockie Scotland **31** G2 57 42N 2 52W
Portland USA **78** G5 45 32N 122 40W
Portland Bill c. England **41** E3 50 31N 2 27W
Port Lincoln Australia **72** D2 34 44S 135 52E
Port Moresby Papua New Guinea **72** E5 9 30S 147 07E
Portnahaven Scotland **32** C3 55 41N 6 31W
Pôrto Alegre Brazil **85** D4 30 03S 51 10W
Port of Ness Scotland **30** C3 58 29N 6 13W
Port of Spain Trinidad and Tobago **79** N2 10 38N 61 31W

Porto Novo Benin **66** C3 6 30N 2 47E
Pôrto Velho Brazil **84** C7 8 45S 63 54W
Portpatrick Scotland **32** D2 54 51N 5 07W
Port Pirie Australia **72** D2 33 10S 138 02E
Portree Scotland **30** C2 57 24N 6 12W
Portrush Northern Ireland **32** C3 55 12N 6 40W
Port Said Egypt **61** D4 31 17N 32 18E
Portsmouth England **38** C1 50 48N 1 05W
Portsmouth u.a. England **38** C1 50 50N 1 04W
Portsoy Scotland **31** G2 57 41N 2 41W
Portstewart Northern Ireland **32** C3 55 11N 6 43W
Port Sudan Sudan **61** D2 19 38N 37 07E
Port Talbot Wales **36** D1 51 36N 3 47W
PORTUGAL **50** A3
Potenza Italy **51** E4 40 38N 15 48E
Potsdam Germany **49** G5 52 24N 13 04E
Powys u.a. Wales **36** D2 52 10N 3 30W
Poyang Hu l. China **59** C2 29 00N 116 30E
Poznań Poland **42** K6 52 25N 16 53E
Prague Czech Republic **42** J6 50 06N 14 26E
Prato Italy **51** C5 43 53N 11 06E
Preston England **34** C2 53 46N 2 42W
Prestwick Scotland **33** E3 55 30N 4 37W
Pretoria Republic of South Africa **67** C2 25 45S 28 12E
Prijedor Bosnia-Herzegovina **51** F6 45 00N 16 41E
Prince Edward Island province Canada **79** N5 46 30N 63 00W
Prince Rupert Canada **78** F6 54 09N 130 20W
Principe i. Gulf of Guinea **66** C3 1 37N 7 27E
Pripet r. Belarus **42** M6 52 00N 28 00E
Providence USA **79** M5 41 50N 71 28W
Providence, Cape New Zealand **73** B1 46 01S 166 28E
Prudhoe Bay tn. USA **78** E7 70 05N 148 20W
Pskov Russia **42** M7 57 48N 28 26E
Pucallpa Peru **84** B7 8 21S 74 33W
Puebla Mexico **79** K2 19 03N 98 10W
Puerto Montt Chile **85** B3 41 28S 73 00W
PUERTO RICO **79** N2
Puig Mayor mt. Balearic Islands **50** G3 39 49N 2 47E
Pukekohe New Zealand **73** C3 37 12S 174 54E
Pune India **58** C2 18 34N 73 58E
Punta Arenas Chile **85** B3 53 10S 70 56W
Pusan South Korea **59** D3 35 05N 129 02E
Puy de Sancy mt. France **48** E2 45 32N 2 48E
Pwllheli Wales **36** C2 52 53N 4 25W
Pyongyang North Korea **59** D3 39 00N 125 47E
Pyrénées mts. France/Spain **50** F5 42 50N 0 30E

Q

Qaidam Pendi (Qaidam Basin) China **59** A4 37 30N 94 00E
Qattara Depression Egypt **61** C3 24 00N 27 30E
Qazvin Iran **61** E4 36 16N 50 00E
Qingdao China **59** D3 36 04N 120 22E
Qinghai Hu l. China **59** B3 37 00N 100 00E
Qiqihar China **59** D4 47 23N 124 00E
Qizil r. Iran **61** E4 36 00N 48 00E
Qom Iran **61** F4 34 39N 50 57E
Quantock Hills England **41** E4 51 05N 3 15W
Québec Canada **79** M5 46 50N 71 15W
Québec province Canada **79** M6 51 00N 75 00W
Queen Charlotte Islands Canada **78** F6 53 30N 131 50W
Queen Elizabeth Islands Canada **78** J8 77 30N 105 00W
Queensland state Australia **72** E3 22 00S 143 00E
Queenstown New Zealand **73** B1 45 02S 168 40E
Quetta Pakistan **58** B4 30 12N 67 00E
Quezon City The Philippines **60** D4 14 39N 121 02E
Qui Nhon Vietnam **60** B4 13 47N 109 11E
Quito Ecuador **84** B7 0 14S 78 30W

R

Raasay i. Scotland **30** C2 57 25N 6 05W
Rabat-Salé Morocco **66** B6 34 02N 6 51W
Rainier, Mount USA **78** G5 46 25N 121 45W
Raipur India **58** D3 21 16N 81 42E
Rajang r. Malaysia **60** C2 2 00N 114 00E
Rakaia r. New Zealand **73** C2 43 00S 172 00E
Ramsey Isle of Man British Isles **33** E2 54 19N 4 23W
Ramsgate England **39** F2 51 20N 1 25E
Randalstown Northern Ireland **32** C2 54 45N 6 19W
Rangitaiki r. New Zealand **73** D3 38 45S 177 00E
Ras Dashen mt. Ethiopia **61** D2 13 15N 38 27E
Rasht Iran **61** E4 37 18N 49 38E
Rathlin Island Northern Ireland **32** C3 55 20N 6 10W
Rathlin Sound Northern Ireland **32** C3 55 20N 6 25W
Rattray Scotland **31** F1 56 36N 3 20W
Ravenna Italy **51** D6 44 25N 12 12E
Rawalpindi Pakistan **58** C4 33 36N 73 04E
Reading England **38** D2 51 28N 0 59W
Reading u.a. England **38** D2 51 27N 0 59W
Recife Brazil **84** F7 8 06S 34 53W
Recklinghausen Germany **49** D4 51 37N 7 11E
Redbridge England **39** E2 51 34N 0 05E
Redcar England **35** D3 54 37N 1 04W
Redcar and Cleveland u.a. England **35** D3/E3 54 30N 1 00W
Redditch England **37** F2 52 19N 1 56W
Rede r. England **33** G3 55 15N 2 20W
Redhill tn. England **38** D2 51 14N 0 11W
Redruth England **40** B3 50 13N 5 14W
Red Sea Middle East **61** D3 27 00N 35 00E
Regensburg Germany **49** G3 49 01N 12 06E
Reggio di Calabria Italy **51** E3 38 06N 15 39E
Reggio nell'Emilia Italy **51** C6 44 42N 10 37E
Regina Canada **78** J6 50 30N 104 38W
Reigate England **38** D2 51 14N 0 13W
Reims France **48** F4 49 26N 1 05E
Remscheid Germany **49** D4 51 10N 7 11E
Renfrewshire u.a. Scotland **33** E3 55 50N 4 40W
Rennes France **48** C4 48 06N 1 40W
Reno USA **79** H4 39 32N 119 49W

REPUBLIC OF IRELAND **28**
REPUBLIC OF SOUTH AFRICA **67** C2
Resistencia Argentina **85** D5 27 28S 59 00W
Reutlingen Germany **49** E3 48 30N 9 13E
Reykjavik Iceland **42** B8 64 09N 21 58W
Rhayader Wales **36** D2 52 18N 3 30W
Rhine r. Europe **49** D4 50 30N 7 30E
Rhode Island state USA **79** M5 41 00N 71 00W
Rhodes i. Greece **42** M3 36 00N 28 00E
Rhondda Wales **36** D1 51 40N 3 30W
Rhondda Cynon Taff u.a. Wales **36** D1 51 40N 3 30W
Rhône r. Switzerland/France **48** F2 45 00N 4 50E
Rhum i. Scotland **30** C1/2 57 00N 6 20W
Rhyl Wales **36** D3 53 19N 3 29W
Ribble r. England **34** C2 53 50N 2 30W
Ribeirão Preto Brazil **84** E5 21 09S 47 48W
Richmond England **34** D3 54 24N 1 44W
Richmond USA **79** M4 37 34N 77 27W
Richmond upon Thames England **38** D2 51 28N 0 19W
Riga Latvia **42** L7 56 53N 24 08E
Rimini Italy **51** D6 44 03N 12 34E
Ringwood England **38** C1 50 51N 1 47W
Rio Branco tn. Brazil **84** C7 9 59S 67 49W
Rio de Janeiro Brazil **84** E5 22 53S 43 17W
Rio Grande tn. Brazil **85** D4 32 03S 52 08W
Rio Grande r. Mexico/USA **79** J3 29 30N 105 00W
Ripon England **34** D3 54 08N 1 31W
River Plate Estuary Uruguay/Argentina **85** D4 35 00S 57 00W
Riyadh Saudi Arabia **61** E3 24 39N 46 46E
Roanne France **48** F3 46 02N 4 05E
Robson, Mount Canada **78** H6 53 08N 118 18W
Rochdale England **34** C2 53 38N 2 09W
Rochester England **39** E2 51 24N 0 30E
Rochester USA **79** M5 43 12N 77 37W
Rockhampton Australia **72** F3 23 22S 150 30E
Rocky Mountains Canada/USA **78/79** F7/J4 46 00N 110 00W
Roebourne Australia **72** B3 20 45S 117 08E
ROMANIA **42** L5
Rome Italy **51** D4 41 53N 12 30E
Romsey England **38** C1 50 59N 1 30W
Ronne Ice Shelf Antarctica **86** 77 00S 60 00W
Rora Head Scotland **29** B1 58 52N 3 26W
Roraima mt. Guyana **84** C8 5 14N 60 44W
Rosario Argentina **85** C4 33 00S 60 40W
Rosehearty Scotland **31** G2 57 42N 2 07W
Rosenheim Germany **51** F3 39 35N 16 38E
Rossano Italy **51** F3 39 35N 16 38E
Ross Ice Shelf Antarctica **86** 80 00S 180 00
Ross of Mull p. Scotland **30** C1 56 20N 6 10W
Ross-on-Wye England **37** E1 51 55N 2 35W
Ross Sea Antarctica **86** 75 00S 180 00
Rostock Germany **49** G6 54 06N 12 09E
Rostov-on-Don Russia **56** D2 47 15N 39 45E
Rotherham England **35** D2 53 26N 1 20W
Rothes Scotland **31** F2 57 31N 3 13W
Rothesay Scotland **32** D3 55 51N 5 03W
Rotorua New Zealand **73** D3 38 08S 176 14E
Rotterdam Netherlands **49** C4 51 54N 4 28E
Rouen France **48** D4 49 26N 1 05E
Rousay i. Scotland **29** B2 59 10N 3 00W
Royal Leamington Spa England **37** F2 52 18N 1 31W
Royal Tunbridge Wells England **39** E2 51 08N 0 16E
Royston England **38** D3 52 03N 0 01W
Ruapehu mt. New Zealand **73** D3 39 18S 175 34E
Rubha Hunish c. Scotland **30** C2 57 40N 6 20W
Rugby England **37** F2 52 23N 1 15W
Rugeley England **37** F2 52 46N 1 55W
Rügen i. Germany **49** G6 54 00N 14 00E
Rukwa, Lake Tanzania **67** D4 8 00S 33 00E
Runcorn England **34** C2 53 20N 2 44W
RUSSIA see RUSSIAN FEDERATION
RUSSIAN FEDERATION (RUSSIA) **56/57**
Rutland u.a. England **38** D3 52 42N 0 35W
Rutland Water l. England **38** D3 52 40N 0 37W
Ruvuma r. Tanzania/Mozambique **67** D3 11 00S 39 00E
Ruwenzori, Mount Congo Dem. Rep./Uganda **67** C5 0 23N 29 54E
RWANDA **67** C4
Ryazan Russia **56** D3 54 37N 39 43E
Rybinsk Russia **56** D3 58 03N 38 50E
Rybinsk Reservoir Russia **43** P7 59 00N 38 00E
Ryde England **38** C1 50 44N 1 10W
Rye England **39** E1 50 57N 0 44E
Ryukyu Islands Japan **59** D2 27 30N 127 30E

S

Saale r. Germany **49** F4 51 15N 12 00E
Saar r. Germany/France **49** D3 49 15N 6 30E
Saarbrücken Germany **49** D3 49 15N 6 58E
Sabadell Spain **50** G4 41 33N 2 07E
Sabah admin. Malaysia **60** C3 5 00N 115 00E
Sabhā Libya **66** D5 27 02N 14 26E
Sacramento USA **79** G4 38 32N 121 30W
Sado i. Japan **59** M2 38 20N 138 30E
Saffron Walden England **39** E2 52 01N 0 15E
Safi Morocco **66** B6 32 20N 9 17W
Sahara Desert North Africa **66** A5/E5 22 50N 0 00
St. Abb's Head c. Scotland **33** G3 55 55N 2 09W
St. Agnes England **40** B3 50 18N 5 13W
St. Albans England **38** D2 51 46N 0 21W
St. Albans Head c. England **41** E3 50 34N 2 04W
St. Andrews Scotland **33** G4 56 20N 2 48W
St. Anton Austria **49** F2 47 09N 10 17E
St. Austell England **40** C3 50 20N 4 48W
St. Bees Head England **34** B3 54 31N 3 39W
St. Bride's Bay Wales **36** B1 51 50N 5 15W
St. Brieuc France **48** B4 48 31N 2 45W
St. Catherine's Point England **38** C1 50 34N 1 18W
St. David's Wales **36** B1 51 54N 5 16W
St. David's Head Wales **36** B1 51 55N 5 19W
St-Denis France **48** E4 48 57N 2 22E
St-Dizier France **48** F4 48 38N 4 58E

Saintes France **48** C2 45 44N 0 38W
St-Étienne France **48** F2 45 26N 4 23E
St. Gallen Switzerland **51** B7 47 25N 9 23E
St. George's Channel British Isles **36** A1/B2 52 00N 6 00W
St. Germain France **48** E4 48 55N 2 08E
St. Gotthard Pass Switzerland **49** E2 46 34N 8 31E
St. Helena i. Atlantic Ocean **5** 15 58S 5 43W
St. Helens England **34** C2 53 28N 2 44W
St. Helier Jersey Channel Islands **41** E2 49 12N 2 07W
St. Ives Cambridgeshire England **38** D3 52 20N 0 05W
St. Ives Cornwall England **40** B3 50 12N 5 29W
Saint John Canada **79** N5 45 16N 66 03W
St. John's Canada **79** P5 47 34N 52 43W
St. John's Point Northern Ireland **32** D2 54 15N 5 40W
St. John's Town of Dalry Scotland **33** E3 55 07N 4 10W
St. Just England **40** B3 50 07N 5 41W
St. Kilda i. Scotland **30** A2 57 49N 8 34W
ST. KITTS AND NEVIS **79** N2
St. Lawrence i. Alaska **78** C7 63 15N 169 50W
St. Lawrence r. Canada/USA **79** M5 47 30N 70 00W
St. Lawrence, Gulf of Canada **79** N5 49 00N 62 30W
St-Lô France **41** F2 49 07N 1 05W
St. Louis Senegal **66** A4 16 01N 16 30W
St. Louis USA **79** K4 38 40N 90 15W
ST. LUCIA **79** N2
St. Magnus Bay Scotland **29** D3 60 25N 1 35W
St-Malo France **48** C4 48 39N 2 00W
St. Martin's i. England **40** A2 49 58N 6 17W
St. Mary's i. England **40** A2 49 55N 6 18W
St. Mary's Loch l. Scotland **33** F3 55 29N 3 12W
St. Matthew i. USA **78** B7 60 30N 172 30W
St. Moritz Switzerland **49** E2 46 30N 9 51E
St-Nazaire France **48** B3 47 17N 2 12W
St. Neots England **38** D3 52 14N 0 17W
St-Omer France **39** G1 50 45N 2 15E
St. Paul USA **79** K5 45 00N 93 10W
St. Peter-Port Guernsey Channel Islands **41** E2 49 27N 2 32W
St. Petersburg Russia **56** D3 59 55N 30 25E
Saint Pierre & Miquelon is. Atlantic Ocean **79** P5 47 00N 56 20W
St-Quentin France **48** E4 49 51N 3 17E
St-Tropez France **48** G1 43 16N 6 39E
ST. VINCENT AND THE GRENADINES **79** N2
Sakhalin i. Russia **57** Q3 50 00N 143 00E
Salado r. Argentina **85** C5 28 30S 62 30W
Salalah Oman **61** F2 17 00N 54 04E
Salamanca Spain **50** C4 40 58N 5 40W
Salcombe England **40** D3 50 13N 3 47W
Sale England **34** C2 53 26N 2 19W
Salem India **58** C2 11 38N 78 08E
Salerno Italy **51** E4 40 40N 14 46E
Salford England **34** C2 53 30N 2 16W
Salisbury England **38** C2 51 05N 1 48W
Salisbury Plain England **38** C2 51 10N 1 55W
Salta Argentina **84** C5 24 46S 65 28W
Saltash England **40** C3 50 24N 4 12W
Saltcoats Scotland **33** E3 55 38N 4 47W
Saltillo Mexico **79** J3 25 30N 101 00W
Salt Lake City USA **79** H5 40 45N 111 55W
Salvador Brazil **84** F6 12 58S 38 29W
Salween r. see Nu Jiang
Salzburg Austria **42** J5 47 48N 13 03E
Salzgitter Germany **49** F5 52 13N 10 20E
Samar i. The Philippines **60** D4 12 00N 125 00E
Samara Russia **56** F3 53 10N 50 10E
Samarinda Indonesia **60** C2 0 30S 117 09E
Samarkand Uzbekistan **56** G1 39 40N 66 57E
Sambre r. France **48** E5 50 15N 3 50E
Samsun Turkey **43** P4 41 17N 36 22E
Sana Yemen Republic **61** E2 15 23N 44 14E
Sanaga r. Cameroon **66** D3 5 00N 14 00E
San Antonio r. USA **79** K3 29 00N 97 00W
San Antonio Abad Balearic Islands **50** F3 38 59N 1 19E
San Benito Islands Mexico **79** H3 28 00N 115 00W
San Cristobal Venezuela **84** B8 7 46N 72 15W
Sandakan Malaysia **60** C3 5 52N 118 04E
Sanday i. Scotland **29** C2 59 15N 2 30W
San Diego USA **79** H4 32 45N 117 10W
Sandown England **38** C1 50 39N 1 09W
San Francisco USA **79** G4 37 45N 122 27W
San Francisco Javier Balearic Islands **50** F3 38 43N 1 26E
San José Costa Rica **79** L1 9 59N 84 04W
San Juan Argentina **85** C4 31 33S 68 31W
San Juan Puerto Rico **79** N2 18 29N 66 08W
Sanliurfa Turkey **43** P3 37 09N 38 49E
San Luis Potosi Mexico **79** J3 22 10N 101 00W
SAN MARINO **51** D5
San Miguel de Tucumán Argentina **85** C5 26 47S 65 15W
San Pedro Sula Honduras **79** L2 15 26N 88 01W
Sanquhar Scotland **33** F3 55 22N 3 56W
San Salvador El Salvador **79** L2 13 40N 89 10W
San Sebastián Spain **50** E5 43 19N 1 59W
Santa Clara Cuba **79** M3 22 25N 79 58W
Santa Cruz Bolivia **84** C6 17 50S 63 10W
Santa Fé Argentina **85** C4 31 35S 60 50W
Santander Spain **50** D5 43 28N 3 48W
Santañy Balearic Islands **50** G3 39 22N 3 07E
Santarém Brazil **84** D7 2 26S 54 41W
Santarém Portugal **50** A3 39 14N 8 40W
Santiago Chile **85** B4 33 30S 70 40W
Santiago r. Mexico **79** J3 104 00N 21 30N
Santiago de Cuba Cuba **79** M3 20 00N 75 49W
Santiago del Estero Argentina **85** C5 27 47S 64 15W
Santo Domingo Dominican Republic **79** N2 18 30N 69 57W
Santos Brazil **84** E5 23 56S 46 22W
São Francisco r. Brazil **84** E6 13 40S 44 00W

ão Luís Brazil **84** E7 2 34S 44 16W
aône r. France **48** F3 47 30N 5 30E
ão Paulo Brazil **84** E5 23 33S 46 39W
ão Tomé i. Gulf of Guinea **66** C3 0 25N 6 35E
ÃO TOMÉ AND PRINCIPE **66** C3
apporo Japan **59** N3 43 05N 141 21E
arajevo Bosnia-Herzegovina **42** K4 43 52N 18 26E
aratov Russia **56** E3 51 30N 45 55E
arawak admin. Malaysia **60** C3 1 00N 111 00E
ardinia i. Italy **51** B4 40 00N 9 00E
arh Chad **66** D3 9 08N 18 22E
ark i. Channel Islands British Isles **41** E2 49 26N 2 22W
askatchewan province Canada **78** J6 55 00N 105 00W
askatchewan r. Canada **78** J6 53 30N 105 00W
askatoon Canada **78** J6 52 10N 106 40W
assari Italy **51** B4 40 43N 8 34E
AUDI ARABIA **61** E3
aumur France **48** C3 47 16N 0 05W
ava r. Europe **51** F6 45 45N 16 15E
avannah USA **79** L4 32 04N 81 07W
awel mt. Northern Ireland **32** B2 54 49N 7 02W
ay'un Yemen Republic **61** E2 15 59N 48 44E
cafell Pike mt. England **34** B3 54 27N 3 14W
calasaig Scotland **32** C4 56 04N 6 12W
calloway Scotland **29** D3 60 08N 1 17W
calpay i. Highland Scotland **30** D2 57 15N 6 00W
calpay i. Western Isles Scotland **30** C2 57 15N 6 00W
capa Scotland **29** C1 58 58N 2 59W
capa Flow sd. Scotland **29** B1 58 55N 3 00W
carba i. Scotland **32** D4 56 45N 5 50W
carborough England **35** E3 54 17N 0 24W
carp i. Scotland **30** B3 58 02N 7 08W
chefferville Canada **78** N6 54 50N 67 00W
chelde r. Netherlands **49** B4/C4 51 00N 4 00E
chwerin Germany **49** F5 53 38N 11 25E
cilly, Isles of i. England **40** A2 49 56N 6 20W
cotland country United Kingdom **28** 56 10N 4 00W
cottish Borders u.a. Scotland **33** F3/G3 55 30N 3 00W
cunthorpe England **35** E2 53 35N 0 39W
eascale England **34** B3 54 24N 3 29W
eaton England **41** D3 50 43N 3 05W
eattle USA **78** G5 47 35N 122 20W
edan France **48** F4 49 42N 4 57E
ee r. France **48** D4 49 15N 1 15E
ekondi Takoradi Ghana **66** B3 4 59N 1 43W
elby England **35** D2 53 48N 1 04W
elkirk Scotland **33** G3 55 33N 2 50W
elsey Bill p. England **38** D1 50 43N 0 48W
elvas geog. reg. South America **84** C7 7 00S 65 00W
emarang Indonesia **60** C2 6 58S 110 29E
emipalatinsk Kazakhstan **56** J3 50 26N 80 16E
endai Japan **59** N2 38 16N 140 52E
ENEGAL **66** A4
enegal r. Senegal/Mauritania **66** A4 16 00N 15 00W
ennar Sudan **61** D2 13 31N 33 38E
ennen England **40** B3 50 03N 5 42W
eoul South Korea **59** D3 37 32N 127 00E
eram i. Indonesia **60** D2 3 30S 129 30E
eram Sea Indonesia **60** D2 2 30S 130 00E
ERBIA AND MONTENEGRO **42** L4
eremban Malaysia **60** B3 2 43N 102 57E
erov Russia **56** G3 59 42N 60 32E
étif Algeria **42** H3 36 11N 5 24E
etúbal Portugal **50** A3 38 31N 8 54W
evastopol Ukraine **56** D2 44 36N 33 31E
evenoaks England **39** E2 51 16N 0 12E
evern r. England **37** E1 51 30N 2 30W
evernaya Zemlya is. Russia **57** K5 80 00N 95 00E
everodvinsk Russia **43** P8 64 35N 39 50E
eville Spain **50** C2 37 24N 5 59W
eward USA **78** E7 60 05N 149 34W
EYCHELLES **5**
fax Tunisia **66** D6 34 45N 10 43E
gurr Mór mt. Scotland **31** D2 57 42N 5 03W
haftesbury England **41** E4 51 01N 2 12W
hakhty Russia **43** Q5 47 43N 40 16E
hanghai China **59** D3 31 06N 121 22E
hanklin England **38** C1 50 38N 1 10W
hannon r. Republic of Ireland **32** B2 54 15N 8 00W
hapinsay i. Scotland **29** C2 59 03N 2 51W
heerness England **39** E2 51 27N 0 45E
heffield England **35** D2 53 23N 1 30W
henyang China **59** D4 41 50N 123 26E
hepton Mallet England **41** E4 51 12N 2 33W
herborne England **41** E3 50 57N 2 31W
herbrooke Canada **79** M5 45 24N 71 54W
heringham England **39** F3 52 57N 1 12E
hetland Islands u.a. Scotland **29** D3 60 00N 1 15W
hiant Islands Scotland **30** C2 57 55N 6 20W
hiel r. Scotland **30** D2 57 09N 5 25E
hijiazhuang China **59** C3 38 04N 114 28E
hikoku i. Japan **59** L1 33 40N 134 00E
hilka r. Russia **57** M3 52 00N 118 00E
himonoseki Japan **59** L1 33 59N 130 58E
hizuoka Japan **59** M1 34 59N 138 24E
hrewsbury England **37** E2 52 43N 2 45W
hropshire co. England **37** E2 52 35N 2 35W
hymkent Kazakhstan **56** G2 42 16N 69 05E
iauliai Lithuania **42** L7 55 51N 23 20E
iberian Lowland Russia **56** H4 60 00N 75 00E
ibu Malaysia **60** C3 2 19N 111 50E
ichuan Basin see Sichuan Pendi
ichuan Pendi (Sichuan Basin) China **59** B3 32 00N 107 00E
icily i. Italy **51** E2 37 00N 14 00E
idi-Bel-Abbès Algeria **42** F3 35 15N 0 39W
idlaw Hills Scotland **31** F1/G1 56 30N 3 10W
idmouth England **41** D3 50 41N 3 15W
iegen Germany **49** E4 50 52N 8 02E
iena Italy **51** C5 43 19N 11 19E
IERRA LEONE **66** A3

Sierra Madre mts. Mexico **79** J3 26 00N 108 00W
Sierra Nevada mts. Spain **50** D2 37 00N 3 20W
Sierra Nevada mts. USA **79** H4 37 00N 119 00W
Simferopol Ukraine **56** D2 44 57N 34 05E
Simplon Pass Europe **49** E2 46 15N 8 03E
Simpson Desert Australia **72** D3 25 00S 137 00E
Sinai, Mount Egypt **61** D3 28 32N 33 59E
SINGAPORE **60** B3
Singkep i. Indonesia **60** B2 0 20S 104 30E
Sinuiju North Korea **59** D4 40 04N 124 25E
Siracusa Italy **51** E2 37 04N 15 19E
Sirte Libya **42** K2 31 13N 16 35E
Sivas Turkey **43** P3 39 44N 37 01E
Skegness England **35** F2 53 10N 0 21E
Skelmersdale England **34** C2 53 55N 2 48W
Skiddaw mt. England **34** B3 54 40N 3 08W
Skikda Algeria **42** H3 36 53N 6 54E
Skipton England **34** C2 53 58N 2 01W
Skopje FYROM **42** L4 42 00N 21 28E
Skye i. Scotland **30** C2 57 20N 6 15W
Sleaford England **35** E1 53 00N 0 24W
Sleat, Sound of Scotland **30** D2 57 00N 5 55W
Slieve Donard mt. Northern Ireland **32** D2 54 11N 5 55W
Slieve Snaght sum. Republic of Ireland **32** B3 55 12N 7 20W
Slough England **38** D2 51 31N 0 36W
Slough u.a. England **38** D2 51 31N 0 36W
SLOVAKIA **42** K5
SLOVENIA **51** E7
Smallwood Reservoir Canada **78** N6 54 10N 63 50W
Smolensk Russia **56** D3 54 49N 32 04E
Snaefell mt. Isle of Man British Isles **33** E2 54 16N 4 28W
Snake r. USA **79** H5 43 00N 114 00W
Snowdon mt. Wales **36** C3 53 04N 4 05W
Snowy Mountains Australia **72** E2 36 24S 148 28E
Soar r. England **37** F2 52 40N 1 10W
Soay i. Scotland **30** C2 57 08N 6 14W
Sochi Russia **43** P4 43 35N 39 46E
Socotra i. Yemen Republic **61** F2 12 05N 54 10E
Sofia Bulgaria **42** L4 42 40N 23 18E
Sokhumi Georgia **43** Q4 43 01N 41 01E
Sokoto Nigeria **66** C4 13 02N 5 15E
Solapur India **58** C2 17 43N 75 56E
Solihull England **37** F2 52 25N 1 45W
Sóller Balearic Islands **50** G3 39 46N 2 42E
SOLOMON ISLANDS **72** F5
Solway Firth est. Scotland/England **34** B3 54 40N 3 40W
SOMALIA **67** E5
Somerset co. England **41** D4/E4 51 10N 3 00W
Somme r. France **48** E4 50 45N 2 30E
Songhua Hu res. China **59** D4 43 30N 126 51E
Songhua Jiang r. China **59** D4 46 30N 129 00E
Songkhla Thailand **60** B3 7 12N 100 35E
Song-koi r. China/Vietnam **59** B2 23 00N 102 00E
Sousse Tunisia **66** D6 35 50N 10 38E
Southampton England **38** C1 50 55N 1 25W
Southampton u.a. England **38** C1 50 54N 1 27W
Southampton Island Canada **78** L7 64 50N 85 00W
South Australia state Australia **72** D3 27 00S 135 00E
South Ayrshire u.a. Scotland **32/33** D2/E3 55 20N 4 40W
South Barrule hill Isle of Man British Isles **33** E2 54 09N 4 40W
South Benfleet England **39** E2 51 33N 0 34E
South Carolina state USA **79** L4 34 00N 81 00W
South China Sea Pacific Ocean **60** C4 15 00N 110 00E
South Dakota state USA **79** J5 45 00N 102 00W
South Downs hills England **38/39** D1/E 150 50N 0 45W
Southend Scotland **32** D3 55 20N 5 38W
Southend u.a. England **39** E2 51 33N 0 45E
Southend-on-Sea England **39** E2 51 33N 0 43E
Southern Alps mts. New Zealand **73** C2 43 07S 171 13E
Southern Ocean **86**
Southern Uplands Scotland **33** E3/G3 55 30N 3 30W
South Esk r. Scotland **31** G1 56 40N 2 40W
South Georgia i. South Atlantic Ocean **85** F2 54 00S 36 00W
South Gloucestershire u.a. England **38** B2 51 30N 2 30W
South Island New Zealand **73** C2 42 30S 172 00E
SOUTH KOREA **59** D3
South Lanarkshire u.a. Scotland **33** E3/F3 55 35N 3 55W
South Molton England **40** D4 51 01N 3 50W
South Orkney Islands Southern Ocean **85** E1 60 00S 45 00W
South Pole Antarctica **86** 90 00S
Southport England **34** B2 53 39N 3 01W
South Ronaldsay i. Scotland **29** C1 58 47N 2 56W
South Shields England **35** D3 55 00N 1 25W
South Uist i. Scotland **30** B2 57 20N 7 15W
South Yorkshire co. England **34/35** D2 53 30N 1 30W
Sovetskaya Gavan Russia **57** Q2 48 57N 140 16E
SPAIN **50** C3
Spalding England **35** E1 52 47N 0 10W
Spencer Gulf Australia **72** D2 34 16S 136 53E
Spennymoor tn. England **34** D3 54 42N 1 35W
Spey r. Scotland **31** F2 57 40N 3 10W
Spilsby England **35** F2 53 10N 0 06E
Spitsbergen i. Arctic Ocean **86** 79 00N 15 00E
Split Croatia **42** K4 43 31N 16 28E
Spokane USA **78** H5 47 40N 117 25W
Spurn Head England **35** F2 53 36N 0 07E
SRI LANKA **58** D1
Srinagar Jammu & Kashmir **58** C4 34 08N 74 50E
Stafford England **37** E2 52 48N 2 07W
Staffordshire co. England **37** E2/F2 52 50N 2 00W

Staines England **38** D2 51 26N 0 30W
Stamford England **35** E1 52 39N 0 29W
Stanley Falkland Islands **85** D2 51 45S 57 56W
Start Bay England **40** D3 50 16N 3 35W
Start Point England **40** D3 50 13N 3 38W
Stavanger Norway **42** H7 58 58N 5 45E
Stavropol Russia **43** Q5 45 03N 41 59E
Stevenage England **38** D2 51 55N 0 14W
Stewart Island New Zealand **73** B1 46 55S 167 55E
Stinchar r. Scotland **33** E3 55 10N 4 45W
Stirling Scotland **33** F4 56 07N 3 57W
Stirling u.a. Scotland **33** E4 56 10N 4 15W
Stockbridge England **38** C2 51 07N 1 29W
Stockholm Sweden **42** K7 59 20N 18 05E
Stockport England **34** C2 53 25N 2 10W
Stockton-on-Tees England **35** D3 54 34N 1 19W
Stockton-on-Tees u.a. England **35** D3 54 33N 1 24W
Stoke-on-Trent England **37** E3 53 00N 2 10W
Stoke-on-Trent u.a. England **37** E3 53 02N 2 10W
Stonehaven Scotland **31** G1 56 58N 2 13W
Stornoway Scotland **30** C3 58 12N 6 23W
Storr, The mt. Scotland **30** C2 57 30N 6 11W
Stour r. Dorset England **41** E3 50 50N 2 18W
Stour r. Suffolk/Essex England **39** E2/F2 51 55N 0 55E
Stourbridge England **37** E2 52 27N 2 09W
Stourport-on-Severn England **37** E2 52 21N 2 16W
Stowmarket England **39** F2 52 11N 1 00E
Stow-on-the-Wold England **38** C2 51 56N 1 44W
Strabane Northern Ireland **32** B2 54 49N 7 27W
Strabane district Northern Ireland **32** B2 54 45N 7 30W
Stralsund Germany **49** G6 54 18N 13 06E
Strangford Lough inlet Northern Ireland **32** D2 54 25N 5 45W
Stranraer Scotland **32** D2 54 55N 5 02W
Strasbourg France **48** G4 48 35N 7 45E
Stratford-upon-Avon England **37** F2 52 12N 1 41W
Strathy Point Scotland **31** E3 58 35N 4 02W
Stroma i. Scotland **31** F3 58 40N 3 08W
Stromness Scotland **29** B1 58 57N 3 18W
Stronsay i. Scotland **29** C2 59 07N 2 37W
Stronsay Firth sd Scotland **29** C2 59 00N 2 55W
Stroud England **38** B2 51 45N 2 12W
Strumble Head c. Wales **36** B2 52 02N 5 04W
Sturt Desert Australia **72** E3 27 00S 139 00E
Stuttgart Germany **49** E3 48 47N 9 12E
Sucre Bolivia **84** C6 19 05S 65 15W
SUDAN **61** C2
Sudbury Canada **79** L5 46 30N 81 01W
Sudbury England **39** E2 52 02N 0 44E
Suez Egypt **61** D3 29 59N 32 33E
Suez Canal Egypt **61** D4 31 30N 32 20E
Suffolk co. England **39** E3/F3 52 10N 1 00E
Sula Islands Indonesia **60** D2 1 50S 124 50E
Sulawesi i. Indonesia **60** D2 2 00S 120 00E
Sullom Voe inlet Scotland **29** D3 60 27N 1 20W
Sulu Sea The Philippines/Malaysia **60** D3 8 00N 120 00E
Sumatra i. Indonesia **60** A3/B2 0 00 100 00E
Sumba i. Indonesia **60** C2 10 00S 120 00E
Sumbawa i. Indonesia **60** C2 8 00S 118 00E
Sumburgh Head Scotland **29** D2 59 51N 1 16W
Sunda Strait Indonesia **60** B2 5 50S 105 30E
Sunderland England **35** D3 54 55N 1 23W
Superior, Lake Canada/USA **79** L5 48 00N 88 00W
Surabaya Indonesia **60** C2 7 14S 112 45E
Surakarta Indonesia **60** C2 7 32S 110 50E
Surat India **58** C3 21 10N 72 54E
SURINAME **84** D8
Surrey co. England **38** D2 51 25N 0 14W
Sutton England **38** D2 51 22N 0 12W
Sutton Coldfield England **37** F2 52 34N 1 48W
Sutton in Ashfield England **37** F3 53 08N 1 15W
Suzhou China **59** D3 31 21N 120 40E
Sverdrup Islands Canada **78** K8 79 00N 96 00W
Swaffham England **39** F2 52 39N 0 41E
Swale r. England **34** D3 54 30N 1 50W
Swanage England **41** E3 50 37N 1 58W
Swansea Wales **36** D1 51 38N 3 57W
Swansea u.a. Wales **36** C1 51 40N 4 05W
SWAZILAND **67** D2
SWEDEN **42** J7/L9
Swilly r. Republic of Ireland **32** B3 55 00N 7 30W
Swindon England **38** C2 51 34N 1 47W
Swindon u.a. England **38** C2 51 32N 1 46W
SWITZERLAND **49** D2/E2
Sydney Australia **72** F2 33 52S 151 13E
Sydney Canada **79** N5 46 10N 60 10W
Syktyvkar Russia **43** S8 61 42N 50 45E
Symbister Scotland **29** D3 60 21N 1 02W
Syr Darya r. Asia **56** G2 45 00N 66 00E
SYRIA **61** D4
Szczecin Poland **42** J6 53 25N 14 32E
Szeged Hungary **42** L5 46 15N 20 09E

T
Tabora Tanzania **67** D4 5 01S 32 48E
Tabriz Iran **61** E4 38 05N 46 18E
Tabuk Saudi Arabia **61** D3 28 33N 36 36E
Tacoma USA **78** G5 47 16N 122 30W
Tadcaster England **35** D2 53 53N 1 16W
Taegu South Korea **59** D3 35 52N 128 36E
Taejon South Korea **59** D3 36 20N 127 26E
Tagus r. Spain/Portugal **50** A3 39 30N 7 00W
Tahat, Mount Algeria **66** C5 23 18N 5 33E
Taif Saudi Arabia **61** E3 21 15N 40 21E
Tai Hu l. China **59** D3 31 15N 120 10E
Taipei Taiwan **59** D2 25 03N 121 30E
TAIWAN **59** D2
Taiyuan China **59** C3 37 50N 112 30E
Ta'izz Yemen Republic **61** E2 13.35N 44 02E
TAJIKISTAN **56** H1
Takamatsu Japan **59** L1 34 20N 134 01E
Takazze r. Africa **61** D2 14 00N 38 00E
Talaud Islands Indonesia **60** D3 4 00N 127 00E
Talca Chile **85** B4 35 28S 71 40W

Talcahuano Chile **85** B4 36 40S 73 10W
Tamanrasset Algeria **66** C5 22 50N 5 28E
Tamar r. England **40** C3 50 35N 4 15W
Tambov Russia **43** Q6 52 44N 41 28E
Tampa USA **79** L3 27 58N 82 38W
Tampere Finland **42** L8 61 32N 23 45E
Tampico Mexico **79** K3 22 18N 97 52W
Tamworth England **37** F2 52 39N 1 40W
Tana, Lake Ethiopia **61** D2 12 20N 37 20E
Tanga Tanzania **67** E4 5 07S 39 05E
Tanganyika, Lake East Africa **67** C4 7 00S 30 00E
Tangier Morocco **66** B6 35 48N 5 45W
Tangshan China **59** C3 39 37N 118 05E
Tanimbar Islands Indonesia **60** E2 7 30S 131 30E
Tanjungkarang Indonesia **60** B2 5 28S 105 16E
TANZANIA **67** D4
Tapajós r. Brazil **84** D7 9 10S 56 20W
Taransay i. Scotland **30** B2 57 55N 7 00W
Táranto Italy **51** F4 40 28N 17 15E
Tarbat Ness c. Scotland **31** F2 57 50N 3 45W
Tarbert Argyll and Bute Scotland **32** D3 55 52N 5 26W
Tarbert Western Isles Scotland **30** C2 57 54N 6 49W
Tarbes France **48** D1 43 14N 0 05E
Tarbet Scotland **33** E4 56 12N 4 43W
Tarim Basin see Tarim Pendi
Tarim He r. China **58** C4 38 00N 77 00E
Tarim Pendi (Tarim Basin) China **58** D4/5 39 00N 84 00E
Tarn r. France **48** E1 44 00N 2 15E
Tarragona Spain **50** F4 41 07N 1 15E
Tashkent Uzbekistan **56** G2 41 16N 69 13E
Tasman Bay New Zealand **73** C2 41 00S 173 14E
Tasmania state Australia **72** E1 42 00S 143 00E
Tasman Sea Pacific Ocean **7** 39 00S 155 00E
Taunton England **41** D4 51 01N 3 06W
Taupo New Zealand **73** D3 38 41S 176 05E
Taupo, Lake New Zealand **73** D3 38 55S 175 49E
Tauranga New Zealand **73** D3 37 41S 176 10E
Tavistock England **40** C3 50 33N 4 08W
Tavy r. England **40** C3 50 35N 4 05W
Taw r. England **40** C4/D3 51 00N 4 00W
Tay r. Scotland **31** F1 56 30N 3 30W
T'bilisi Georgia **56** E2 41 43N 44 48E
Te Anau, Lake New Zealand **73** B1 45 13S 167 45E
Tébessa Algeria **42** H3 35 21N 8 06E
Tees r. England **35** D3 54 30N 1 25W
Tegucigalpa Honduras **79** L2 14 05N 87 14W
Tehran Iran **61** F4 35 40N 51 26E
Teifi r. Wales **36** C2 52 03N 4 30W
Teign r. England **40** D3 50 33N 3 30W
Teignmouth England **40** D3 50 33N 3 30W
Tel Aviv-Yafo Israel **61** D4 32 05N 34 46E
Telford England **37** E2 52 42N 2 30W
Telford and Wrekin u.a. England **37** E2 52 45N 2 30W
Teme r. England **37** E2 52 20N 2 30W
Temuco Chile **85** B4 38 45S 72 40W
Tenby Wales **36** C1 51 41N 4 43W
Tenerife i. Canary Islands **66** A5 28 15N 16 35W
Tennant Creek tn. Australia **72** D4 19 38S 134 12E
Tennessee r. USA **79** L4 36 00N 89 00W
Tennessee state USA **79** L4 35 00N 87 00W
Teramo Italy **51** D5 42 40N 13 43E
Teresina Brazil **84** E7 5 09S 42 46W
Terni Italy **51** D5 42 34N 12 39E
Terracina Italy **51** D4 41 17N 13 15E
Test r. England **38** C2 51 10N 1 30W
Tétouan Morocco **66** B6 35 34N 5 22W
Teviot r. Scotland **33** G3 55 30N 2 45W
Tewkesbury England **38** B2 51 59N 2 09W
Texas state USA **79** K4 31 00N 100 00W
THAILAND **60** B4
Thailand, Gulf of Asia **60** B4 10 50N 101 00E
Thame England **38** C2 51 45N 0 59W
Thame r. England **38** D2 51 45N 1 00W
Thames r. England **39** E2 51 30N 0 05E
Thar Desert India **58** C3 27 30N 72 00E
The Hague Netherlands **49** C5 52 05N 4 16E
The Needles rocks England **38** C1 50 39N 1 35W
The Peak mt. England **37** F3 53 24N 1 51W
The Solent sd. England **38** C1 50 45N 1 25W
Thessaloniki Greece **42** L4 40 38N 22 58E
Thetford England **39** E3 52 25N 0 45E
The Vale of Glamorgan u.a. Wales **36** D1 52 30N 3 30W
The Wrekin pk. England **37** E2 52 41N 2 32W
Thimphu Bhutan **58** D3 27 32N 89 43E
Thionville France **48** G4 49 22N 6 11E
Thirsk England **35** D3 54 14N 1 20W
Thornaby-on-Tees England **35** D3 54 34N 1 18W
Thornhill Scotland **33** F3 55 15N 3 46W
Three Kings Islands New Zealand **73** C4 34 10S 172 07E
Thunder Bay tn. Canada **79** L5 48 27N 89 12W
Thurrock England **39** E2 51 28N 0 20E
Thurrock u.a. England **39** E2 51 30N 0 23E
Thurso Scotland **31** F3 58 35N 3 32W
Thurso r. Scotland **31** F3 58 35N 3 35W
Tianjin China **59** C3 39 08N 117 12E
Tibetan Plateau Tibet **58** D4 33 00N 85 00E
Tibesti mts. Chad **66** D5 21 00N 17 00E
Tien Shan mts. China C5/D5 41 00N 76 00E
Tierra del Fuego i. Chile/Argentina **85** C2 54 00S 67 30W
Tighnabruaich Scotland **32** D3 55 56N 5 14W
Tigris r. Iraq **61** E4 34 00N 44 00E
Tijuana Mexico **79** H4 32 29N 117 10W
Tilburg Netherlands **49** C4 51 34N 5 05E
Timaru New Zealand **73** C2 44 24S 171 15E
Timişoara Romania **42** L5 45 45N 21 15E
Timor i. Indonesia **60** D2 9 00S 125 00E
Timor Sea Australia **72** C4 12 30S 127 00E
Tiranë Albania **42** K4 41 20N 19 49E
Tiree i. Scotland **30** C1 56 30N 6 55W
Titicaca, Lake Peru/Bolivia **84** C6 16 00S 69 30W
Tiverton England **41** D3 50 55N 3 29W
Tivoli Italy **51** D4 41 58N 12 48E
Tizi Ouzou Algeria **50** H2 36 44N 4 05E
Toamasina Madagascar **67** E3 18 10S 49 23E

Tobago i. Trinidad and Tobago **84** C9 11 15N 60 40W
Tobermory Scotland **30** C1 56 37N 6 05W
Tobol r. Russia **56** G3 56 00N 66 00E
Tocantins r. Brazil **84** E7 8 40S 48 00W
TOGO 66 C3
Tokoroa New Zealand **73** D3 38 14S 175 52E
Tokyo Japan **59** M2 35 40N 139 45E
Toledo USA **79** L5 41 40N 83 35W
Toliara Madagascar **67** E2 23 20S 43 41E
Tol'yatti Russia **56** E3 53 32N 49 24E
Tombouctou Mali **66** B4 16 49N 2 59W
Tomsk Russia **56** J3 56 30N 85 05E
Tonbridge England **39** E2 51 12N 0 16E
Tone r. England **41** D4/E4 51 00N 3 00W
Tone r. Japan **59** N2 36 00N 140 00E
TONGA 5
Toowoomba Australia **72** F3 27 34S 151 58E
Torbay England **40** D3 50 27N 3 30W
Torbay u.a. England **40** D3 50 26N 3 30W
Tordesillas Spain **50** C4 41 30N 5 00W
Torfaen u.a. Wales **36** D1 51 45N 3 03W
Toronto Canada **79** M5 43 42N 79 46W
Toros Dağlari mts. Turkey **43** N3 36 00N 33 00E
Torpoint tn. England **40** C3 50 22N 4 11W
Torre del Greco Italy **51** E4 40 46N 14 22E
Torrens, Lake Australia **72** D2 30 58S 137 52E
Torreón Mexico **79** J3 25 34N 103 25W
Torres Strait Australia **72** E5 9 30S 142 00E
Torridge r. England **40** C3 50 55N 4 15W
Tortosa Spain **50** F4 40 49N 0 31E
Tory Island Republic of Ireland **32** A3 55 16N 8 14W
Tory Sound Republic of Ireland **32** A3 55 15N 8 05W
Totnes England **40** D3 50 25N 3 41W
Totton England **38** C1 50 56N 1 29W
Tottori Japan **59** L2 35 32N 134 12E
Toubkal, Mount Morocco **66** B3 31 03N 7 57W
Touggourt Algeria **66** C6 33 08N 6 04E
Toulon France **48** F1 43 07N 5 55E
Toulouse France **48** D1 43 33N 1 24E
Tours France **48** D3 47 23N 0 42E
Towcester England **38** D3 52 08N 1 00W
Townsville Australia **72** E4 19 17S 146 48E
Toyama Japan **59** M2 36 42N 137 14E
Trabzona Turkey **43** P4 41 00N 39 43E
Trent r. England **37** G3 53 30N 0 50W
Trento Italy **51** C7 46 04N 11 08E
Tresco i. England **40** A2 49 57N 6 20W
Trevose Head England **40** B3 50 33N 5 01W
Trier Germany **49** D3 49 45N 6 39E
Trieste Italy **51** D6 45 39N 13 47E
Trincomalee Sri Lanka **58** D1 8 34N 81 13E
Trinidad i. Trinidad and Tobago **84** C9 11 00N 61 30W
TRINIDAD AND TOBAGO 79 N2
Tripoli Lebanon **43** N4 34 27N 35 50E
Tripoli Libya **66** D6 32 54N 13 11E
Tristan da Cuhna i. Atlantic Ocean **5** 37 15S 12 30W
Trivandrum India **58** C1 8 30N 76 57E
Tromsø Norway **42** K9 69 42N 19 00E
Trondheim Norway **42** J8 63 36N 10 23E
Troon Scotland **33** E3 55 32N 4 40W
Trowbridge England **38** B2 51 20N 2 13W
Troyes France **48** F4 48 18N 4 05E
Trujillo Peru **84** B7 8 06S 79 00W
Trujillo Spain **50** C3 39 28N 5 53W
Truro England **40** B3 50 16N 5 03W
Tsimlyansk Reservoir Russia **43** Q5 47 30N 43 00E
Tsugaru Channel Japan **59** N3 41 30N 140 30E
Tubruq Libya **66** E6 32 05N 23 59E
Tucson USA **79** H4 32 15N 110 57W
Tula Russia **56** D3 54 11N 37 38E
Tulsa USA **79** K4 36 07N 95 58W
Tunis Tunisia **66** D6 36 50N 10 13E
TUNISIA 66 C6
Turin Italy **51** A6 45 04N 7 40E
Turkana, Lake Ethiopia/Kenya **67** D5 4 00N 36 00E
TURKEY 43 N3
TURKMENISTAN 56 F1
Turks and Caicos Islands West Indies **79** M3 21 30N 72 00W
Turku Finland **42** L8 60 27N 22 15E
Turpan Depression China **58** D5/E5 42 40N 89 30E
Turriff Scotland **31** G2 57 32N 2 28W
TUVALU 5
Túy Spain **50** A5 42 03N 8 39W
Tver Russia **56** D3 56 49N 35 57E
Tweed r. Scotland/England **33** G3 55 45N 2 10W
Tynda Russia **57** N3 55 10N 124 35E
Tyndrum Scotland **31** E1 57 27N 4 44W
Tyne r. England **34** D3 54 58N 2 00W
Tyne and Wear co. England **35** D3 54 55N 1 20W
Tynemouth England **35** D4 55 01N 1 24W
Tyrrhenian Sea Europe **51** C4/D4 40 00N 12 00E
Tyumen Russia **56** G3 57 11N 65 29E
Tywi r. Wales **36** C1 51 45N 3 20W

U

Uberaba Brazil **84** E6 19 47S 47 57W
Uberlândia Brazil **84** E6 18 57S 48 17W
Ucayali r. Peru **84** B7 7 30S 75 00W
Udine Italy **51** D7 46 04N 13 14E
Uele r. Congo Dem. Rep. **67** C5 4 00N 26 00E
Ufa Russia **56** F3 54 45N 55 58E
UGANDA 67 D5
Ujung Pandang Indonesia **60** C2 5 09S 119 28E
Ukhta Russia **43** S8 63 33N 53 44E
UKRAINE 56 D2
Ulan Bator Mongolia **57** L2 47 54N 106 52E
Ulan-Ude Russia **57** L3 51 55N 107 40E
Ullapool Scotland **30** D2 57 54N 5 10W
Ullswater l. England **34** C3 54 35N 2 55W
Ullung Island South Korea **59** L2 37 30N 132 00E
Ulm Germany **49** F3 48 24N 10 00E
Ulva i. Scotland **30** C1 56 30N 6 15W

Ul'yanovsk Russia **56** E3 54 19N 48 22E
Umeå Sweden **42** L8 63 50N 20 15E
Unimak Island USA **78** C6 55 00N 164 00W
UNITED ARAB EMIRATES 61 F3
UNITED KINGDOM 42 F6
UNITED STATES OF AMERICA (USA) **79**
Unst i. Scotland **29** E3 60 45N 0 55W
Upper Lough Erne l. Northern Ireland **32** B2 54 15N 7 30W
Uppsala Sweden **42** K7 59 55N 17 38E
Ural Mountains Russia **56** F3 57 00N 60 00E
Ural'sk Kazakhstan **56** F3 51 19N 51 20E
Ure r. England **34** D3 54 20N 2 00W
Urmia, Lake Iran **61** E4 37 20N 45 55E
URUGUAY 85 D4
Uruguay r. South America **85** D5 28 30S 55 30W
Ürümqi China **58** D5 43 43N 87 38E
Usk Wales **36** D1 51 59N 3 35W
Ustinov Russia **56** E3 53 19N 53 11E
Ust-Kut Russia **57** L3 56 48N 105 42E
Utah state USA **79** H4 39 0N 112 00W
Utrecht Netherlands **49** C5 52 05N 5 07E
Utsunomiya Japan **59** M2 36 33N 139 52E
Uttoxeter England **37** F2 52 54N 1 52W
UZBEKISTAN 56 G2

V

Vaal r. Republic of South Africa **67** C2 27 30S 25 00E
Vaasa Finland **42** L8 63 06N 21 36E
Vadodara India **58** C3 22 19N 73 14E
Vaduz Liechtenstein **49** E2 47 08N 9 32E
Valdepeñas Spain **50** D3 38 46N 3 24W
Valdivia Chile **85** B4 39 46S 73 15W
Valence France **48** F2 44 56N 4 54E
Valencia Spain **50** E3 39 29N 0 24W
Valencia Venezuela **84** C9 10 14N 67 59W
Valenciennes France **48** E5 50 22N 3 32E
Valladolid Spain **50** C4 41 39N 4 45W
Valletta Malta **51** E1 35 54N 14 32E
Valognes France **41** F2 49 31N 1 28W
Valparaiso Chile **85** B4 33 05S 71 40W
Vancouver Canada **78** G5 49 13N 123 06W
Vancouver Island Canada **78** G5 48 55N 124 33W
Vänern, Lake Sweden **42** J7 59 00N 13 30E
Van, Lake Turkey **43** Q3 38 33N 42 46E
Vannes France **48** B3 47 40N 2 44W
Vantaa Finland **42** L8 60 20N 24 50E
VANUATU 5
Varanasi India **58** D3 25 20N 83 00E
Varaždin Croatia **51** F7 46 18N 16 21E
Varna Bulgaria **42** M4 43 12N 27 57E
VENEZUELA 84 C8
Venice Italy **51** D6 45 26N 12 20E
Veracruz Mexico **79** K2 19 11N 96 10W
Verdun France **48** F4 49 10N 5 24E
Verkhoyansk Russia **57** P4 67 35N 133 25E
Vermont state USA **79** M5 44 00N 73 00W
Verona Italy **51** C6 45 26N 11 00E
Versailles France **48** E4 48 48N 2 07E
Vesuvius mt. Italy **51** E4 40 49N 14 26E
Veurne Belgium **39** G2 51 04N 2 40E
Vicenza Italy **51** C6 45 33N 11 32E
Vichy France **48** E3 46 07N 3 25E
Victoria Canada **78** G5 48 26N 123 20W
Victoria r. Australia **72** D4 17 00S 131 00E
Victoria state Australia **72** E2 47 00S 143 00E
Victoria Falls Zambia/Zimbabwe **67** C3 17 55S 25 51E
Victoria Island Canada **78** H4 70 45N 115 00W
Victoria, Lake East Africa **67** D4 2 00S 33 00E
Vienna Austria **42** K5 48 13N 16 22E
Vienne r. France **48** D3 46 30N 0 30E
Vientiane Laos **60** B4 17 59N 102 38E
Vierzon France **48** E3 47 14N 2 03E
VIETNAM 60 B4
Vigo Spain **50** A5 42 15N 8 44W
Vijayawada India **58** D2 16 34N 80 40E
Villach Austria **51** D7 46 37N 13 51E
Vilnius Lithuania **42** M6 54 40N 25 19E
Viña del Mar Chile **85** B4 33 02S 71 35W
Vinh Vietnam **60** B4 18 42N 105 41E
Vinnytsya Ukraine **56** C2 49 11N 28 30E
Vinson Massif mts. Antarctica **86** 78 02S 22 00W
Vire r. France **41** F2 49 15N 1 05W
Virginia state USA **79** M4 38 00N 77 00W
Virgin Islands West Indies **79** N2 18 00N 64 30W
Visakhapatnam India **58** D1 17 42N 83 24E
Vitória Brazil **84** E5 20 20S 40 18W
Vitoria Spain **50** D5 42 51N 2 40W
Vitsyebsk Belarus **56** D3 55 10N 30 14E
Vladikavkaz Russia **43** Q4 43 02N 44 43E
Vladimir Russia **56** E3 56 08N 40 25E
Vladivostok Russia **57** P2 43 09N 131 53E
Volga r. Russia **56** E3 51 30N 48 00E
Volgograd Russia **56** E2 48 45N 44 30E
Vologda Russia **56** D3 59 10N 39 55E
Volta, Lake Ghana **66** B3 7 30N 0 30W
Vorkuta Russia **56** G4 67 27N 64 00E
Voronezh Russia **56** D3 51 40N 39 13E
Vosges mts. France **48** G4 48 10N 6 50E
Vyrnwy r. Wales **36** D2 52 45N 3 10W
Vyrnwy, Lake Wales **36** D2 52 47N 3 30W

W

Waal r. Netherlands **49** C4 51 50N 5 00E
Waddington, Mount Canada **78** G6 51 22N 125 14W
Wadebridge England **40** C3 50 32N 4 50W
Wadi Halfa Sudan **61** D3 21 55N 31 20E
Wad Medani Sudan **61** D2 14 24N 33 30E
Waiau r. New Zealand **73** B1 46 00S 167 40E
Waigeo i. Indonesia **60** E2 0 15S 130 45E
Waikato r. New Zealand **73** D3 38 30S 175 30E
Wairau r. New Zealand **73** C2 42 00S 173 00E
Waitaki r. New Zealand **73** C2 44 45S 170 30E
Wakatipu, Lake New Zealand **73** B1 45 06S 168 31E

Wakayama Japan **59** M1 34 12N 135 10E
Wakefield England **35** D2 53 42N 1 29W
Wakkanai Japan **59** N4 45 26N 141 43E
Wales country United Kingdom **36** D2 52 40N 3 30W
Wallasey England **34** B2 53 26N 3 03W
Walls Scotland **29** D3 60 14N 1 34W
Walsall England **37** F2 52 35N 1 58W
Waltham Forest England **38** D2 51 36N 0 00
Walton on the Naze England **39** F2 51 51N 1 16E
Walvis Bay tn. Namibia **67** B2 22 59S 14 31E
Wanaka, Lake New Zealand **73** B2 44 28S 169 09E
Wanganui New Zealand **73** D3 39 56S 175 03E
Wanganui r. New Zealand **73** D3 39 30S 175 00E
Wansbeck r. England **35** D4 55 10N 1 50W
Wantage England **38** C2 51 36N 1 25W
Ward Hill Scotland **29** B1 58 54N 3 20W
Ward's Stone hill England **34** C3 54 03N 2 38W
Wareham England **41** E3 50 41N 2 07W
Warley England **37** F2 52 30N 1 59W
Warminster England **38** B2 51 13N 2 12W
Warrenpoint tn. Northern Ireland **32** C2 54 06N 6 15W
Warrington England **34** C2 53 24N 2 37W
Warrington u.a. England **35** D2 53 23N 2 37W
Warsaw Poland **42** L6 52 15N 21 00E
Warwick England **37** F2 52 17N 1 34W
Warwickshire co. England **37** F2 52 15N 1 40W
Washington England **34** D3 54 54N 1 31W
Washington state USA **78** G5/H5 47 00N 120 00W
Washington D.C. USA **79** M4 38 55N 77 00W
Wash, The b. England **35** F1 52 55N 0 10E
Waterlooville England **38** C1 50 53N 1 02W
Water of Luce r. Scotland **32/33** E2 54 55N 4 55W
Watford England **38** D2 51 39N 0 24W
Waveney r. England **39** F3 52 30N 1 30E
Wau Papua New Guinea **72** E5 7 22S 146 40E
Weald, The geog. reg. England **39** E2 51 05N 0 25E
Wear r. England **34** C3 54 40N 2 05W
Weddell Sea Southern Ocean **86** 71 00S 40 00W
Wei He r. China **59** B3 34 00N 106 00E
Welland r. England **38** D3 52 30N 0 40W
Wellingborough England **38** D3 52 19N 0 42W
Wellington England **41** D3 50 59N 3 15W
Wellington New Zealand **73** C2 41 17S 174 46E
Wells England **41** E4 51 13N 2 39W
Wells-next-the-Sea England **39** E3 52 58N 0 51E
Welshpool Wales **36** D2 52 40N 3 09W
Welwyn Garden City England **38** D2 51 48N 0 13W
Wenlock Edge hills England **37** E2 52 30N 2 45W
Wensum r. England **39** F3 52 45N 1 05E
Weser r. Germany **49** E5 52 30N 9 00E
West Berkshire u.a. England **38** C2 51 30N 1 17W
West Bromwich England **37** F2 52 31N 1 59W
Westbury England **38** B2 51 16N 2 11W
West Dunbartonshire u.a. Scotland **33** E3/4 56 03N 4 30W
Western Australia state Australia **72** 25 00S 123 00E
Western Ghats mts. India **58** C2 15 30N 74 00E
Western Isles u.a. Scotland **30** B2/C3 57 30N 7 00W
WESTERN SAHARA 66 A5
West Friesian Islands Netherlands **49** C5 53 25N 5 15E
West Lothian u.a. Scotland **33** F3 55 50N 3 36W
West Midlands co. England **37** E2/F2 52 28N 1 40W
Weston-super-Mare England **41** E4 51 21N 2 59W
Westport New Zealand **73** C2 41 45S 171 36E
Westray i. Scotland **29** B2/C2 59 18N 3 00W
Westray Firth sd. Scotland **29** B2/C2 59 15N 3 00W
West Rift Valley Africa **67** D4 0 00 30 00E
West Sussex co. England **38** D1 51 00N 0 25W
West Virginia state USA **79** L4 39 00N 81 00W
West Yorkshire co. England **34/35** D2 53 45N 1 30W
Wetherby England **35** D2 53 56N 1 23W
Weymouth England **41** E3 50 37N 2 25W
Whakatane New Zealand **73** D3 37 58S 176 59E
Whalsay i. Scotland **29** E3 60 22N 0 59W
Whangarei New Zealand **73** C3 35 43S 174 19E
Wharfe r. England **34** C3 54 10N 2 05W
Whernside sum. England **34** C3 54 14N 2 23W
Whitby England **35** E3 54 29N 0 37W
Whitchurch England **37** E2 52 58N 2 41W
Whiteadder Water r. Scotland/England **33** G3 55 50N 2 10W
Whitehaven England **34** B3 54 33N 3 35W
Whitehorse Canada **78** F7 60 41N 135 08W
White Nile r. Sudan **61** D2 11 00N 32 00E
White Sea Russia **42** P9 66 00N 37 30E
Whithorn Scotland **33** E2 54 44N 4 25W
Whitley Bay tn. England **35** D4 55 03N 1 25W
Whitney, Mount USA **79** H4 36 35N 118 17W
Whyalla Australia **72** D2 33 02S 137 35E
Wichita USA **79** K4 37 43N 97 20W
Wick Scotland **31** F3 58 26N 3 06W
Wicklow Republic of Ireland **32** A2 52 59N 6 03W
Widnes England **34** C2 53 22N 2 44W
Wiesbaden Germany **49** E4 50 05N 8 15E
Wigan England **34** C2 53 33N 2 38W
Wigston England **37** F2 52 36N 1 05W
Wigton England **34** B3 54 49N 3 09W
Wigtown Scotland **33** E2 54 10N 4 26W
Wigtown Bay Scotland **33** E2 54 10N 4 20W
Wilhelmshaven Germany **49** E5 53 32N 8 07E
Wilkes Land geog. reg. Antarctica **86** 68 00S 105 00E
Wiltshire co. England **38** B2/C2 51 20N 1 52W
Wimborne Minster England **41** F3 50 48N 1 59W
Wincanton England **41** E4 51 04N 2 25W
Winchester England **38** C2 51 04N 1 19W
Windermere England **34** C3 54 23N 2 54W
Windermere l. England **34** C3 54 20N 2 57W
Windhoek Namibia **67** B2 22 34S 17 06E
Windsor England **38** D2 51 29N 0 38W
Windsor & Maidenhead u.a. England **38** D2 51 30N 0 45W

Winnipeg Canada **79** K5 49 53N 97 10W
Winnipeg, Lake Canada **78** K6 53 00N 97 00W
Winsford England **34** C2 53 11N 2 31W
Winterthur Switzerland **49** E2 47 30N 8 45E
Wisbech England **39** E2 52 40N 0 10E
Wisconsin state USA **79** K5 45 00N 90 00W
Wishaw Scotland **33** F3 55 47N 3 56W
Witham England **39** E2 51 48N 0 38E
Witham r. England **35** E2 53 05N 0 10W
Witney England **38** C2 51 48N 1 29W
Wittenberg Germany **49** G5 51 53N 12 39E
Woking England **38** D2 51 20N 0 34W
Wokingham England **38** D2 51 25N 0 51W
Wokingham u.a. England **38** D2 51 24N 0 51W
Wolfsburg Germany **49** F5 52 27N 10 49E
Wolverhampton England **37** E2 52 36N 2 08W
Wonsan North Korea **59** D3 39 07N 127 26E
Woodbridge England **39** F3 52 06N 1 19E
Wooler England **33** G3 55 33N 2 01W
Worcester England **37** E2 52 11N 2 13W
Worcestershire u.a. England **37** E2 52 13N 2 13W
Workington England **34** B3 54 39N 3 33W
Worksop England **35** D2 53 18N 1 07W
Worms Head Wales **36** C1 51 34N 4 20W
Worthing England **38** D1 50 48N 0 23W
Wrangel i. Russia **57** U5 61 30N 180 00
Wrath, Cape Scotland **31** D3 58 37N 5 01W
Wrexham Wales **36** D3 53 03N 3 00W
Wrexham u.a. Wales **36** D3 53 00N 3 00W
Wrocław Poland **42** K6 51 05N 17 00E
Wuhan China **59** C3 30 35N 114 19E
Wuppertal Germany **49** D4 51 15N 7 10E
Würzburg Germany **49** E3 49 48N 9 57E
Wye r. England/Wales **37** E1 51 40N 2 40W
Wymondham England **39** F3 52 34N 1 07E
Wyndham Australia **72** C4 15 28S 128 06E
Wyoming state USA **79** J5 43 00N 108 00W
Wyre r. England **34** C2 53 50N 2 50W

X

Xi r. China **60** C5 23 00N 112 00E
Xi'an China **59** B3 34 16N 108 54E
Xi Jiang r. China **59** C5 22 00N 111 00E
Xingu r. Brazil **84** D7 5 30S 52 40W
Xining China **59** B3 36 35N 101 55E
Xuzhou China **59** C3 34 17N 117 18E

Y

Yakutsk Russia **57** N4 62 10N 129 50E
Yamagata Japan **59** N2 38 16N 140 16E
Yamoussoukro Côte d'Ivoire **66** B3 6 50N 5 20W
Yangon Myanmar **58** E2 16 47N 96 10E
Yangtze r. see Jinsha Jiang (upper course), Chang Jiang (lower course)
Yaoundé Cameroon **66** D3 3 51N 11 31E
Yarlung Zangbo Jiang (Tsangpo) r. China **58** D3 30 00N 90 00E
Yaroslavl Russia **56** D3 57 34N 39 52E
Yarrow Water r. Scotland **33** F3 55 35N 3 05W
Yazd Iran **61** F4 31 54N 54 22E
Yekaterinburg Russia **56** G3 56 52N 60 35E
Yell i. Shetland Islands Scotland **29** D3 60 35N 1 10W
Yellowknife Canada **78** H7 62 30N 114 29W
Yellow Sea China **59** D3 35 30N 122 30E
Yell Sound Scotland **29** D3 60 30N 1 15W
YEMEN REPUBLIC 61 E2
Yenisey r. Russia **57** J4 64 00N 88 00E
Yeo r. England **41** E4 51 00N 2 45W
Yeovil England **41** E3 50 57N 2 39W
Yerevan Armenia **43** Q4 40 10N 44 31E
Yes Tor sum. England **40** C3 50 42N 4 00W
Yogyakarta Indonesia **60** C2 7 48S 110 24E
Yokkaichi Japan **59** M1 34 58N 136 38E
Yokohama Japan **59** M2 35 27N 139 38E
York England **35** D2 53 58N 1 05W
York u.a. England **35** D2 53 56N 1 02W
York, Cape Australia **72** E4 10 41S 142 32E
Yorkshire Wolds hills England **35** E3 54 00N 0 45W
York, Vale of England **35** D3 54 10N 1 20W
Ypres see Ieper
Yucatan Channel Caribbean Sea **79** L3 21 00N 85 00W
Yucatan Peninsula Mexico **79** L2/3 19 00N 89 00W
Yukon r. Canada/USA **78** D7 65 00N 155 00W
Yukon Territory Canada **78** F7 62 00N 135 00W

Z

Zagreb Croatia **42** K5 45 48N 15 58E
Zagros Mountains Iran **61** E4/F3 32 45N 48 50E
Zahedan Iran **61** G3 29 32N 60 54E
Zahlé Lebanon **43** P2 33 50N 35 55E
Zambezi r. Southern Africa **67** D3 17 00S 34 00E
ZAMBIA 67 C3
Zamboanga The Philippines **60** D3 6 55N 122 05E
Zanzibar Tanzania **67** D4 6 10S 39 12E
Zaporizhzhya Ukraine **43** P5 47 50N 35 10E
Zaragoza Spain **50** E4 41 39N 0 54W
Zaria Nigeria **66** C4 11 01N 7 44E
Zarqa Jordan **43** P2 32 04N 36 05E
Zaysan, Lake Kazakhstan **56** J2 48 00N 84 00E
Zealand i. Denmark **42** J6 55 00N 12 00E
Zeebrugge Belgium **49** B4 51 20N 3 13E
Zhambyl Kazakhstan **56** H2 42 50N 71 25E
Zhangjiakou China **59** C4 40 51N 114 59E
Zhangye China **59** B3 38.58N 100.30E
Zhanjiang China **59** C2 21 10N 110 24E
Zhengzhou China **59** C3 34 45N 113 38E
Zhytomyr Ukraine **42** M6 50 18N 28 40E
Zibo China **59** C3 36 51N 118 01E
Ziel, Mount Australia **72** D3 23 30S 132 24E
ZIMBABWE 67 C3
Zinder Niger **66** C4 13 46N 8 58E
Zonguldak Turkey **43** N4 41 26N 31 47E
Zürich Switzerland **49** E2 47 23N 8 33E
Zwickau Germany **49** G4 50 43N 12 30E